Methodological Issues in Psychology

Methodological Issues in Psychology is a comprehensive text that challenges current practice in the discipline and provides solutions that are more useful in contemporary research, both basic and applied.

This book begins by equipping the readers with the underlying foundation pertaining to basic philosophical issues addressing theory verification or falsification, distinguishing different levels of theorizing, or hypothesizing, and the assumptions necessary to negotiate between these levels. It goes on to specifically focus on statistical and inferential hypotheses including chapters on how to dramatically improve statistical and inferential practices and how to address the replication crisis. Advances to be featured include the author's own inventions, the a priori procedure and gain-probability diagrams, and a chapter about mediation analyses, which explains why such analyses are much weaker than typically assumed. The book also provides an introductory chapter on classical measurement theory and expands to new concepts in subsequent chapters. The final measurement chapter addresses the ubiquitous problem of small effect sizes in psychology and provides recommendations that directly contradict typical thinking and teaching in psychology, but with the consequence that researchers can enjoy dramatically improved effect sizes.

Methodological Issues in Psychology is an invaluable asset for students and researchers of psychology. It will also be of vital interest to social science researchers and students in areas such as management, marketing, sociology, and experimental philosophy.

David Trafimow is a Distinguished Achievement Professor of psychology at New Mexico State University, a Fellow of the Association for Psychological Science, Executive Editor of the *Journal of General Psychology*, and for *Basic and Applied Social Psychology*. He received his PhD in psychology from the University of Illinois at Urbana-Champaign in 1993. His current research interests include attribution, attitudes, cross-cultural research, ethics, morality, philosophy and philosophy of science, methodology, potential performance theory, the a priori procedure, and gain-probability diagrams.

Methodological Issues in Psychology
Concept, Method, and Measurement

David Trafimow

NEW YORK AND LONDON

First published 2024
by Routledge
605 Third Avenue, New York, NY 10158

and by Routledge
4 Park Square, Milton Park, Abingdon, Oxon, OX14 4RN

Routledge is an imprint of the Taylor & Francis Group, an informa business

© 2024 David Trafimow

The right of David Trafimow to be identified as author of this work has been asserted in accordance with sections 77 and 78 of the Copyright, Designs and Patents Act 1988.

All rights reserved. No part of this book may be reprinted or reproduced or utilised in any form or by any electronic, mechanical, or other means, now known or hereafter invented, including photocopying and recording, or in any information storage or retrieval system, without permission in writing from the publishers.

Trademark notice: Product or corporate names may be trademarks or registered trademarks, and are used only for identification and explanation without intent to infringe.

Library of Congress Cataloging-in-Publication Data
Names: Trafimow, David, author.
Title: Methodological issues in psychology : concept, method, and measurement / David Trafimow.
Description: New York, NY : Routledge, 2023. | Includes bibliographical references and index.
Identifiers: LCCN 2023007447 (print) | LCCN 2023007448 (ebook) | ISBN 9781032429816 (hardback) | ISBN 9781032429786 (paperback) | ISBN 9781003365167 (ebook)
Subjects: LCSH: Psychology--Research--Methodology.
Classification: LCC BF76.5 .T727 2023 (print) | LCC BF76.5 (ebook) | DDC 150.72--dc23/eng/20230415
LC record available at https://lccn.loc.gov/2023007447
LC ebook record available at https://lccn.loc.gov/2023007448

ISBN: 978-1-032-42981-6 (hbk)
ISBN: 978-1-032-42978-6 (pbk)
ISBN: 978-1-003-36516-7 (ebk)

DOI: 10.4324/9781003365167

Typeset in Times New Roman
by Deanta Global Publishing Services, Chennai, India

Several people were influential in my writing this book. I thank Bas Verplanken who first suggested the idea decades ago, and it has been in the back of my mind ever since. I also thank Michael Hyman for helping me spread scientifically revolutionary ideas to top business journals, a desirable expansion. And Tonghui Wang and the mathematics group have been fantastic at helping me translate conceptual ideas into precise mathematical formulation. Finally, and most of all, I thank my wife Sabine Trafimow who not only tolerates, but even encourages, my extreme focus on improving the social and behavioral sciences.

Contents

Acknowledgments ix
Preface x

PART I
General Methodological Issues 1

1 A Philosophical Foundation 3

2 The Reality underneath the Reality: Examples from the Hard Sciences 18

3 The TASI Taxonomy and Implications 30

4 Why We Should Not Engage Null Hypothesis Significance Testing 47

5 How to Think about Replicating Findings 62

6 The A Priori Procedure (APP) 74

7 Gain-Probability Diagrams 89

8 The Unfortunate Dependence of Much Social Science on Mediation Analysis 106

PART II
Measurement Issues 123

9 The Classical Theory and Implications 125

10 Potential Performance Theory 144

11 Auxiliary Validity 161

12	Unit Validity and Why Units Matter	171
13	A Tripartite Parsing of Variance	182
14	Shocking Measurement Implications	195

References *209*
Index *217*

Acknowledgments

There are many people to thank for their influence on this book. Most of all, my wife, Sabine, who provided all the beautiful artwork as well as constant encouragement. In addition, I thank two wonderful friends, Mike and Stacey. Mike did a wonderful job providing high resolution scanning and aid transmitting huge files to the publisher. Stacey was a consistent source of support. In addition, I thank the many people who have collaborated with me on research and thereby aided me in thinking through some of the ideas presented in the book.

Then too, others have contributed less directly but nevertheless importantly. My parents, Alice and Jordan, provided much of my education and especially the lesson that the questions one asks may be as, or even more, important than the answers. I also thank my brother, Jonnie, and sister, Janet, for the advice, support and help provided over the years. I have also benefitted from my sister-in-law, Elsa, and my brother-in-law Uli who has had innumerable conversations with me about my research and helped me sharpen my thinking. My friends Butch, Doris, and Joy also provided encouragement. Finally, my acknowledgments would be incomplete without mentioning my good friend Bas, who has been encouraging me to write this book for years and is already after me to write another book.

Preface

I have long felt that the social and behavioral sciences are not doing well, and not doing nearly as well as they ought to do. To dramatize the point—and I am an opera fanatic, so I love drama—imagine being in graduate school 150 years ago, when psychology was starting to become a formal science. Suppose someone asked you to make a prediction about how much progress there would be in psychology by the year 2023. When I imagine myself in this scenario, my strong belief is that I would have predicted much more progress than has been attained. That is, I would not only have been wrong, but way wrong!

All would be well if I were way wrong in the good direction, the direction of underpredicting progress. But being way wrong in the bad direction, the direction of overpredicting progress, is intolerable even though my wrongness is completely hypothetical. Of course, it is easy to make excuses, and I have heard many of them.

- Psychology is too multi-causal.
- There is no way to observe mental processes.
- Psychology is too young a science.
- Etcetera.

Although one or more of the bullet-listed excuses may sound reasonable, and may even be true, I do not buy any of them. Making excuses is too easy. Why not instead try to figure out how to make impressive progress despite the obstacles?

And that brings us to this book. My main premise is that the social and behavioral sciences are not nearly as impressive as they should be after all this time, an issue explained in detail in Chapter 2. We not only ought to do better, but can do better, and the goal of this book is to push the social and behavioral sciences in the direction of improved progress. Hence, I do not rehash what other methodology textbooks say—these have not sufficiently stimulated progress. Rather, this book is very much about how we can do better than what we are doing, and you will find many places where I disagree with traditional or textbook thinking and suggest superior alternative thinking. Put simply, this is a book about what I think, not about methodological traditions, and so there is no attempt at methodological coverage. This is a selfish book in the sense that it is about what I want to say for improving research, not about what anyone else has said.

Consequently, this was an easy book to write as most of it is from my own mind. There was little reason for external research, which is what usually causes writing a book to be a difficult process. There is nothing like a labor of love to render writing easy. I hope you gain as much from reading the book as I did from writing it.

David Trafimow
January 11, 2023

Part I
General Methodological Issues

1 A Philosophical Foundation

Imagine the theory that attitudes—the extent to which people like or dislike performing behaviors—cause behaviors (e.g., Fishbein, 1980; Fishbein & Ajzen, 1975; 2010). The theory might be true or false. The obvious course of action is to test the theory in some way by comparing

DOI: 10.4324/9781003365167-2

or contrasting it against observations. To use a convenient term that means the same thing, an attitude researcher would wish to submit the theory to an *empirical* test (an observation or set of observations that bear on the theory). If the results of the empirical test are in line with the theory, then the theory is supported; but if the results of the empirical test contradict the theory, then the theory is not supported.

For now, let us postpone questioning how a researcher traverses the distance from the theory to an empirical test, and instead focus on the strength with which the findings obtained from the empirical test justify conclusions concerning the theory. To continue with attitudes, imagine that a researcher randomly assigns participants to read or not read an essay in favor of wearing seatbelts. The researcher intends that reading the pro seat belt essay will increase positive attitudes towards wearing seatbelts relative to not reading it. In psychology terminology, the essay group—the group that gets the treatment—is called the *experimental group* or *experimental condition*, whereas the other group is called the *control group* or *control condition*. The prediction is that participants in the experimental condition will wear seatbelts more than participants in the control condition.

Suppose that the researcher's prediction pans out; participants in the experimental condition do wear seatbelts more than participants in the control condition. Is the researcher justified in concluding that the theory is true?

Unfortunately, this happy conclusion is premature. Perhaps the prediction panned out for a reason other than that the essay caused attitude change that, in turn, caused behavior change. For example, perhaps the researcher simply got lucky and the participants in the experimental condition just happened to be more prone to wearing seatbelts than participants in the control condition, even notwithstanding any influence on the part of the essay. Or perhaps the essay worked by influencing something other than attitudes, such as affect towards the behavior (the essay made people happier about wearing seatbelts). In general, the fact that an empirical test pans out in the desired way is insufficient for concluding that the theory is true. The best one can conclude is that the empirical test supports, but does not prove, the theory.

Philosophers sometimes use logic to make this point. Consider the following *syllogism* (conclusion drawn from two premises).

Syllogism 1
If the theory is true, then the prediction should occur. (Premise 1)
The prediction occurs. (Premise 2)
Therefore, the theory is true. (Conclusion)

Of course, the syllogism is flawed because, as we have seen, the prediction could have been confirmed for a reason other than the theory, thereby compromising the ability of the confirmed prediction to prove the theory. Philosophers often term syllogisms that are problematic in this way invalid. A *valid* syllogism is one where if the premises are true, the conclusion must be true (e.g., Syllogism 2, coming up soon); and an *invalid* syllogism is one where even giving the truth of the premises fails to prove the conclusion (e.g., Syllogism 1). In addition, a syllogism can be *sound* or *unsound*. A syllogism is sound if (a) it is valid and (b) the premises are true. Otherwise, the syllogism is unsound. Syllogism 1 is both invalid and unsound. An example of a valid (good logic) but unsound (a false premise) syllogism is the following: if the moon exists, it is made of green cheese; the moon exists; therefore, the moon is made of green cheese.

But now let us switch courses and imagine that the prediction does not pan out; the researcher observes no difference in seatbelt wearing between participants in the experimental condition and participants in the control condition. Does the failed prediction validly prove the theory false? Interestingly, from the point of view of strict logic, it does, though we will see later that strict logic has limitations. To see this, let us rewrite the foregoing syllogism but adjusting for the fact that we are now supposing that the prediction fails.

Syllogism 2
If the theory is true, then the prediction should occur.	(Premise 1)
The prediction does not occur.	(Premise 2)
Therefore, the theory is not true.	(Conclusion)

In contrast to Syllogism 1, where assuming the truth of the two premises fails to validly prove the truth of the conclusion, in Syllogism 2, the truth of the two premises does prove the truth of the conclusion. And so, we have an asymmetry where predictions that pan out do not prove the theory true, but predictions that fail prove the theory false.

Lest the invalidity of Syllogism 1 and the validity of Syllogism 2 are elusive to the reader, it may be more intuitive to think in terms of more concrete entities. Consider a rewritten Syllogism 1, that has the same form as the original Syllogism 1, but in terms of rain and sidewalks instead of in terms of theories and predictions.

Rewritten Syllogism 1
If it is raining, then the sidewalks are wet.	(Premise 1)
The sidewalks are wet.	(Premise 2)
Therefore, it is raining.	(Conclusion)

The problem with Syllogism 1 is obvious immediately: someone might have left the sprinkler system on, thereby causing the sidewalks to be wet, even in the absence of rain. An easy way to check the validity of any syllogism is to change the entities to rain and sidewalks but keeping the form the same. Let us now move to Syllogism 2 and rewrite it similarly.

Rewritten Syllogism 2
If it is raining, then the sidewalks are wet.	(Premise 1)
The sidewalks are not wet.	(Premise 2)
Therefore, it is not raining.	(Conclusion)

There is clearly no way for both premises to be true and the conclusion to be false; thus, Syllogism 2 is valid. As a test, consider a contrary argument that perhaps a tarp is covering the sidewalks thereby keeping them dry even when it is raining. But the problem with the contrary argument is that if a tarp is covering the sidewalks, then Premise 1 is false. And if one of the premises is false, then we do not have a fair test of validity which, to remind the reader, is that if the premises are true, then the conclusion must be true.

Now that we see that Syllogism 1 is invalid, even when rewritten to feature rain and sidewalks, and that Syllogism 2 is valid, even when similarly rewritten, what follows? To reiterate, there is an asymmetry: it is not possible to prove theories with confirmed predictions, but it is possible to disprove theories with disconfirmed predictions. This asymmetry suggests that it might be better, or at least more definitive, to have predictions fail to pan out than have them succeed. After all, a successful prediction is insufficient to draw a strong conclusion, such as that the theory is true. However, a failed prediction is sufficient to draw a strong conclusion, that the theory is false. Theory disconfirmation is logically possible whereas theory confirmation is not, and it is better to do that which is possible than that which is not possible. Thus, many philosophers, most notably Karl Popper (e.g., 1963; 1972), have argued that it is better to try to disconfirm theories than to try to confirm them.

However, if it is only possible to disconfirm theories, and not possible to confirm them, one might wonder how it is possible to make progress in science. Progress may seem impossible if there is no way to prove theories true. Popper suggested an interesting solution. According to Popper, science can progress by disconfirming theories and replacing them with better theories. The scientific program, then, is one where researchers propose theories and subject them to empirical tests. If the predictions pan out, no conclusion is drawn, though the theory can be said to have at least withstood a test. But failed predictions disconfirm theories, which can be replaced with better theories, to the betterment of science. Sometimes philosophers claim that failed predictions *falsify* theories (prove them false), and the larger program of falsifying theories to replace them with better ones can be considered a *falsificationist* program or philosophy of science. In summary, the asymmetry the syllogisms illustrate implies that falsifying theories is better than verifying them because the former is logically possible whereas the latter is not.

Popper's falsificationist program implies something interesting about scientific theories that has had a strong influence in psychology, including at the level of introductory textbooks. Put simply, if the goal of a research scientist ought to be to falsify theories, so they can be replaced with better ones, an implication is that the theories must be capable of being shown wrong in the first place. In a word, theories must be *falsifiable*. Theories that are not falsifiable cannot be shown wrong, by definition, and so the falsificationist program cannot proceed. In contrast, theories that are falsifiable allow the falsificationist program to proceed. For this reason, the methodology chapter of many psychology textbooks includes some sort of statement about how theories must be falsifiable to be of value to psychology (or any field that considers itself to be a science). Unfortunately, although many textbooks extol the importance of having falsifiable theories, they do not explain the underlying justification for the claim, particularly the asymmetry illustrated by Syllogism 1 and Syllogism 2.

What would be an example of an unfalsifiable theory? A typical example would be the theory that God created the world. It is difficult to imagine a way to subject this theory to an empirical test that would have a chance of disconfirming the theory. The falsificationist argument would not be that the theory is wrong, only that it is unfalsifiable and consequently of no use to scientists.

There is one last point to be made. Many philosophers distinguish between theories that have been falsified, theories that have not been falsified but are falsifiable in principle, and theories that are not falsifiable in principle. It is only the theories that are not falsifiable in principle that are not considered useful in science. The theory that God created the world is considered unfalsifiable in principle because it is difficult to imagine a way to submit that theory to an empirical test. However, the foregoing arguments need not be the last word.

Contrary Arguments

We have thus far only considered strict logic, but there is more to science than that. For example, Kuhn (1962) invoked the notion of *incommensurability*, to be explained shortly, to argue that there is no way to have crucial (definitive) experiments to falsify theories. Aside from Kuhn, a limitation is that logic is strongly subject to the nature of the premises, with different premises supporting different conclusions. Another limitation is that the premises might not be true, at least not without modification. In that case, as we have seen, syllogisms with at least one false premise are unsound, even if logically valid. The subsequent subsections address each of these issues, in turn.

Kuhnian Incommensurability

Put briefly, Kuhn (1962) argued that there is a prescientific phase where there is no dominant *paradigm*, that is, no dominant way to perform research. Once there is a dominant paradigm, then researchers use that paradigm to solve all sorts of problems, many of which may not have been considered by the original inventors of the paradigm. Kuhn termed this "normal science" where researchers solve small puzzles but do not question foundational assumptions. However, even with a dominant paradigm, there may be one or more cases where an empirical prediction fails to pan out. Such empirical anomalies may pile up as experiments continue to be performed. At some point, researchers may propose a different theory to handle the anomalies, and the new theory may be in competition with the old theory. The obvious course of action would be for researchers to test the two theories against each other, to determine the best one. However, Kuhn argued that researchers cannot take this obvious course of action. The reason is that either different theories use different words or, even if they use the same words, the words have different meanings in the competing theories. Because of the different meanings, there is no way to directly compare the theories, and no way to subject them to competitive testing.

To see this in detail, let us consider the use of the word 'mass' from a Newtonian (1642–1727) and Einsteinian (1879–1955) perspective. An important characteristic of mass, for Newton, is that it does not change with velocity. For example, the same rocket ship traveling through space would have the same mass regardless of whether it would be traveling at 5,000 miles per hour or 50,000 miles per hour. In contrast, for Einstein, mass does change depending on velocity, with more velocity implying more mass. So, a rocket ship traveling at 50,000 miles per hour would have slightly more mass than a rocket ship traveling at 5,000 miles per hour. Thus, the word has different meanings for Newton and Einstein, and the two theories are, to use Kuhn's (1962) famous word, incommensurable. That is, despite using the same words, they are not speaking the same language, and there is no way either theory can be used to understand the other. There is no way to relate crucial terms, such as mass, as used in one theory, to the other theory. Without the ability to relate crucial terms across theories, there is no way to design definitive ways to test the theories against each other. And if there is no way to perform definitive empirical tests, there is no way to falsify either theory. (A related complication, glossed over here for the sake of brevity, but explained in the Appendix on Definitions at the end of this chapter, is the lack of explicit definitions.)

Because of the impossibility of falsifying either theory, Kuhn (1962) argued that the theory that comes out on top does so largely due to sociological factors. As aficionados of the older theory retire or die, they are replaced with new scientists who are more likely to have been indoctrinated in the newer paradigm or who are otherwise more open to it. Thus, what Kuhn considered revolutionary science is largely a matter of a process where new paradigms are developed to handle empirical anomalies, the new paradigms are incommensurable with older ones thereby precluding empirical tests from being definitive, and sociological factors largely determine the winning paradigm. In this Kuhnian scheme, there is no way for the falsificationist program to work.

However, it is possible to criticize Kuhnian incommensurability. Consider an experiment where two clocks are synchronized. One clock is placed in an airplane which, after taking off, is moving considerably faster than the clock that remains on the ground. According to Newton, there is no reason for the two clocks to be become out of synch during the flight. However, according to Einstein, greater velocity implies a slower passage of time. Therefore, the clock that was on an airplane should be slightly behind the other clock due to its faster velocity. The moral of this empirical story is that even if there is incommensurability at the theoretical level, there need not be incommensurability at the empirical level. A Newtonian scientist and an Einsteinian scientist may disagree about the meaning of mass, but they can agree on clock readings. Hence, it is possible to perform definitive empirical tests despite theoretical incommensurability.

Or consider another test, concerning the precession of the perihelion of Mercury (how the point of closest approach of Mercury to the sun changes). The value is different for Newton and Einstein, and Einstein's value is closer to the empirically determined one (see Einstein, 1961, for details). Although the theories may be incommensurable, distance and angular distance measurements are not incommensurable, any more than time measurements are incommensurable in the clocks example. Aficionados of different theories can agree on measurements despite their theoretical disagreements. Thus, theoretical incommensurability need not translate into empirical incommensurability. In turn, if theories are empirically commensurable, regardless of theoretical incommensurability, then falsification is possible after all. Therefore, Kuhnian incommensurability constitutes an insufficient reason to reject the falsificationist program. The following two subsections will be more problematic for the falsificationist program.

The Form of the Major Premise

Consider again the first premise in Syllogisms 1 and 2, sometimes termed the *major* premise because it is a general statement: "If the theory is true, then the prediction should occur." However, there is no law requiring that the major premise be stated in that form, as I pointed out in a recent article (Trafimow, 2020). We might state the major premise in a different way: "If the theory is not true, then the prediction should not occur." And if we change the major premise in this way, it is easy to show that Syllogism 1, which used to be invalid, now becomes valid. And Syllogism 2, which used to be valid, now becomes invalid. In turn, because the previous argument made in favor of a falsificationist philosophy of science depended on the invalidity of Syllogism 1, and the validity of Syllogism 2, reversing these is inconvenient, to say the least.

Let us commence with Syllogism 1, but with the new major premise.

Syllogism 1 With the New Major Premise
If the theory is not true, then the prediction should not occur.	(Premise 1)
The prediction occurs.	(Premise 2)
Therefore, the theory is true.	(Conclusion)

Perhaps surprisingly, when we change the form of the major premise so that falsity of the theory implies that the empirical prediction fails, the entire syllogism that verifies the theory suddenly becomes valid. We have the opposite of that which was argued previously because now theory confirmation is logically possible.

And we can play a similar game with Syllogism 2. However, substituting the new major premise for the old one makes what used to be a valid syllogism now invalid.

Syllogism 2 with the New Major Premise
If the theory is not true, then the prediction should not occur.	(Premise 1)
The prediction does not occur.	(Premise 2)
Therefore, the theory is not true.	(Conclusion)

If a prediction fails, the old Syllogism 2 shows that the failure disconfirms the theory. And this demonstration is logically valid. In contrast, the new Syllogism 2, with the new major premise, is not logically valid. It does not provide a sufficient reason to reject theories.

Well, then, if stating the major premise in one way supports falsifying theories as more logical than verifying them but stating the major premise in a different way supports verifying theories as more logical than falsifying them, it places the researcher who wishes to be logical in a quandary. Is it better to try to falsify theories or is it better to verify them? Both are equally logical or illogical, depending on how the major premise is stated.

Worse yet, the issue of how the major premise is stated imposes only one sort of problem. Matters become more complex when we consider syllogism soundness, and the necessity to consider auxiliary assumptions.

Auxiliary Assumptions

Let us return to our theory, that attitudes—the extent to which people like or dislike performing behaviors—cause behaviors. We have thus far ignored the issue of how one traverses the distance between the theory and an empirical test. It is now convenient to address that issue. As will become clear eventually, addressing that issue has a knock-on effect of influencing our syllogisms, which, in turn, influences how we should think about falsification and verification. To alert the reader, this will be a long subsection, but a crucial one that will figure strongly in subsequent chapters.

To commence, consider that the focal construct in the theory—attitude—cannot be directly observed. There is no known way to look at a person and see that person's attitude. Thus, attitude is a *nonobservational* term. In contrast, in the case of our hypothetical experiment involving an essay designed to influence attitudes, it is possible to observe the essay. Likewise, as a generality, behavior cannot be observed, though a single behavior, such as wearing a seatbelt, can be observed. Thus, attitude and behavior are nonobservational terms that can be distinguished from the essay designed to manipulate attitude or the single way a researcher measures behavior, both of which can be observed. Stated more generally, theories contain nonobservational terms (e.g., attitude and behavior), whereas empirical predictions contain observational terms (the essay and the single behavior measure can be observed). Another way to say the same thing, that will be convenient throughout this book, is to term the empirical prediction an *empirical hypothesis*. Using the new term, we could say that theories contain nonobservational terms, empirical hypotheses contain observational terms, and the hope is that the observational terms in the empirical hypothesis have something to do with the nonobservational terms in the theory. With respect to attitudes and behaviors, the hope is that the essay really does manipulate attitudes and that the measure of the extent to which people wear seatbelts really does measure behavior. To foreshadow, the issue of measurement will be the focus of Part II of this book.

Of course, the distinction between observational terms and nonobservational terms is an oversimplification because there are various degrees to which it is possible to observe entities. To illustrate, consider that germ theory includes the notion of germs, which could not be observed prior to the invention of microscopes, but could be, and were, observed afterwards. The extent to which germs should be considered nonobservational (because they cannot be observed directly) or observational (because they can be observed with microscopes) is not completely clear. Nevertheless, the ambiguity is not important for present purposes, though it will become important in subsequent chapters. For now, it is sufficient that terms in empirical hypotheses are more observational than terms in theories. Because it is awkward to speak in terms of entities being more observational, or less observational, I will continue to refer to theoretical terms as nonobservational and empirical terms as observational, but please keep on mind that these are relative terms.

Well, then, if theories contain nonobservational terms and empirical hypotheses contain observational terms, how do we traverse the distance from theories to empirical hypotheses? Obviously, something needs to be added to the system that connects nonobservational terms in theories to observational terms in empirical hypotheses. That entity is termed auxiliary assumptions.

Returning to attitudes and an essay designed to increase attitude positivity towards wearing seatbelts, why should we believe that the essay does that which it was designed to do? Let us consider two examples and your own intuitions.

For the first example, consider the following sentences that might be part of a larger essay.

> There is much evidence that wearing seatbelts can prevent injuries and can reduce the probability of being killed in a car accident. Statistics indicate that wearing seatbelts reduces the probability of injury in a car accident by more than 50%. Statistics also indicate that wearing seatbelts reduces the probability of death by 67%.

The second example is similar in form, but with an obvious change.

> There is much evidence that wearing hats can prevent injuries and can reduce the probability of being killed in a car accident. Statistics indicate that wearing hats reduces the probability of injury in a car accident by more than 50%. Statistics also indicate that wearing hats reduces the probability of death by 67%.

As you doubtless have noticed, the difference between the two essays is that the first one features wearing seatbelts whereas the second one features wearing hats. Both essays provide the same statistics, which I made up for the examples.

Which essay do you believe is more likely to influence attitudes towards wearing seatbelts? Probably, you would choose the first essay over the second essay. A reason is that the first essay features wearing seatbelts, which is relevant to attitudes towards wearing seatbelts, whereas the second essay features wearing hats, which is irrelevant to attitudes towards wearing seatbelts. Using more general language, the first essay includes the mention of the observational term of importance in the empirical hypothesis, but the second essay does not. Therefore, the first essay is more likely to change the relevant attitude than is the second essay. And we now arrive at an auxiliary assumption, that the first essay is relevant to the type of attitude we wish to manipulate but the second essay is not relevant to the type of attitude we wish to manipulate. It bears emphasis that the theory, itself, does not say anything about essays or about essay relevance; this is an assumption that we must add to the theory to arrive at the empirical hypothesis. It is an auxiliary assumption that connects the theoretical term—attitude—with the essay that can be observed.

Of course, the assumption of relevance is not the only auxiliary assumption. There are many more. To see this, let us return to the first essay and consider reasons why it might not work, despite its relevance. One potential problem is that people might not care about injury and death statistics, and if they do not care about these statistics, there is little reason for them to change their attitudes. Thus, another auxiliary assumption is that participants care about injury and death statistics.

Another potential problem might be that even if participants care about injury and death statistics, they might not believe that the statistics apply to them. Thus, even if the essay convinces participants that people ought to wear seatbelts, in general, that general prescription does not apply to them specifically. In turn, if the general prescription does not apply to them specifically, then they need not wear seatbelts. Thus, another auxiliary assumption is that participants will see the prescription in the essay as applying to them.

Worse yet, even if participants are convinced that they ought, themselves, to wear seatbelts, they might not be interested in doing what they ought to do. Their attitudes—what they like or dislike—might be completely uninfluenced by what they ought to do. Thus, yet another auxiliary assumption is that people's attitudes become consistent with what they feel they ought to do.

Finally, there are seeming trivial issues, such as the assumption that the researcher hands participants the correct forms. Or if the experiment is performed via computer or cellphone, that the program causes the correct forms to appear on participants' computer or cellphone screens. Obviously, if participants do not get the correct forms, the experiment is unlikely to be successful. An auxiliary assumption, though often an implicit one, is that participants get the correct forms.

We have seen that many auxiliary assumptions, often unstated, are necessary to connect nonobservational terms in theories with observational terms in empirical hypotheses. But that is not the only function auxiliary assumptions serve. Another function is that they set initial conditions. For example, consider that to perform the experiment properly, it is necessary to randomly assign participants to conditions. We will explore the statistical implications of random assignment in a subsequent chapter. For now, however, it is sufficient that random assignment provides reason to believe that the experimental and control conditions are approximately equivalent with respect to causally relevant factors. One of these might be initial attitudes towards wearing seatbelts. Although we would expect that different people would differ in their initial attitudes, we would at least hope that the mean initial attitudes in the two randomly assigned conditions would be approximately equal. If that is so, then the anticipated difference in mean seatbelt wearing between the two conditions, if obtained, could not reasonably be attributed to an initial difference in the two conditions. The assumption of initial equality increases our confidence that the anticipated effect, if obtained, is due to reading the essay versus not reading it. In contrast, suppose we were to doubt that the process of randomly assigning participants to conditions successfully induces an initial equivalence of mean attitudes in the two conditions. In that case, we would be wary of concluding that the anticipated effect, if obtained, would be due to reading the essay versus not reading it. Thus, although our focus will be more on the ability of auxiliary assumptions to bridge the gap between nonobservational terms in theories and observational terms in empirical hypotheses than on setting initial conditions, both matter and matter a lot.

Once we understand that empirical hypotheses come not just from theory, but from auxiliary assumptions too, a crucial implication is that Syllogism 2, the one that is used to justify the falsificationist program, is unsound despite being logically valid. To see why, consider this syllogism again, copied for you below.

Syllogism 2
If the theory is true, then the prediction should occur.   (Premise 1)
The prediction does not occur.   (Premise 2)
Therefore, the theory is not true.   (Conclusion)

Our understanding of the importance of auxiliary assumptions renders Premise 1, the major premise, untrue. Rather, the premise should be amended to say that if the theory is true and the auxiliary assumptions leading to the empirical hypothesis are true, then the prediction should occur. But once we amend Premise 1 accordingly, the conclusion no longer follows. Rather, the best we can conclude from a failed prediction is that either the theory is false or at least one auxiliary assumption is false. This is an immense distance away from what had seemed a definitive conclusion that the theory is false. In turn, if we cannot definitively conclude that the theory is false, then we cannot carry through the falsificationist program.

To nail down this point, let us rewrite Syllogism 2 with the amended Premise 1 and the amended conclusion.

Amended Syllogism 2 with Auxiliary Assumptions
If the theory is true and the auxiliary assumptions are true,
   then the prediction should occur. (Premise 1)
The prediction does not occur. (Premise 2)
Therefore, the theory is not true or at least one auxiliary
   assumption is not true. (Conclusion)

The good news about the amended Syllogism 2 is that it is logically valid; if Premise 1 and Premise 2 are true, then the conclusion must be true. However, the bad news, as we have seen, is that the conclusion is insufficient for falsificationist needs. To make the falsificationist program work, it is necessary to be able to falsify the theory so it can be replaced with a better theory. However, the conclusion is insufficient to falsify the theory because an auxiliary assumption could be to blame for the failed prediction.

Before saying more about the implications of auxiliary assumptions for falsification, it is worth inserting a quick note that auxiliary assumptions are a problem for verification as well as for falsification. Just as a failed prediction can be blamed either on the theory or on at least one auxiliary assumption, a successful prediction can be credited to either the theory or at least one auxiliary assumption (Trafimow, 2017a). An important consequence is that a successful prediction does not unambiguously support the theory because one or more powerful auxiliary assumptions might be responsible. Therefore, the necessity to have auxiliary assumptions renders absolute falsifiability (or absolute verifiability) impossible. The best we can do is talk about some sort of 'reasonable' falsifiability that would be limited by our confidence in the correctness of the relevant auxiliary assumptions. The impossibility of absolute proof, either way, is widely accepted (e.g., Duhem, 1954; Lakatos, 1978; Meehl, 1990; Trafimow, 2009).

We have seen that widening our discussion to include auxiliary assumptions, exemplified in the Amended Syllogism 2, creates a problem for the falsificationist program because there is now no way to unambiguously disprove theories. However, there is another problem that has not received much attention but may be equally or even more important. To see the problem, recall an earlier point that theories must be falsifiable, in principle, to be of scientific value. A theory that is not falsifiable cannot be eliminated to make room for, and be replaced by, another theory. An example of such a theory, as we saw earlier, is the creation theory, that God created the world.

However, an imaginative consideration of auxiliary assumptions suggests that we should, perhaps, rethink whether the creation theory is unfalsifiable. To set up the forthcoming argument, consider a common belief among scientists in the 1850s, that theories about the chemical composition of stars are unfalsifiable, in principle. Why? Because there is no way to travel to a star and gather samples of star material for chemical analysis. Soon after, however, the science of spectroscopy was invented, and it became possible to test theories about the chemical composition of stars based on the light stars emit. Moreover, the history of science is replete with similar examples of seemingly unfalsifiable theories that were later subjected to convincing experimental tests and were shown to be reasonably falsified (but not falsified absolutely because it could have been that one or more auxiliary assumptions were to blame).

Let us now return to the creation theory: God created the world. I will now argue that although the theory is currently unfalsifiable, it is not unfalsifiable in principle under the umbrella of reasonable falsifiability. To see this, imagine that a devotee invents a prayer that causes God to appear and answer questions truthfully. The devotee asks God the following question: "God, did you create the world?" God retorts: "Of course I did not create the world; if I had created the world, I would have done a much better job!" God's retort, if it were to happen, would falsify the creation theory. The falsification is not absolute because we can question various auxiliary assumptions, such as whether the being that answered the prayer really is God; whether the being, even if it really is God, wanted to avoid responsibility for having done a poor job with creation by denying having been responsible; and so on. Nevertheless, within the limits of the auxiliary assumptions, there would be some degree of reasonable falsification, and so the creation theory is reasonably falsifiable, despite the seeming impossibility of testing it. Hence, critics of the creation theory who claim it is not falsifiable, even in principle, are on shaky grounds. This is not to say that the creation theory is a good theory, but at least the falsifiability argument is insufficient for discrediting it.

There is a reason for having emphasized that the creation theory is falsifiable, in principle, despite many pronouncements that it is not. There is a fashion in psychology that ought to be changed. Inevitably, if a theory survives long enough, someone will declare it unfalsifiable. However, the creation example shows that it is practically impossible to have a theory that is unfalsifiable, in principle. This is because there is no way of knowing whether a clever scientist will invent the requisite auxiliary assumptions that allow the allegedly unfalsifiable theory to be subjected to convincing empirical testing. We saw this in physics with the example of theories of the chemical composition of stars. The invention of spectroscopy provided the necessary auxiliary assumptions to allow convincing (though not absolute) tests of theories of the chemical composition of stars. The creation example shows how, in principle, it is practically always possible to invent the requisite auxiliary assumptions to test theories under the rubric of reasonable falsification.

Psychology Examples of Unfalsifiable Theories that Were Falsified

There is one psychology theory that has been deemed unfalsifiable in more textbooks than any other, and that theory is Freud's psychodynamic theory (1955; 1959). Why is this theory alleged to be unfalsifiable? The answer is that Freud's stages of psychosexual development are replete with statements about unconscious processes that are typically pronounced untestable. After all, how do we know there even is an unconscious, and even if we did know that, how can we know what goes on there when there is no way for participants to tell us?

And yet, I was involved in what I consider a reasonably definitive test of this allegedly unfalsifiable theory. To understand the test, it is first necessary to understand something about psychosexual development, according to Freud (see Sarnoff, 1976, for an accessible description). Without going through all five of Freud's stages, the crucial point is that parents have much power over young children and much less power as children grow older, especially when they enter adolescence. And there are two reasons. The first reason is that very young children are at a severe disadvantage compared to their parents with respect to both physical and mental maturity. The second reason is that it takes time to develop effective defense mechanisms against one's own unconscious feelings of guilt that are tied to previous parental behavior. Young children have not had time to develop such defense mechanisms, whereas they are well developed by adolescence. Both because of the issue of development of physical and mental maturity, and because of the issue of development of defense mechanisms, young children should mostly do what their parents think they should do, whereas adolescents should be better able to do what they want to do. In social psychology terminology, the behavior of young children should be influenced mostly by subjective norms (what one thinks important others, such as parents, think they should do) and the behavior of adolescents should be influenced mostly by attitudes (what people like or want to do). I and some students and colleagues tested the idea by measuring children's attitudes, subjective norms, and behavioral intentions (what people intend to do) for thirty behaviors (Trafimow et al., 2002). If Freud is correct, subjective norms should best predict behavioral intentions for young children, whereas attitudes should best predict behavioral intentions for older children and adolescents. In contradiction to Freud, attitudes best predicted behavioral intentions no matter the age of the children, nor did the extent of the prediction depend on age. Thus, despite the vaunted impossibility, in principle, of testing Freud's theory, we not only tested it but falsified it too.

Another example concerns the theory of reasoned action (e.g., Fishbein, 1980). According to Greve (2001), the theory is not falsifiable. For example, Fishbein (1980) argued against separate cognitive (thinking) and affective (feeling) components of attitudes, thereby potentially rendering the theory unfalsifiable because of the lack of specification of the nature of attitudes. However, I and a colleague were nevertheless able to provide a strong test of the theory (Trafimow & Sheeran, 1998). We made an auxiliary assumption that it would be possible for participants to distinguish between cognitive and affective beliefs about the potential consequences of behaviors that cause attitudes. During attitude formation, cognitive beliefs are compared or contrasted, thereby resulting in the formation of a cognition about the behavior; and affective beliefs are compared or contrasted, thereby resulting in the formation of an affect about the behavior. The consequence of these processes is the formation of associations between cognitive beliefs and other cognitive beliefs, between affective beliefs and other affective beliefs, but not between cognitive and affective beliefs. Thus, the retrieval of a cognitive belief should stimulate the participant to follow an association to another cognitive belief, whereas the retrieval of an affective belief should stimulate the participant to follow an association to another affective belief. In contrast, because there is a lack of associations between cognitive and affective beliefs, it should be unlikely that a participant would retrieve an affective belief after a cognitive belief, or a cognitive belief after an affective belief. We tested this reasoning by simply having people write down their beliefs about behaviors and looking at the order of the retrieved items. If Fishbein is correct in assuming a lack of distinction between the two kinds of beliefs (or between cognition and affect), then the order of retrieval should be random. In contrast, according to our reasoning, because of the pattern of associations among the beliefs, retrieved items should exhibit a clustered order, where cognitive beliefs tend to be retrieved together and affective beliefs tend to be retrieved together. The data strongly supported the latter prediction, thereby falsifying the lack of distinction between cognition and affect assumed by the theory. Interestingly, a later version of the theory incorporated the distinction (Ajzen & Fishbein, 2005).

Thus, two examples of how psychology theories that had been evaluated as unfalsifiable, in principle, not only turned out to be falsifiable, but were falsified too. Of course, these successful falsifications were under the umbrella of reasonable falsification. There remains the possibility of a false auxiliary assumption, though nobody has suggested that (at least not yet). The larger lesson, though, is that practically every theory is reasonably falsifiable, though not falsifiable absolutely, provided one thing—and it is a very important thing. The proviso is that the researcher must be sufficiently creative to think of the necessary auxiliary assumptions that render a seemingly unfalsifiable theory falsifiable. If the required creative thinking is lacking, alleged unfalsifiable theories will remain unfalsified. And this will be a theme throughout the book. It is insufficient to "learn the methodological rules." Much more important than the rules themselves are the philosophical principles underlying them. A focus on the underlying philosophical principles, with critical evaluation concerning their soundness, can potentially increase creativity dramatically. In the end, creativity is the most important factor that contributes to research successes.

Chapter Summary

We commenced by considering the extent to which empirical testing provides good reason to believe theories verified or falsified. Commencing from the major premise, "If the theory is true, then the prediction should occur," we saw that it is logically valid to use failed empirical predictions to disconfirm theories (Syllogism 2), but it is logically invalid to use failed empirical predictions to confirm theories (Syllogism 1). Consequently, it is possible to argue that scientists should do that which is logically valid—namely, falsifying theories—and eschew that which is logically invalid (verifying theories). In turn, according to this falsificationist program, science progresses when scientists use empirical tests to falsify theories and replace those falsified theories with better ones.

However, we also discussed three arguments against the falsificationist program. According to Kuhnian incommensurability, theories cannot be contrasted against each other, thereby precluding sound empirical testing capable of distinguishing between them. If 'mass' has a different meaning for Einstein than for Newton, how can we test the two theories against each other and use the falsification of one to corroborate (but not prove) the other? There is an answer, however, which is that Kuhnian incommensurability at the theoretical level need not manifest at the empirical level. If researchers can agree on clock readings, distance measurements, and so on, they can determine whether the evidence is more consistent with one theory than another, even giving Kuhn incommensurability at the theoretical level. Thus, Kuhnian incommensurability, though not trivial, is insufficient to provide a strong challenge to the falsificationist program.

A greater challenge is provided by an explicit consideration of the importance of how the major premise is stated. Consider the first bullet-listed item below, where the major premise of Syllogism 2 is repeated, and the second bullet-listed item where it is changed.

- "If the theory is true, then the prediction should occur."
- "If the theory is not true, then the prediction should not occur."

There is no good prior reason why either of the bullet-listed premises is automatically superior to the other. And recognizing that both may have value implies an interesting quandary for researchers. As we saw earlier, the first bullet-listed major premise implies that theory falsification is more logical than theory verification; but the second bullet-listed major premise implies that theory verification is more logical than theory falsification. Thus, from a purely logical perspective, accompanied by a recognition that logic is limited by how the major premise is stated, there is no strong reason to prefer theory falsification to theory verification, or to prefer theory verification to theory falsification.

Finally, there is the issue of auxiliary assumptions. Theories contain observational terms whereas empirical hypotheses contain nonobservational terms. To traverse the distance from nonobservational terms in theories, to observational terms in empirical hypotheses, it is necessary to employ auxiliary assumptions. But the necessity to employ auxiliary assumptions entails consequences. One consequence is that the major premise must be changed to include auxiliary assumptions: "If the theory is true and the auxiliary assumptions are true, then the prediction should occur." Once the change is made, there is no way to know to know if a failed prediction should be blamed on the theory or whether it should be blamed on one or more auxiliary assumptions. This constitutes an important challenge to the falsificationist program. Likewise, if an empirical prediction is confirmed, it is unclear whether the empirical victory should be credited to the theory or to one or more auxiliary assumptions. Auxiliary assumptions can be problematic for falsifying or verifying theories.

A second consequence of admitting the importance of auxiliary assumptions is the difficulty in pronouncing unfalsified theories as being unfalsifiable, in principle. Empirical predictions depend on both theory and auxiliary assumptions. If sufficiently creative thinking is employed at the level of auxiliary assumptions, it is possible that theories previously deemed unfalsifiable may nevertheless be subjected to tough empirical testing. A hard science example was how the discovery of spectroscopy enabled strong empirical tests of theories of the chemical composition of stars that had been previously considered unfalsifiable. The creation example showed how even theories with reference to the supernatural (God) are falsifiable, in principle. And the examples of Freud's sociosexual stages and Fishbein's attitude theory provided psychology instances of how theories that had been pronounced unfalsifiable previously were nevertheless falsified upon the performance of sufficiently creative thinking at the level of auxiliary assumptions.

It seems appropriate to end this chapter by repeating the advice that what matters most in science is creativity. The foregoing material focused on creativity at the level of auxiliary assumptions, but there are other levels to be considered too, as you will see in future chapters. I still remember vividly a particular realization that I had had in graduate school that unfortunately was not taught explicitly in any graduate courses. The realization is the one explained in this chapter: auxiliary assumptions are crucial in the research process and strongly influence whether experiments succeed or fail. Once I made a strong effort to be as explicit as possible about auxiliary assumptions, and to consider alternative ones to those that are obvious, my ability to perform experiments that worked increased dramatically. I hope that the present chapter gives you the same happy experience.

Appendix on Definitions

For both Newton and Einstein, mass is a nonobservational term that should not be confused with weight, which is observational. To see that they are different, consider that the same object would have the same mass on Earth and Moon, but would have different weights. However, although Newton and Einstein agreed that mass is a nonobservational term, they disagreed on what mass means, though neither defined it. The lack of definitions may seem puzzling. After all, it seems obvious that scientists ought to define their terms. But the Nobel Laureate, Leon Lederman (1993), argued that Newton's famous equation, *force = mass · acceleration*, is the most important equation in the history of physics despite the lack of a definition of mass.

Furthermore, the great science philosopher, Carl Gustav Hempel (1965), argued that definitions are generally problematic. Here is the problem, applied to Newton's mass.

Suppose that Newton had defined mass. He would have had to have used another word. In turn, we could ask what that word means, which would require yet another word, and so on indefinitely. Alternatively, Newton could have defined mass by using other words in his equation. By simple algebraic manipulation, he could have defined mass as follows: *mass = force/acceleration*. But there is a problem here too, as defining each word in the equation, in terms of other words in the equation, is blatantly circular. The third option, and the option Newton chose (correctly in my opinion), was to treat mass as a primitive concept, without definition. However, the lack of a definition does not render mass meaningless. Terms in theories that are not defined gain meaning from the way they are used in the theories. Newton's theory and Einstein's theory use mass very differently, as the main text describes, so the term has meaning, but the meaning is different in each theory. The different meanings lead back to the main text, and the alleged incommensurability between Newton's use of mass and Einstein's use of mass.

2 The Reality underneath the Reality
Examples from the Hard Sciences

You doubtless have heard, on many occasions, that the social sciences are different from sciences such as physics, chemistry, and other so-called hard sciences. Some social scientists have an inferiority complex because successes in the social sciences are few and far between relative to successes in the hard sciences. The usual social science apology is that the subject matter in the social sciences is more difficult than in the hard sciences. Nothing is more difficult to study than aspects of the mind, such as attitudes, mental states, and so on which cannot be seen or touched, and so it is unfair to expect the social sciences to produce spectacular successes like the hard sciences do. Recognizing the greater difficulties that social scientists face necessitates that we "cut them a break."

Then, too, the apology goes, the hard sciences have *empirical laws* whereas the social sciences lack them. An empirical law might be something like: "Whatever comes up eventually comes down unless it has reached escape velocity." In the happy cases where scientists have empirical laws, they are then in a good position to theorize about possible causes. Thus, empirical laws could be argued a prerequisite for successful theories. Because the hard sciences have empirical laws, and the social sciences allegedly do not, of course researchers in the hard sciences have discovered better theories than researchers in the social sciences. As in the previous paragraph, the task is easier in the hard sciences than in the social sciences, so it is again necessary to cut social scientists a break.

The alleged greater difficulty of performing social science research, as opposed to performing research in the hard sciences, may seem ample reason for social science pessimism. However, it is possible to hold that the foregoing arguments imply a misunderstanding of the difficulty of performing research in the hard sciences. In turn, if the hard sciences are approximately as difficult to perform as the social sciences, the many successes in the hard sciences can be taken to imply that comparable successes in the social sciences are possible, after all. A searching review of some hard science successes may confer an added benefit. A typical social sciences argument is that the social sciences are concerned with *unobservable* entities whereas the hard sciences are concerned with *observable* ones. Therefore, again the social sciences are at a disadvantage and again we need to cut social scientists a break. On the contrary, however, as we saw to some degree in Chapter 1, theories in the hard sciences contain nonobservational terms (e.g., mass, not to be confused with weight), just as theories in the social sciences contain nonobservational terms (e.g., attitudes).

It is possible to be dramatic about this. Consider the state of physics for almost two millennia after Aristotle (384–322 BC). Progress in physics was very slow as researchers continued to believe that objects fall because it is in their nature to fall and that all planets orbit the Earth (not the Sun). It is not difficult to argue that progress in psychology over the last century, however slow compared to progress in the hard sciences in modern times, nevertheless was at least faster than in physics during the two millennia after Aristotle. Well, then, if progress in physics was so agonizingly slow for almost two millennia, but then snapped out of the malaise with an amazing spurt of progress that has continued and even accelerated for several subsequent centuries, perhaps psychology can do so too. An optimistic view might be that a century of slow progress is not nearly as bad as two millennia of slow progress, and so psychology has much less of a negative tradition of slow progress to overcome than physics had. With less negativity to overcome, psychology may be at an advantage compared to physics in the two millennia after Aristotle. Put in the form of a question, if physics was able to overcome two millennia of slow progress, why cannot psychology overcome a mere century of slow progress?

The obvious answer to the question is, again, that physics research is easier to conduct than is psychology research due to the alleged fact that physicists are concerned with observable entities and social scientists are concerned with unobservable entities. The following sections describe how natural philosophers (we call them physicists today) made spectacular progress despite not being able to observe crucial entities. The goal of these sections is not to be complete—they are far from that—but rather to render salient the importance of imagination in physics and particularly a willingness to probe underneath *commonsense perception* to find the reality underneath the reality. That is, the willingness to posit imaginary universes that are blatantly not real, to discover that which is more basic and perhaps even contradictory to commonsense perception.

The Shape of the Earth

Perhaps you can remember times when you could see for long distances without your view being blocked by buildings, mountains, and so on. Perhaps you were at sea and enjoyed a vista of seemingly unlimited ocean with the sky appearing to stretch downward to meet it in the distance. Or perhaps you were in a midwestern cornfield or prairie where the sky appeared to stretch downward to meet the distant expanse of land. It is no wonder that the book of Genesis speaks of a "firmament" dividing the waters of the Earth from the waters of the Heavens. Of course, today we know that outer space is not replete with water, nor that there is a firmament between the Earth and outer space. But nevertheless, the description in the book of Genesis accords well with commonsense perception. It is not surprising, then, that prior to the advances in science pertaining to the shape of the Earth, many people believed that the Earth was flat, perhaps a flat disk, and that if one sailed far enough there would be the risk of falling off the edge.

But let us attempt to move beyond commonsense perception. We might ask, as the ancient Greeks did, about what it is that holds up the Earth, under the assumption that the Earth is a flat disk. We might propose that the Earth is resting on the back of a giant turtle. However, this answer leads to a further question: "What holds up the giant turtle?" We might propose that the giant turtle is swimming in a giant ocean, but this leads to a further query about what holds up the giant ocean. As the ancient Greeks recognized, we could go on like this forever; we have the problem of an *infinite* series of questions and answers. And the ancient Greeks disliked such problems. Was there a way out?

There was. The ancient Greeks realized that a way out is to dispense with the assumption that the Earth is a flat disk, and instead assume that the Earth is a sphere. If we assume that the Earth is a sphere and define 'down' as towards the center of the Earth, we have solved the infinity problem. We need posit no outside entities to hold up the earth and so there is no need to keep querying, in turn, about that which holds up an infinite series of subsequent entities. Let us pause, for a moment, and marvel at the power of reason to correct commonsense perception. According to commonsense perception, the Earth is flat. But even lacking the benefit of pictures from cameras situated in outer space showing plainly that the Earth is not flat, the ingenious reasoning the ancient Greeks employed nevertheless made a strong case that the Earth is approximately spherical, not flat.

The ancient Greeks also used empirical evidence. For example, if the Earth is flat, a ship that sails into the distance should be visible until it sails too far away not to be visible. However, if the Earth is approximately spherical, then one would expect the hull to disappear first, and the sail to disappear later. Of course, the latter is what the ancient Greeks observed.

Then, too, if the Earth is flat, there is little reason to believe that the shadow that the Earth casts upon the Moon would be curved. In contrast, if the Earth is approximately spherical, then it would make sense that the shadow the Earth casts upon the Moon would be curved. In fact, the shadow the Earth casts upon the Moon is curved. Thus, the empirical evidence supports the evidence obtained using non commonsensical reason (theorizing), and the combination provides a strong case for believing the Earth is approximately spherical, not a flat disk.

Let us reconsider the shape of the Earth from the point of view of the psychology pessimism in the first few paragraphs of this chapter. We might ask the following bullet-listed questions.

- Was it possible to observe the shape of the Earth?
- Was there an empirical law to provide a basis for theorizing about the shape of the Earth?

The answer to both bullet-listed questions is a resounding "no." There was no way to observe the shape of the Earth. Nor was there any useful empirical law. In fact, at best, what we might consider the one existing empirical law is that the Earth appeared flat to everyone, but this empirical law pointed in the wrong direction. Remembering that the main reasons proffered why we need to cut social scientists a break is because of (a) the impossibility of observing the phenomena of interest (e.g., attitudes, mental states, or the mind more generally) and (b) the alleged lack of empirical laws, we see that the ancient Greeks were under precisely the same disadvantages as today's social scientists. Nevertheless, the ancient Greeks came out of it in fine style with respect to the shape of the Earth. Perhaps we need not cut social scientists a break after all!

The Circumference of the Earth

Imagine yourself living in the times of the ancient Greeks. You want to know how big the Earth is, but how can you measure it? In ancient times, there were no cellphones, no way to bounce radiation off different parts of the Earth to gain an idea of distances, no global positioning systems, nor was there a way to travel around the Earth to make measurements. The ancient Greeks were stuck. Or were they?

Eratosthenes (276–194 BC) had access to information about Syene and Alexandria (500 miles north of Syene) during the summer solstice. During the summer solstice, the Sun was almost directly overhead in Syene, but not in Alexandria. Hence, a stick thrust into the ground at Alexandria cast a shadow on the ground and it was possible to measure the angle of the shadow. Assuming that the Earth is a sphere (see previous section), Eratosthenes was able to use geometry to calculate the circumference of the Earth. That is, Eratosthenes knew how many miles (about 500) corresponded to how many degrees of angle that the shadow from the stick cast on the ground in Alexandria. Because the Earth is a sphere, it has 360 degrees. Thus, Eratosthenes merely had to ask if 500 miles (or rather the Greek equivalent to 500 miles) corresponds to the measured angle of the shadow cast by the stick in Alexandria, then how many miles corresponds to 360 degrees? He came up with approximately 25,000 miles, which is quite close to the truth. According to modern measurements, the circumference around the equator is a little over 24,902 miles. Eratosthenes scored a bullseye!

Let us again consider this advance in the context of the two main social science complaints, that social science entities of interest cannot be observed, and there is an alleged dearth of empirical laws. There was no way for Eratosthenes to observe the circumference of the Earth, nor were there clear empirical laws pertaining to the circumference of the Earth. Thus, according to the two main psychology apologies, Eratosthenes should have been stuck, but he nevertheless managed to unstick himself. As in the previous section, we see again that reasoning was better than commonsense perception. If Eratosthenes could do it, perhaps we can do it too.

Falling Objects

The shape and circumference of the Earth were warm-ups as the issue of falling objects is perhaps the most telling for psychology; consequently, this will be a long section. We might start with the ancient Greeks, in general, and with Aristotle, specifically. The ancient Greeks noticed, as it is easy to imagine everyone did, that heavy objects fall more quickly than do light objects. If you drop a heavy iron skillet and a light feather from the same height at the same time, the iron skillet will contact the ground before the feather does. Although the ancient Greeks did not perform formal experiments involving dropping objects of different weights from different heights, they nevertheless had what might be considered an empirical law: heavy objects fall more quickly than do light objects. Based on this empirical law, Aristotle theorized that the reason objects fall is because it is their nature to fall, and heavy objects have more of this nature than do light objects. It is differences in the amount of nature to fall—we can make up a word, 'fallingness'—that distinguishes how different objects fall. In psychology terms, fallingness would be a trait that objects have to more of a degree or to less of a degree. In fact, the great psychology researcher, Robert Wicklund (1941–2020), pointed out in his wonderful book, *Zero-variable theories and the psychology of the explainer* (1990), that Aristotle's theory is very much like personality theories today. Why do people behave the way they do? Because of the extent to which they possess the relevant trait. Returning to falling objects, why do objects fall the way they do? Because of the extent to which they possess the relevant trait of fallingness. It is worth emphasizing, here, that Aristotle's theory accorded well with commonsense perception.

Let us now skip ahead almost two thousand years, during which there was little progress on the issue of falling objects. Our hero is Galileo (1564–1642), who made advances on multiple fronts and is rightly regarded as one of the greatest scientists who ever lived. I especially recommend Galileo's classic: *Dialogue concerning the two chief world systems, Ptolemaic & Copernican* (1632/1953), with a foreword and annotations by Einstein (1879–1955). Despite Galileo's stature, few appreciate his innovative thinking about how to think. Galileo did not trust commonsense perception and he might even have thought about it as 'uneducated perception.' Reason is needed to correct how commonsense or uneducated perception could lead us astray. With respect to falling objects, for example, could it be that commonsense perception is not getting at the truth of what is really happening at a more basic level? To see the issue, let us return to what we learned in Chapter 1 about theories and auxiliary assumptions. We have seen that Aristotle proposed a trait theory of falling objects; an iron skillet will fall faster than a feather because the iron skillet has more fallingness than a feather. However, could it be that the iron skillet falls faster than the feather for some other reason? Possibly, the feather is more susceptible to air resistance, and that is why it falls more slowly than the iron skillet. Not because the feather lacks fallingness. Well, then, if the feather falls more slowly than the iron skillet, due to susceptibility to air resistance, then the observation fails to provide strong support for Aristotle's theory. Aristotle needs what might be considered a hidden auxiliary assumption, that objects do not differ in their susceptibility to air resistance. If the hidden auxiliary assumption is false—and today we know that it is—then our experience with falling objects fails to provide impressive support for Aristotle's trait theory of falling objects.

But we have only started to plumb heights of Galileo's brilliance. Galileo used the device of a thought experiment to make further progress. To perform the thought experiment, imagine a heavy object attached to a light object by a rope. These are dropped from the same height at the same time. According to Aristotle's theory, it is not clear what to predict. On the one hand, we might suppose that the slower falling speed of the lighter object would impede the normally greater falling speed of the heavier object, so that the combination of objects falls more slowly than the heavy object would by itself. Alternatively, we might consider that the weight of the heavy object plus the weight of the light object exceeds the weight of the heavy object alone. Thus, it is possible to consider both objects and the rope, together, as a single extremely heavy object. This extremely heavy object has more weight than the heavy object alone, more fallingness, and hence falling speed should exceed that of the heavy object alone. Based on Aristotelian thinking alone, there is no way to know what prediction to make, and Galileo saw this clearly.

Yet another way Galileo was brilliant is that he realized that the goal is not to describe the real world, but to uncover its underlying essences, the reality underneath the reality. The problem with the real world is that everything has multiple causes, and there is a necessity to distinguish that which is more basic from that which is less basic. As we have seen, the Earth's atmosphere influences the velocity with which falling objects descend, but Galileo felt that although this might be of practical importance, it is not of theoretical importance, and it would be desirable to think in terms of *idealized* objects not subject to this limitation.

Galileo came up with the unprecedented innovation of rolling balls of different weights down slightly inclined planes. Why slightly? For multiple reasons. One reason is that the effect of air resistance is reduced to triviality for slowly moving balls. Another reason is that having the balls move slowly made the speed of descent easier to measure, an important consideration given the imprecise time measurements that were available in Galileo's day. A third reason is that the angle of inclination could be varied, thereby providing Galileo the opportunity to relate angle of inclination and speed of descent. The punchline is that Galileo found that the weight of the balls had no discernable effect on speed of descent. A further punchline is that Galileo was able to establish an empirical law, fitting a simple equation, relating angle of inclination to speed of descent. Once Galileo had the law, it was easy to imagine free fall (90 degrees of inclination), and calculate what the speed of falling must be, even though there was no way for him to measure it directly (again, time measurement was too imprecise).

With Galileo's rolling balls experiments strongly disconfirming Aristotle's trait theory of falling objects, the door opened for Galileo to propose an alternative theory. Galileo proposed the principle of inertia which, stated briefly, is that objects in motion tend to remain in motion and objects at rest tend to remain at rest, unless acted on by an outside force. Newton later coopted this idea as his first law of motion. So, returning to falling objects, it is true that gravitational force is more relevant for heavier objects than for lighter objects, however, heavier objects also have more inertia and so it takes more force to make them fall faster. The two factors balance out exactly, thereby rendering falling speeds completely uninfluenced by the weight of objects. It is worth stressing that this is under ideal conditions where air resistance does not apply. It is also worth mentioning that although I remained with 'heavier' or 'lighter' objects to remain consistent with ancient Greek thinking, in terms of modern scientific thinking it would be better to use 'more mass' or 'less mass,' as mass is an enduring property of objects whereas weight changes depending on where one is doing the weighing. An object weighs less on top of a mountain, or on the Moon, than at sea level on Earth.

Let us consider the Galilean advance from the perspective of a typical psychology professor. In fact, imagine yourself telling your advisor that you want to form a theory using idealized people that are not influenced by real world causes in a variety of ways. Your advisor would probably consider you crazy and say something like the following: "Of course, you must theorize about real people in the real world. We are doing science, not fantasy." Perhaps some of the lack of progress in psychology is due to an insistence on focusing on commonsense or uneducated or apparent reality, instead of focusing on the reality underneath the reality. Had Galileo followed traditional psychology advice, he would not have theorized in the absence of air resistance, would not have performed his experiments rolling balls down slightly inclined planes, and would not have overturned almost 2000 years of Aristotelian dominance. Although air resistance is an undeniable and important aspect of reality on the Earth, it would have been a mistake for Galileo to allow it to disturb his elegant theorizing.

What's more, let us emphasize that Galileo was not able to observe an idealized universe sans air resistance, and his notion of inertia was no more directly observable than psychology notions such as attitude. If Galileo was able to succeed, despite these limitations, it is not clear why social science researchers cannot succeed either. Perhaps a problem is too much dogmatism about remaining with uneducated reality, and insufficient imagination with respect to idealized worlds. If social scientists were to embrace imagination, perhaps we too could be as innovative as Galileo. Instead of pessimism, let us be optimistic, but realistically so, keenly appreciating that out-of-the-box thinking is crucial for spectacular advances.

Galilean Relativity

The word, 'relativity,' is usually associated with Albert Einstein, who well deserves his place in the pantheon of all-time great scientists. However, in one way, Galileo beat him to the draw by several centuries. Again, Galileo succeeded by using his imagination.

Suppose you have a perfect ship that sails perfectly smoothly parallel to a coastline. Of course, such perfect ships do not exist, but there is no reason for us to be limited to observable and uneducated reality; we can imagine a perfect ship. Suppose Joe is standing high up near the top of the mast and drops an object. How does the object fall? Well, it falls straight down, or at least so it seems to Joe. Now, however, suppose that Sarah is standing on the coastline and with her excellent vision sees Joe drop the object. For Sarah, the object does not drop in a straight line, due to the motion of the ship. From Sarah's point of view, the object negotiates a curved path on its way to the deck of the ship. Why the difference? Returning to Joe, he is moving with the ship, and so the movement of the ship is irrelevant to him. Thus, for Joe, there is only one kind of motion to consider, which is the falling of the object. But from Sarah's perspective, the ship is moving (one kind of motion), and the object is falling (another kind of motion), and she sees the combination of the two kinds of motion.

So, who is right? Is it Joe or Sarah? Galileo's answer is that both are right (or wrong), depending on where you are standing. If you are standing high up on the mast of the ship, then Joe is right. But if you are standing on shore, then Sarah is right. Rightness is defined by where you are standing.

Why should you care? Consider the issue of whether the Sun orbits the Earth or whether the Earth orbits the Sun. The former view is the traditionally 'correct' view whereas the latter view was famously put forth by Copernicus (1473–1543). An important reason for disbelieving Copernicus, and going with the traditional view, was the seemingly unanswerable question: "If the Earth moves, why don't we feel it?" But Galilean relativity provides an answer to this seemingly unanswerable question. The reason we don't feel it is because we are moving with the Earth. Therefore, relative to us, the Earth is not moving. The Earth moves only if one takes an outside perspective, such as imagining being situated among the stars.

As in the other sections, let us consciously acknowledge that in Galileo's day, researchers did not have direct access to whether the Sun orbits the Earth or whether the Earth orbits the Sun. At that time, scientists could not observe orbits any more than modern psychologists can observe attitudes. Nevertheless, people such as Copernicus and Galileo made astounding progress. This was not by thinking in the same old ways, but with wild flights of fancy into the realms of imagination. If psychologists refuse to be imaginative, and even insist on throwing roadblocks in the way of those few psychologists who are, we should not cut them a break for failing to make impressive progress. Again, it is possible to be optimistic, and understand that out-of-the-box thinking is not only not a bad thing, but it is both desirable and required for the social sciences to have spectacular successes such as we have seen in the hard sciences.

Newton

Newton (1642–1726/27) provides another example of the benefits of investigating the reality underneath the reality. As explained earlier, he coopted Galileo's inertia as his first law. His second law is that the acceleration of an object depends on both the mass of the object and the amount of force applied. This is basically a restatement of the principle of inertia. The more massive an object, the more force it takes to induce it to accelerate to a desired extent. Finally, his third law is that every action is associated with an equal and opposite reaction. Sometimes the third law is stated in causal terms, that an action 'causes' an equal and opposite reaction. The reason I replaced 'causes' with 'is associated with' is because the usual expression seems to imply that first the action happens, and then the reaction happens. But this is not true. What Newton termed the action and reaction occur simultaneously. For example, when someone fires a gun, the bullet does not get fired first and then the gun recoils. Rather, the recoil is simultaneous with the emission of the bullet. The thing to note, thus far, is the tacit assumption of an idealized universe where, for example, there is no air resistance. Although the laws may seem rather dry at first, they are the product of Newton's imaginative flights of fancy. And we will see more along that line.

Now let us consider gravity. According to Newton, gravity is a function of both objects involved. When the proverbial apple falls to the ground, it is not just because the Earth attracts the apple, but because the apple attracts the Earth too. But why should you care about Newton's laws of motion and his notion of gravity?

Well, we saw earlier that Galilean relativity provides a compelling answer as to why we do not feel the Earth's movement. But it might not be clear why the planets orbit the Sun, or why the Moon orbits the Earth. One thing to note is that the natural tendency of an orbiting planet, if gravity were suddenly to cease existing, would be to continue to fly off in a straight path along a tangent to the orbit. The reason the planet does not do so is because gravity does not cease to exist, but rather continues to exist. Or, we can imagine, for a moment, that the planet's inertia could somehow cease to exist. In that case, the planet would fall into the Sun (well, and the Sun would be attracted to the planet too as we saw with the example of the apple and the Earth). Because gravity continues to exist and inertia continues to exist, these balance each other out so that the planet continues to orbit the Sun, though there is a complication.

Newton's thinking clarifies that, if we insist on being precise, the Moon does not orbit the Earth as we were taught in grade school. Rather, the Moon and the Earth both orbit the center of gravity of the Earth–Moon system (not worrying, for now, about the Sun or other planets). However, because the Earth is so much more massive than the Moon, that center of gravity happens to be within the volume of the Earth. A consequence is that the Earth itself undergoes a tiny orbit around that center of gravity. Thus, it appears that the Moon orbits the Earth and for most purposes this is a good enough approximation. However, it is not strictly true.

A similar statement could be made about how the planets orbit the Sun. Strictly speaking, they do not orbit the Sun. Rather, the planets and the Sun orbit the center of gravity of the solar system which, due to the extreme mass of the Sun, happens to reside within the volume of the Sun.

It is both fun and enlightening to consider the vast distances across which gravity works. There is the distance between the Moon and the Earth, between the planets and the Sun, and even between galaxies that are many thousands of light years apart. This can be construed as quite unreasonable. How is it that objects so far apart can affect each other? Some have considered gravity to be 'spooky' action at distances and even Newton was uncomfortable with it. Modern physicists have proposed that objects gravitationally attracted to each other do so by exchanging gravitons or gravity waves. It is too early to discern the ultimate utility of such ways around spooky action at distances.

Let us now contemplate Newton from a psychology perspective. Newton's thinking is replete with entities that cannot be observed. There is Galileo's inertia, mass (not to be confused with weight, which can be observed as Chapter 1 explained), and gravity, to name a few of them. Worse yet, there is spooky action at distances. That Newton was able to achieve so much, admittedly with the immense boost provided by Copernicus, Galileo, and others that predated him, might seem incredible given that Newton's theorizing is replete with nonobservational terms, the alleged bugaboo for the social sciences. If Newton was able to get it done, despite having to deal with entities that cannot be observed, social scientists might to be able to do it too. A proper understanding of the seemingly intractable problems the great physicists have faced, and the wild flights of fancy necessary to overcome these problems, suggests that we, too, can overcome the problem of unobservable entities provided that social science culture changes to render wildly creative thinking socially acceptable.

Social Science Thinking and the Real World

If you have performed research with a social science professor, the desire for a large effect of the manipulation on the dependent variable, a large correlation coefficient, a large variance-accounted-for value, and so on, has probably not escaped your notice. In later chapters I will formally define effect size, correlation coefficient, variance, and so on. For the present, informal characterizations are sufficient. In an experimental context, an effect size indexes the degree to which the manipulation influences scores on the dependent variable. A correlation coefficient indexes the extent to which scores on one variable can be predicted from scores on another variable. Variance provides an index of how scores differ, and researchers typically hope that variance in one variable—say, the dependent variable—can be accounted for by variance in another variable. The more variance one variable can account for in another variable, the better the support for whatever the researcher is proposing, at least under typical circumstances.

However, it is now time to temporize. On the one hand, it is true that impressive effect sizes, correlation coefficients, and variance-accounted-for values, all support that the researcher who hoped for such effects indeed got it right. On the other hand, the physics examples suggest that there is a larger sense in which this is not the right way to go. Consider again falling objects.

Let us pretend that a social science trained researcher wished to support the Aristotelian view that objects fall because it is in their nature to fall, and heavier objects have more of this nature (what we termed 'fallingness' earlier) than lighter objects. Suppose the researcher finds 100 objects at random, weighs them, and drops each of them from the height of 10 feet off the ground and measures the time it takes for each of them to contact the ground. The researcher uses a common statistical package to explore the extent to which object weight correlates with time to contact the ground. Doubtless, the researcher would find a substantial correlation and conclude that Aristotle's trait theory of falling objects is strongly supported. Or the researcher might calculate the variance in times to contact the ground and show that such variance is well accounted for by variance in object weights, again supporting Aristotle's theory. As an experimental alternative, the researcher might manipulate whether the objects are iron skillets or feathers and show that mean ground contact times are much faster for iron skillets than for feathers. Whether the researcher uses correlation coefficients, variance-accounted-for, or experimentally derived effect sizes does not matter. All these ways of performing empirical research will provide impressive support for Aristotle's theory, but not because Aristotle was right. Unfortunately, Aristotle's theory will only seem right because the lighter objects (e.g., feathers) are more susceptible to air resistance, not because lighter objects have less fallingness.

Worse yet, the results of all these research projects will strongly disconfirm Galileo, according to whom all objects should have equal ground contact times. And if an aficionado of Galileo tried to argue that all these studies were performed wrongly, and that it is necessary to depart from real world conditions by using Galileo's paradigm, a vacuum, or performing the studies in outer space, he or she might be subject to a strong retort:

> We are interested in the real world, not in a fantasy world. Instead of arguing with us based on a flight of fancy, you should accept the strength of our findings and the fact that we replicate so consistently. The Galilean theory you favor predicts no effects, we consistently get strong effects, and you need to get with the program!

Now, perhaps, you see why I took so much trouble over the physics examples. Our pretended Aristotelian studies, that all come out in favor of Aristotle, and the interpretation that this, in fact, is so, are subject to problems that social scientists rarely realize. One problem is that all the studies depend on an incorrect auxiliary assumption, though a tacit one, that air resistance is not a relevant factor. This error should be a strong hint to you that you should always pay careful attention to auxiliary assumptions, especially the tacit ones or ones that elicit wide agreement. Speaking from my own experience, when I had internalized, strongly, the importance of auxiliary assumptions, my own studies commenced working much better.

A second problem is the assumption that successful replication necessitates that a strong case has been made. This is not so. If all the replications, despite using different methodologies, nevertheless embrace the same wrong auxiliary assumption, even one million successful replications need not provide definitive evidence for the touted theory. I will say more about replications in Chapter 5. I have made this point in a journal article too and in greater detail (Trafimow, 2019b).

A third problem, and a crucial one despite its subtlety, is the insistence on remaining in the seeming real world. The professor who stated the quoted retort is guilty of focusing exclusively on commonsensical or uneducated perception, despite having a PhD degree. As explained earlier, it is necessary to look beyond commonsensical or uneducated perception, to the reality beyond the reality. And although the professor was sarcastic about flights of fancy, this is precisely what was needed, and what Galileo provided.

A fourth but related problem pertains to a decision that social science researchers ought to make but do not. To see this, suppose you were deciding about what to include in your theory of falling objects. Let us suppose that you know about (a) inertia and (b) air resistance. Both matter and matter a lot, and so you will get the strongest results by including both in your theory. This is the course of action that practically any social scientist would take, but it is nevertheless the wrong course of action. Galileo purposely included inertia in his theory and consciously decided not to include air resistance. And for good reason. Consider that inertia is always relevant; even if a falling objects study is performed in outer space, a vacuum, or a moon without an atmosphere, inertia continues to matter. In contrast, air resistance sometimes is not relevant, such as if the study is performed in outer space, a vacuum, or a moon without an atmosphere. Because inertia is always relevant, whereas air resistance is not always relevant, inertia should be included in the theory whereas air resistance should be relegated to the level of auxiliary assumptions. This is not to say that Galileo did not consider air resistance at all; on the contrary, he considered it carefully in devising his slightly inclined ramps. Rather, Galileo carefully distinguished between that which deserved to feature in the theory and that which did not. There are many things that matter but nevertheless do not deserve to be in the theory, a lesson that social scientists have yet to learn as they continue to cram everything that might matter into their theories.

To reinforce this last point, consider that Newton agreed with Galileo about not including air resistance in his theory, and he relegated this issue to the level of auxiliary assumptions too. And to this day, air resistance does not feature in any physics theories. This is not to say that air resistance is unimportant. It is extremely important for both practical accomplishments and even theory tests, which well justifies the attention devoted to it by engineers. But importance is not the issue, domain of relevance is. And to reiterate, inertia is always relevant and therefore deserves to be in the theory. Air resistance is not always relevant and therefore deserves relegation to the level of auxiliary assumptions. The lack of discussion in the social sciences about what deserves to be in the theory and what deserves to be relegated to the level of auxiliary assumptions exemplifies the profound degree to which social scientists have failed to think about this issue. If social scientists wish to enjoy the spectacular successes that litter the post-Galilean history of physics, they had best learn to distinguish that which should be included in their theories from that which should not.

Summary

We commenced by considering the typical social science apology, that social scientists are concerned with mental entities that cannot be observed. Because the physical sciences are allegedly concerned with that which can be observed, they have a strong advantage over social scientists and so it is not to be wondered at that progress is faster in the physical sciences than in the social sciences. However, when we looked more closely at spectacular physics advances concerning the shape and circumference of the Earth, falling objects, Galilean relativity, and Newton's laws and gravity, we saw that the great physicists faced challenges at least as difficult as those that social scientists face. In particular, the entities of concern, in each case, were every bit as unobservable as in the social sciences. For example, the circumference of the Earth was no more observable when Eratosthenes lived than an attitude is observable by a social psychologist today. Yet, the challenges were met and defeated, with resulting spectacular victories for the physical sciences.

Nor does recourse to empirical laws change the argument much. There were no relevant empirical laws to help determine the shape or circumference of the Earth in ancient Greek times. And when it comes to falling objects, the empirical law—heavy objects fall more quickly than do light objects—gave Galileo a head start all right, but in the wrong direction! There is no way to argue plausibly that Galileo was benefitted by any empirical laws other than the one he created relating angle of inclination to speed of descent. Therefore, an apology with recourse to empirical laws fails.

So, if the usual apologies fail to explain spectacular hard science advances, what does explain them? There may be more than one explanation. As we have seen, Galileo's and Newton's advances required imagining a simplified universe—an admittedly non-real universe—where issues such as air resistance were not at play. I stress that to have such a simplified universe, it is crucial to exclude much from the theory, even if that which is excluded matters greatly in the real universe, such as air resistance. It may seem counterintuitive to argue that the best way to understand the real universe is to go underneath it to an imaginary universe where many factors that are considerations in the real universe are rendered irrelevant in the imagined universe. And yet, that is what has worked in the hard sciences and, for the most part, that is a strategy that most social scientists are unwilling to embrace.

Another explanation might be that social scientists are too superficial at the philosophical level and pay insufficient attention to auxiliary assumptions. To render this point salient, we imagined social scientists performing studies to support the Aristotelian theory about falling objects and coming to poor conclusions based on social science research strategies. Specifically, it is easy to imagine that social science type correlation effect sizes, correlation coefficients, and variance-accounted-for would strongly support the Aristotelian theory. This is because air resistance would make these findings come out in a way that supports the Aristotelian theory even though it is wrong. The moral of that story is that a sophisticated examination of auxiliary assumptions, including, or perhaps especially, the tacit ones, is crucial for performing high-quality research that leads to spectacular advances.

Finally, I had one last goal in writing this chapter. Knowing the pressures that undergraduate students, and perhaps graduate students even more, are under to think in the ways you are told to think, the most important goal of this chapter is to help you resist those pressures. In short, the most important goal is to give you permission to think for yourself!

3   The TASI Taxonomy and Implications

In Chapter 1, we saw that theories contain nonobservational terms that refer to unobservable entities. Therefore, there is no way to test theories directly. In Chapter 2, we saw that this is just as much of a problem in the hard sciences as in the social sciences. In all sciences, the only way out is to add auxiliary assumptions (e.g., Duhem, 1954/1914; Lakatos, 1978; Quine, 1952). Thus, it is the theory plus auxiliary assumptions, and not just the theory itself, that leads to empirical hypotheses. The advantage of empirical hypotheses is that they contain observational terms that refer to entities that can be observed. Thus, if a theory, combined with auxiliary assumptions, results in an empirical hypothesis that pans out, that is a victory for the theory. Alternatively, if the empirical hypothesis does not pan out, that is a defeat for the theory. However, a crucial caveat is that an empirical victory can be credited to the auxiliary assumptions, rather than the theory, so it need not be definitive. Likewise, an empirical defeat can be blamed on the auxiliary assumptions, rather than the theory, so an empirical defeat need not be definitive either (Trafimow, 2017a). The examples in both previous chapters illustrate the interaction between theory and auxiliary assumptions, especially in physics. There will be one more quick illustration below, and then we will move to the social sciences. As shall become clear, the social sciences necessitate some complications.

Remaining, for the moment, in the tradition of Chapter 2, consider the comet that made Edmund Halley (1656–1742) famous and now bears his name. There had been historical records of comets that had appeared in previous times, and Halley's insight was that these might be reappearances of the same comet, rather than different comets. Based on Newton's theory (see Chapter 2) and auxiliary assumptions pertaining to the current position of the comet, the effects of gravitationally relevant astronomical bodies, and so on, Halley successfully predicted the approximate time of reappearance of the comet. For this empirical victory, the French astronomer, Nicolas-Louis de Lacaille (1713–1762) first named the comet in Halley's honor in 1759.

The episode of Halley's comet reinforces that Newton's theory, alone, was completely incapable of predicting the reappearance of the comet. This is because Newton's theory contains general principles, not specific information about any comets, or even about any planets. Newton's theory contains nonobservational terms. It required Halley's brilliance to figure out the high-quality auxiliary assumptions needed to reduce Newton's theory to a specific prediction about the comet. There are two morals to Edmund Halley's story. The first moral is that creativity can take place at more than one level: it can take place at the theoretical level (e.g., Newton) but it can also take place at the level of auxiliary assumptions (e.g., Halley). The second moral is that auxiliary assumptions really are required to gain the necessary level of specificity to render empirical predictions. However, we might ask two more questions:

- Is it possible that for some purposes, especially in the social sciences, even more specificity is required?
- If more specificity is required, how do we get it?

Statistical Assumptions: Going Beyond Theoretical and Auxiliary Assumptions

We are finally ready to switch to the social sciences, and the easiest way to proceed is with an illustrative example. There are various 'threat' theories of prejudice, and they have in common the assumption that feeling threatened by an outgroup increases prejudice against the outgroup. An example of such a threat theory is the one by Stephan and Stephan (2000). Clearly, 'threat' and 'prejudice' are nonobservational terms, and so there is no direct way to test the threat theory. However, it is possible to manipulate threat, and this could be accomplished in a variety of ways. One way would be to provide an essay that describes how members of the outgroup are stealing jobs from the ingroup. We could randomly assign participants to read the essay or not read the essay. Then there is the problem that prejudice cannot be observed any more than threat can, but we might address this by providing participants with a prejudice scale, say from –3 (extreme lack of prejudice) to +3 (extreme prejudice) (measurement issues will be discussed extensively in Part II of this book). The nice characteristic our essay and prejudice scale have is they are observable. We can read the essay and we can observe the check marks participants make on the prejudice scale. The empirical hypothesis, in this case, is not that threat causes prejudice. It is that being exposed to the essay or not influences scores on the observable scale. If this empirical hypothesis is verified, we hope to make the mental leap to asserting the theory that threat causes prejudice. Of course, in reducing threat to a particular essay that is hoped to be threatening, and in reducing prejudice to a particular scale that we hope measures prejudice, we are making auxiliary assumptions, even if tacitly. We assume that reading about an outgroup stealing jobs really does make participants feel threatened, and we assume that a check mark on the blank labelled '3' really does indicate more prejudice than a check mark on any of the other blanks in the prejudice scale. Then, too, there are countless other assumptions that the research assistant distributed the correct forms to the participants, the participants were able to read and understand the essay, the participants responded honestly, and so on. If any of these assumptions is incorrect, it is possible to assert that the experiment does not provide a fair test of the theory.

Suppose that we generously take all assumptions, both stated and tacit, as true. Does our generosity solve all our problems? Well, it depends. In the case of Halley's comet, where Halley made a one-off prediction, our generosity really does solve most problems for Halley, and it helps Newton too because Halley's spectacularly successful prediction provides a nice piece of support for the worth of Newton's theory. However, in the case of our prejudice experiment, we are not making a one-off prediction. We are making a more complicated prediction and it is necessary to see clearly exactly what the complications are.

Based on threat theory and auxiliary assumptions, we predicted that participants who receive the threat essay should have higher scores on the prejudice scale than should participants who do not receive the threat essay. At first glance, this seems quite clear. But appearances are deceiving. What do we mean when we say that prejudice scores in the essay condition should exceed prejudice scores in the no essay condition? Are we predicting that every score in the essay condition should exceed every score in the no essay condition? Probably, this is too extreme a prediction. But if we are not predicting that, then we must be predicting something else. For example, perhaps we wish to predict that the mean score in the essay condition should exceed the mean score in the no essay condition. This would be typical in the social sciences, but there are alternatives. Rather than predicting a difference in means, we might rather predict a difference in medians. It is possible that there would be a difference in means, but not a difference in medians, or the reverse. Given the information thus far provided, it is not clear whether we should trust a difference in means more than a difference in medians, or whether we should trust a difference in medians more than a difference in means. And matters can become yet more complex.

Statistical Interlude

Before continuing, it is necessary to explain some basic statistical concepts: mean, standard deviation, and skewness. You are probably used to calculating means to figure your grades. To do so, you add all the scores and divide by the number of scores. In mathematical notation, we might consider two expressions, one at the sample level and one at the population level. Much more will be said about populations in the next section and especially Chapter 4, but for now, it is sufficient to consider a sample subset of a larger number of cases, with the larger number of cases termed a population. Usually, it is not feasible to test whole populations and so we are

The TASI Taxonomy and Implications   33

forced to use subsets; that is, we are forced to use samples. Equation 1 formally defines the mean of a sample, and Equation 2 formally defines the mean of a population:

$$M = \frac{\sum_{i=1}^{n} x_i}{n}, \tag{3.1}$$

$$\mu = \frac{\sum_{i=1}^{n} x_i}{n}. \tag{3.2}$$

Let us take our time and make sure to understand the mathematical notation. The obvious difference between the two equations is that Equation 1 features an English letter, M whereas Equation 2 features a Greek letter μ (Mu). Usually, Greek letters are preferred for population parameters whereas this is not necessarily so for sample statistics. Thus, both equations tell us how to compute the mean, but Equation 1 tells us how to compute the sample mean (M) whereas Equation 2 tells us how to compute the population mean (μ).

Both equations include a denominator that features n. This refers to the number of scores. Finally, the most complex part of the equations is the expression in the numerator: $\sum_{i=1}^{n} x_i$. Each successive score is indexed by i (i would be 1, 2, ..., n), so that x_i is the score at a particular value for i (this would be $x_1, x_2, ..., x_n$) and the whole expression means that one takes the sum of the scores. For example, suppose the scores are test scores, and the first score is 90, the second score is 80, and the third score is 85. Thus, the first score, when $i = 1$, is 90; the second score, when $i = 2$, is 80; and the third score, when $i = 3$, is 85. Therefore, the sum is 90 + 80 + 85 = 255. And so, to finish the example, the mean of the three scores is as follows: $\frac{90+80+85}{3} = 85$. And, by the way, because the median is defined as the middle score, it would be 85 too in this example, though the median and mean will differ if scores are not symmetric.

The standard deviation is the square root of the variance, so let us discuss what we mean by variance. In Chapter 2, variance was loosely characterized in terms of scores differing, but now we will be formal. As we saw with means, there can be a sample variance and a population variance. However, unlike means, we need different formulas for the sample variance and population variance. This is because, for reasons described in most statistics textbooks, but too far afield to describe here, the sample variance does not provide the best possible estimate of the population variance, unless an adjustment is made (e.g., see Hays, 1994, for a description). In the case of means, of course, no adjustment is needed. Equation 3 renders the population variance:

$$\sigma^2 = \frac{\sum_{i=1}^{n} (x_i - \mu)^2}{n}. \tag{3.3}$$

The Greek letter σ (Sigma) denotes the standard deviation, so that σ^2 denotes the variance. And, as usual, n denotes the sample size. The complex part is, again, the numerator, where instead of summing individual scores, we are summing the differences between individual scores and the mean.

To remain with the example of three scores: 90, 80, and 85 (remembering that the mean is 85), the numerator now is as follows: $(90-85)^2 + (80-85)^2 + (85-85)^2 = 50$. Dividing by the denominator, which remains 3, we have the following: $\dfrac{(90-85)^2 + (80-85)^2 + (85-85)^2}{3} = \dfrac{50}{3} = 16.67$.

Why would we want to make this calculation? You may recall from Chapter 2 that it is useful to have a way of indexing how scores differ, so that we can see how well our touted manipulation or predictor variable accounts for those differences. But the numerator of Equation 3 allows us to be more precise than we were in Chapter 2 because it specifies that we are looking at how much each score deviates from the mean, and the summing those deviations. Thus, to be extremely precise, the variance is not quite about how much the scores differ from each other, but rather how much the scores differ from the mean.

You might find the squaring in the numerator of Equation 3 confusing; why use squares? There are multiple reasons, but the simplest one suffices for present purposes. Suppose that we do not use squares in the numerator of Equation 3, but instead simply take differences. Because there are three scores, there are three differences: $90-85 = 5$, $80-85 = -5$, $85-85 = 0$. Put more simply, the differences are 5, −5, and 0, and if we sum these, we get $5 - 5 + 0 = 0$. The problem is that the positive differences cancel out the negative differences, with the net result being zero. One way, though not the only way, to avoid this problem is to square the differences. Thus, a difference of 5 becomes a squared difference of 25, a difference of −5 becomes a squared difference of 25, and a difference of 0 becomes a squared difference of 0, and so the sum of the squared differences is $25 + 25 + 0 = 50$, as we saw a couple of paragraphs ago.

Why divide by n? For the same reason as when we calculated means. We want the average squared deviation from the mean, not the totality of squared deviations, and that is why we divide by n.

Finally, to get the standard deviation, it is merely necessary to find the square root of the variance. So, $\sigma = \sqrt{\sigma^2} = \sqrt{\dfrac{\sum_{i=1}^{n}(x_i - \mu)^2}{n}}$. To continue with the present example, where the variance is 16.67, the standard deviation is the square root of that, or $\sqrt{16.67} = 4.08$.

Thus far, we have imagined that the three scores compose the whole population of scores and so we were able to use Equation 3. But suppose that rather than composing the population, we had simply chosen the three scores randomly from the population of scores. In that case, we likely do not care about the three scores per se, rather, we care about the population of scores from which the sample of three scores was chosen. Hence, we only care about the three scores in our sample as a conduit to estimating the population variance and standard deviation. Unfortunately, if we were to use Equation 3 for this purpose, we would tend to underestimate the population variance. Equation 4 renders the sample variance that gives the best estimate of the unknown population variance:

$$s^2 = \dfrac{\sum_{i=1}^{n}(x_i - \mu)^2}{n-1}. \tag{3.4}$$

Equation 4 departs from Equation 3 in two important ways. First, because we are at the sample level, rather than at the population level, we use the English letter s instead of the Greek letter σ. Second, the denominator of Equation 4 features $n-1$ whereas the denominator for Equation

3 only features n. Using $n-1$ instead of n decreases the size of the denominator. And because dividing by a smaller number increases the size of the whole quantity, Equation 4 gives a larger variance than does Equation 3. Thus, Equation 3, though correct at the population level, underestimates the population variance if used on a sample of data. The upshot, then, is that Equation 3 should be used for populations whereas Equation 4 should be used for samples.

In turn, the sample standard deviation is not $\sigma = \sqrt{\sigma^2} = \sqrt{\dfrac{\sum_{i=1}^{n}(x_i - \mu)^2}{n}}$, as this is the population standard deviation. Rather the sample standard deviation is the square root of the sample variance, where we again use $n-1$ instead of n: $s = \sqrt{s^2} = \sqrt{\dfrac{\sum_{i=1}^{n}(x_i - \mu)^2}{n-1}}$.

The typical assumption is that distributions of scores are symmetric; that is, they differ similarly to the left of the mean and to the right of the mean. But distributions of scores need not be symmetric. They can be asymmetric, with a longer tail either on the left side of the mean or on the right side of the mean. Or to say this another way, distributions can be left-skewed or right-skewed. There is some debate about the best way to calculate sample skewness, and there is no need to get into the mathematical details here. What is necessary is to emphasize that it is possible to compute a skewness statistic and most statistical packages and even some spreadsheets will make the calculation easily. In addition, if the distribution is left skewed, the mean will be less than the median, whereas if the distribution if right skewed, the mean will exceed the median.

Why the Statistical Interlude?

Let us return to the point that researchers rarely care about sample statistics for their own sake. Rather, they care about sample statistics as a conduit to estimating population parameters that are unknown. For example, a sample mean is rarely interesting for its own sake but might be very useful if it provides a good estimate of the corresponding population mean. Similarly, a sample variance or standard deviation is rarely interesting for its own sake but might be very useful for providing good estimates of the corresponding population variance or standard deviation. The separate presentation of equations for computing population parameters versus sample statistics underscores the difference.

But another point needs to be made about populations. Although we generally do not know all the scores in a population, nor do we know the parameters, a consideration of population distributions is relevant to which sample statistics it would be desirable to calculate. To see this, consider that the typical assumption in the social sciences is that the population is normally distributed (bell shaped) or can be transformed thusly. Well, then, normal distributions have two parameters and—you guessed it—these are the population mean and population standard deviation. If you know that the population is normally distributed, and you know the population mean and population standard deviation, then you know everything there is to know about the distribution. Hence, it is not surprising that researchers tend to focus on means and standard deviations, as these are all one needs to know under the assumption of normality!

But hold on. I brought normally distributed populations into play under the excuse that most social science researchers assume normality. However, that most social science researchers assume normality need not indicate that it is a correct assumption. On the contrary, papers by Blanca et al. (2013), Ho and Yu (2015), and Micceri (1989) all provide a very strong case that very few distributions are normally distributed and that there is usually skewness, either to the left or to the right. If a distribution is skewed, then it may no longer be true that if one knows the mean and the standard deviation, one knows everything there is to know about it. For example, there is a family of distributions under the umbrella of skew normality, as Azzalini (2014) detailed in his complex mathematical analysis. It is convenient to talk about skew normal distributions because normal distributions are a small subset of the much larger set of skew normal distributions. In contrast to normal distributions, skew normal distributions have three parameters (not two), and none of them is the mean or standard deviation. Rather, the mean is replaced by a parameter called the 'location,' the standard deviation is replaced by a parameter called the 'scale,' and there is a third parameter called the 'shape' parameter. If the shape parameter equals zero, then the distribution is normally distributed, the location equals the mean, and the scale equals the standard deviation. Thus, the convenience of assuming normality should be clear. However, if the shape parameter does not equal zero, then the distribution is skew normally distributed, the location does not equal the mean, and the scale does not equal the standard deviation.

Why am I bothering you with skew normal distributions? Let us return to our experiment where participants are randomly assigned to read the threatening essay or not, and then everyone is measured on the prejudice scale. Prior to the statistical interlude, we asked the question: Given that participants in the essay condition are predicted to score higher on the prejudice scale than participants in the no essay condition, what do we mean when we talk about higher scores? To reiterate, we probably do not mean that all scores in the essay condition should exceed all scores in the no essay condition. The typical meaning is that the mean score should be higher in the essay than no essay condition. But the foregoing discussion indicates (a) that most distributions are skewed and (b) skew normal distributions have different parameters (location, scale, and shape) than the parameters of normal distributions (mean and standard deviation). Considering skew normal distributions opens the possibility that the prediction need not be that the mean in the essay condition should exceed the mean in the no essay condition. An alternative prediction could be that the location in the essay condition should exceed the location in the no essay condition. Furthermore, there are other distributions with yet other parameters, but there is no need to engage that complexity as skew normal distributions are sufficient to make the present point. And that point, to say it bluntly, is that it is necessary to make some sort of assumption about distributions to have a good reason to state the hypothesis in terms of means, medians, locations, or something else.

To really nail this down, let us put some values on the essay and no essay conditions. Suppose that the data in both conditions come not from normal distributions, but from skew normal distributions and suppose further that the skewness in the experimental condition is –0.10 and it is 0.10 in the control condition. These skewness values are so close to 0 that most researchers would characterize the data as approximately normal in both conditions if they bothered to look at skewness at all. In addition, suppose that mean prejudice is +2 in the experimental condition, +1 in the control condition, and the standard deviation is 2 in both conditions. Practically any social science researcher would conclude that the experiment worked. After all, the mean is half a standard deviation larger in the essay condition than in the no essay condition: $\frac{2-1}{2} = 0.5$.

However, running out the calculations for estimates of skew normal parameters, rather than normal parameters, gives the following estimated locations (see Trafimow, Wang, & Wang, 2019 for how to make the calculations): experimental condition (0.77) and control condition

(2.23). Notice that the effect is in the opposite direction from before. When we looked at means, we noticed that the mean was substantially larger in the essay condition than in the no essay condition, consistent with our prediction. However, when we look at locations, the location is substantially larger in the no essay condition than in the essay condition, in contradiction to our prediction. Looking at means, the substantive story is that the threatening essay does, indeed, cause higher scores on the prejudice scale, thereby supporting the theory that threat causes prejudice. But moving to locations, the substantive story is that the threatening essay decreases scores on the prejudice scale, thereby contradicting the theory and supporting an opposing theory that threat decreases prejudice. And all this because of a seemingly minute difference in skewness (0.1 versus –0.1) that almost all researchers would consider as not making a whit of difference.

To make sure you do not lose the big picture, let us summarize thus far. We start with theories. Assumptions in theories—that is, *theoretical assumptions*—have nonobservational terms. It is necessary to add *auxiliary assumptions* to traverse the distance from nonobservational theoretical terms to observational terms in empirical hypotheses. Auxiliary assumptions also can be useful for setting initial conditions (e.g., assessing the present location of Halley's comet in the interest of predicting when it will reappear). But in the present section, we have also seen that for most social science purposes, empirical hypotheses lack the specificity we need. For example, the empirical hypothesis that scores in the essay condition should exceed scores in the no essay condition could be cashed out through means, medians, locations, or other summary statistics. It is necessary to make further assumptions—called *statistical assumptions*—to reach the requisite level of specificity. An example, as we have seen, is assumptions about distribution shapes. It is through statistical assumptions that an empirical hypothesis can be further specified as a statistical hypothesis. As if all this is not enough, there is yet one more category of assumptions.

Inferential Assumptions

Doubtless you have heard of significance testing and you may even have calculated P-values in an introductory statistics class or methods class. But why perform a significance test?

To answer the question, let us return to our experiment randomly assigning participants to read a threatening essay or not, with measurement on our prejudice scale. Suppose that the mean in the essay group is 2.20 and the mean in the no essay group is 2.19. Obviously, these values are very close to each other, and the difference is small (2.20 – 2.19 = 0.01), though in the predicted direction. Could we say that the experiment strongly supports the statistical hypothesis, the empirical hypothesis, or the theory? The smallness of the difference might prompt a critic to complain that perhaps we just got lucky.

Nor does the concern only come up for true experiments. Suppose we performed a correlational study where we measure perceptions of threat and prejudice under the prediction that the two should be positively correlated (positively related to each other). In addition, suppose that the correlation coefficient we obtain is 0.01, which is not very different from 0.00, though the very small correlation coefficient is in the predicted direction. Again, an obvious rejoinder to our claim that the obtained correlation coefficient supports our thinking is that we just got lucky.

It is to counter the inconvenient alternative explanation of having gotten lucky that researchers perform significance tests. This is not to say that researchers ought to perform significance tests, only that they can do it. Although I will argue strenuously against significance tests in Chapter 4, for now let us pretend to favor them to clarify what *inferential assumptions* are and the necessity to make them.

Let us return to our threat-and-prejudice experiment and consider that one gets lucky or not relative to a population. Let us suppose that the population of threatened people really is more prejudiced than the population of not threatened people. In that case, getting a difference in the hypothesized direction would not be lucky; the sample data would reflect the true state-of-affairs at the population level. In contrast, if there is no difference between the two populations, then getting a difference in the hypothesized direction really would be due to our getting lucky. Thus, that which constitutes luck at the level of our sample is relative to the population. To attempt to decrease the plausibility of getting lucky as an alternative explanation, researchers pose inferential hypotheses with respect to populations, and it is worth emphasizing the contrast between statistical and inferential hypotheses.

For the sake of simplicity, let us go ahead and assume normal distributions for the essay condition and the no essay condition, though the assumption is almost certainly wrong. Our statistical hypothesis is that the mean in the essay group should exceed the mean in the no essay group. Our inferential hypothesis is that the mean in the essay group should exceed the mean in the no essay group. But these seem to be the same hypothesis! Am I pulling something on you?

Well, yes, I am pulling something on you because I neglected to tell you, when giving the hypotheses, that one of them concerns sample means, and the other concerns population means. Here is where symbols can really help. At the statistical level, the hypothesis is that the sample mean in the essay group should exceed the sample mean in the no essay group. In symbols, the statistical hypothesis is: $M_{essay} > M_{no\ essay}$. In contrast, the inferential hypothesis is that the population mean from which the essay condition was sampled exceeds the population mean from which the no essay condition was sampled. In symbols, the inferential hypothesis is: $\mu_{essay} > \mu_{no\ essay}$. So, you see that despite initial appearances, the two hypotheses differ with respect to whether they concern a difference in sample means or a difference in population means.

In significance testing, the typical practice is to propose a null hypothesis, that the population means either are not different, or differ by some stated value. For present purposes, it is sufficient to use a null hypothesis that the population means are not different. In symbols, the null hypothesis is: $\mu_{essay} = \mu_{no\ essay}$. Our goal in performing a significance test is to disconfirm the null hypothesis, so that we can support the alternative hypothesis. The underlying notion is that the two hypotheses cannot both be true, so if we can disconfirm one of them, we have better reason to believe the other. Thus, if it is not true that $\mu_{essay} = \mu_{no\ essay}$, then one of the following must be true: either $\mu_{essay} > \mu_{no\ essay}$ or $\mu_{essay} < \mu_{no\ essay}$. If the sample mean in the essay condition is reasonably larger than the mean in the no essay condition, and if the result is "statistically significant," then most researchers would draw the desired conclusion: $\mu_{essay} > \mu_{no\ essay}$.

But I have glossed over much. For example, what does it mean to obtain a statistically significant result? The procedure involves assuming that the null hypothesis is true, assuming many other things that will become clear presently, and making a calculation based on all those assumptions about the probability of the obtained test statistic, or a more extreme one. If that probability is below a threshold level, usually set at 0.05, then the researcher rejects the null hypothesis in favor of the touted hypothesis, and all seems well.

The issue of whether any of this is sensible will have to await Chapter 4. For now, what matters is to bring out the assumptions. For example, as has been well documented in the literature (Berk & Freedman, 2003; Hirschauer et al., 2020), practically all significance tests assume that the researcher has randomly selected from the population. This assumption is almost never true except perhaps in a very limited sense. If the researcher has randomly assigned participants to conditions, then it could be argued that the researcher has randomly selected one randomization from the population of potential ways participants could have been assigned to conditions. That said, however, most researchers wish to generalize to populations of people, not populations of potential randomizations, and such generalization would require random selection from a population of people, which is practically never the case. The assumption of random selection from a population is one of many inferential assumptions.

Then, too, in the section on statistical assumptions, we discussed assumptions about distributions as being statistical assumptions. As we are now on the section on inferential assumptions, it is worth emphasizing that assumptions about population distributions can be inferential assumptions too.

Summary

We have seen that there are theoretical assumptions that compose theories. In addition, there are auxiliary assumptions that traverse the distance between nonobservational terms in theories and observational terms in empirical hypotheses. Then, too, there are statistical assumptions that bring empirical hypotheses down to the desired level of specificity to enable researchers to posit statistical hypotheses. Finally, there are inferential assumptions that enable inferential hypotheses. Thus, there are four kinds of theories or hypotheses: theories, empirical hypotheses, statistical hypotheses, and inferential hypotheses. And there are four kinds of assumptions on which each is based: **T**heoretical assumptions, **A**uxiliary assumptions, **S**tatistical assumptions, and **I**nferential assumptions. Putting the boldfaced letters together renders TASI, or what will henceforth be termed the TASI taxonomy. The TASI taxonomy will come up again and again both here and in future chapters. So, if you feel your understanding is not completely firm, it would be worthwhile to re-read the foregoing content before continuing.

Internal and External Validity

The TASI taxonomy implies many items, some of which will be explored in future chapters. However, perhaps the most basic application is to the issues of internal and external validity. This would be a good place to fasten your mental seatbelt, because we are going to see that conventional internal and external validity wisdom is wrong (also see Trafimow, in press). Yet, let us commence with conventionality.

Researchers usually consider internal validity to reflect the degree to which one can be confident that the effect in an experiment is due to the alleged cause. Randomized control trials do well, here, because they maximize the difficulty in positing alternative explanations, thereby increasing confidence that the difference between conditions on the dependent variable really is due to the experimental manipulation. Vazire, Schiavone, and Bottesini (2022) summarized this conventional view by stating that internal validity is "the validity of causal inferences" (p. 165).

In contrast, Vazire et al. (2022) described external validity as follows:

> External validity is the validity of inferences about how the observed effect will generalize beyond the specific conditions of the study. This includes generalizations to other people (or populations of whatever unit was sampled, if not people), other stimuli, other operationalizations or research designs, and other settings or times.
>
> (p. 166)

Conventionally, it is obvious that internal and external validity are in tradeoff. To maximize internal validity, it is necessary to abstract phenomena of interest out of their social contexts to achieve experimental control. However, abstracting the phenomena of interest out of their social contexts necessarily decreases the extent to which researchers can expect experimental effects to generalize to those social contexts. Indeed, authorities across decades have pronounced various versions of what henceforth will be termed the 'Received View,' that procedures taken to maximize internal validity do so at the expense of external validity, and procedures taken to maximize external validity do so at the expense of internal validity. Lest you suspect I am exaggerating about the extent to which practically everyone accepts the Received View, consider the following quotations across decades.

- "Both types of criteria are obviously important, even though they are frequently at odds in that features increasing one may jeopardize the other" (Campbell & Stanley, 2015/1963, p. 5).
- "Many of the choices among alternatives within each domain involve trade-offs or dilemmas" (Brinberg & McGrath, 1985, p. 42).
- "It is a well-known methodological truism that in almost all cases there will be a trade-off between internal validity and external validity" (Cartwright, 2007, p. 220).
- "When designing experiments and interpreting findings, the tension between experimentation goals and validity becomes apparent: Experiments provide the most direct way for determining causal effects and test theories because they maximize control and internal validity by simplifying, isolating, and making tractable even the most complex phenomena (Manzi, 2012; Pearl & Mackenzie, 2018), but these concessions are made at the cost of reducing external validity or the generalizability of the findings" (Lin, Werner, & Inzlicht, 2021, p. 855).

Not surprisingly, the Received View has given rise to conventional advice for researchers. It is best to perform multiple studies, some with an emphasis on internal validity, recognizing that these will not have external validity, and some with an emphasis on external validity, recognizing that these will not have internal validity. It is the set of studies, not any single study, that confers both internal and external validity.

In my view, there is an alternative way to think about internal and external validity that suggests the Received View is incorrect and that the standard advice is plain bad advice. I will attempt to convince you of this in the following pages.

To commence, consider that there is another way to think about internal validity and external validity. As we have seen, the conventional view, what I will term the *Sense 1* view, is that internal validity concerns the ability to unambiguously deem the effect on the dependent variable as due to the independent variable. However, we can consider an alternative view that emanates from the TASI taxonomy emphasis on theories, termed the *Sense 2* view, that internal validity concerns the ability to unambiguously deem the effect on the dependent variable as due to having occurred for the theoretically correct reason. This may seem confusing. After all, if the effect on the dependent variable is due to the independent variable, isn't that the same thing as saying that the effect occurred for the theoretically correct reason?

To see why this is not necessarily so, consider again the threat-and-prejudice experiment. Let us suppose we perform the experiment, and it works—mean prejudice scores are higher in the essay condition than in the no essay condition. Let us further assume that the essay manipulation really does cause the effect on the prejudice scale. However, there remains a question: Does the essay manipulation cause the effect because of threat (the theoretically correct reason) or does the essay manipulation cause the effect for some other reason? For example, perhaps the reason the essay manipulation works is not because of threat, but because the negativity in the threatening essay causes participants to experience a mood change for the worse. In turn, it is the mood change rather than the threat that causes the effect on the prejudice scale.

Returning to Sense 1 internal validity versus Sense 2 internal validity, suppose that the mood change explanation is correct and the threat explanation incorrect. In that case, the effect remains due to the manipulation, so Sense 1 internal validity is achieved. However, the effect is not due to the theoretically correct reason (threat), but rather it is due to a theoretically incorrect reason (mood change). Therefore, there is no Sense 2 internal validity. The experiment has achieved Sense 1 internal validity but has not achieved Sense 2 internal validity.

Let us now move on to Sense 1 and Sense 2 external validity. The Sense 1 view of external validity is the conventional view that external validity concerns generalizing the study finding. In contrast, the Sense 2 view of external validity, again consistent with the TASI taxonomy emphasis on theory, is that external validity is achieved when the theory, not necessarily the finding, generalizes. To see the difference, imagine two versions of the threat-and-prejudice experiment, one in the United States and one in China. Let us suppose that the experiment works in the United States, and suppose it works for the right theoretical reason too, so there is both Sense 1 and Sense 2 internal validity. Now, suppose it works in China too, but for a different theoretical reason such as mood change rather than threat. In this case, there would be Sense 1 external validity because the effect generalizes, but there would be a lack of Sense 2 external validity, because the effect generalizes for the wrong theoretical reason.

Or suppose that the effect does not generalize when the experiment is performed in China, because that which induces threat in the United States does not induce threat in China. A different way to manipulate threat is necessary in China. Imagine that, in addition to the experiment failing when performed in China, an additional experiment, with a culturally appropriate threat manipulation, does work in China. In that case, we have Sense 1 external invalidity because the original experiment does not work in China. However, the reason for the Sense 1 external invalidity is not that the theory is wrong. It is because of a problem with the auxiliary assumption level of the TASI taxonomy: the threat essay fails to induce feelings of threat in China. Hence, the experiment fails to bear on Sense 2 external validity due to its failure to provide a proper test of the theory. However, to reiterate, the second experiment in China, where the essay is changed to adopt to the cultural difference so that it really does induce threat, works. The fact of this second experiment in China working supports Sense 2 external validity. In addition, however, it is possible to argue that the failed experiment in China also supports Sense 2 external validity. How so? Consider that one would not expect the theory to predict correctly when combined with one or more faulty auxiliary assumptions. Because the failed experiment is based on a faulty auxiliary assumption, that the original essay increases feelings of threat in China, the lack of a result is consistent with enlightened expectations. As experiments can fail for many reasons, the failure, by itself, can be considered quite weak support for Sense 2 external validity. However, when this failure—when failure would be expected—is combined with the success—when success would be expected—in the second experiment conducted in China, the combination can be considered reasonably strong support for Sense 2 external validity. To reiterate with fewer words, failure when expected, combined with success when expected, provides a reasonably strong case that the theory generalizes. Social science researchers often fail to understand that it is possible to turn Sense 1 external validity failures into Sense 2 external validity successes.

Now that we have Sense 2 internal and external validity to contrast against Sense 1 (conventional) internal and external validity, what are the implications for the Received View? The proper answer involves proceeding through the TASI taxonomy but, before we do that, let us consider a preliminary argument. Suppose we know that the effect in an experiment is because of the theoretically correct reason, that is, we have Sense 2 internal validity. Our confidence that the theory is correct should increase accordingly. In turn, our increased confidence in the theory ought to increase our confidence that the theory, though not necessarily the finding, should generalize. Hence, although the Received View has something to it with respect to Sense 1 internal validity and Sense 1 external validity, it is dead wrong with respect to Sense 2 internal validity and Sense 2 external validity. And we can go in the opposite direction too. Suppose we know that a theory generalizes (Sense 2 external validity). That increases our confidence that we have the theory right to begin with; if the theory is wrong to begin with, it would be less likely to generalize. To state the point in general terms, rather than internal and external validity being in tradeoff, as the Received View states, they go together provided we are talking about Sense 2 internal validity and Sense 2 external validity.

Why should you prefer Sense 2 internal and external validity to Sense 1 internal and external validity? The reason hearkens back to why social scientists are conducting their studies in the first place; the goal is to test the theory. Because the goal is to test the theory, we do not care about Sense 1 internal and external validity if we can have Sense 2 internal and external validity. My point is not that Sense 1 validities do not matter at all, only that the reason they matter—to the extent that they do—is because of their potential to aid in achieving Sense 2 validities. For example, although it is more valuable to know that an effect is for the theoretically correct reason (Sense 2 internal validity) than to know it is because of the manipulation (Sense 1 internal validity), our ability to attribute the effect to the manipulation may aid in ultimately attributing the effect to the theoretically correct reason. Still, however, what we really want is Sense 2 validities much more than Sense 1 validities.

A caveat might concern so-called atheoretical research. Obviously, if there is no theory, Sense 2 internal and external validity are out of the question. I will address this in Chapter 4. For now, though, let us not lose our focus on basic research where the goal is to test theories.

The argument becomes more specific as we proceed through the TASI taxonomy. Let us first consider the combination of theory and auxiliary assumptions. Suppose we had certain knowledge that all auxiliary assumptions are correct. In that case, if the experiment works, we have better reason to be confident that the experiment works for the theoretically correct reason too and, ultimately, better reason to believe the theory. In turn, we would have better reason to believe that the theory generalizes as well. We have already seen all this illustrated by the threat-and-prejudice example.

It is useful to consider another example. The theory of reasoned action (e.g., Ajzen & Fishbein, 1980; Fishbein, 1980; Fishbein & Ajzen, 1975), with later versions being the theory of planned behavior (e.g., Ajzen, 1988), or reasoned action approach (Fishbein & Ajzen, 2010), states that people's attitudes towards their performing behaviors cause corresponding intentions to perform them. The theory states many other items too, but for present purposes, the simplified version is sufficient. In a typical theory of reasoned action study, a researcher might obtain a correlation between attitudes and intentions with respect to, say, wearing seatbelts. This finding is weak from a Sense 1 and Sense 2 internal validity perspective, because correlation coefficients can be explained in many ways. One explanation would be the preferred one, that the correlation between attitudes and intentions is because attitudes cause intentions. However, an alternative is that intentions cause attitudes. Finally, there could be something else, not considered in the study, that causes both attitudes and intentions.

Do matters improve from an external validity perspective? It depends. From a Sense 1 external validity perspective, the finding might or might not replicate in other contexts of interest. If not,

Sense 1 external validity is weakened but if so, Sense 1 external validity is strengthened. From a Sense 2 external validity perspective, there is a problem no matter whether the finding replicates in other contexts because there is so little evidence that the effect—whether in the original or replication study—is for the theoretically correct reason (attitudes cause intentions). Thus, we see that if Sense 2 internal validity is weak, so is Sense 2 external validity.

Or suppose a stronger research paradigm is used, so that participants are randomly assigned to a pro-seatbelt essay condition or not. And suppose we have good reason to believe that the manipulation really does influence attitudes, and not other causally relevant constructs. In this case, both Sense 1 and Sense 2 internal validity would be strengthened. But what about external validity? Let us imagine a situation not too different from the threat-and-prejudice example. Suppose a replication attempt in a different culture does not work. This would be immediately problematic for Sense 1 external validity. However, it need not be problematic for Sense 2 external validity if there is reason to believe the manipulation inappropriate for the different culture. This would be especially so if a culturally appropriate manipulation were to work for the different culture. In that case, Sense 1 external invalidity would remain because the finding still fails to replicate in the different culture, but Sense 2 external validity would be supported as there would be good reason to believe that the theory generalizes to the different culture. As we saw before, although Sense 1 internal and external validity may be in tradeoff, as the Received View stipulates, Sense 2 internal and external validity are in unison. When Sense 2 internal or external validity is weak, either weakness renders the other weaker too, but when Sense 2 internal or external validity is strong, that strength tends to render the other stronger too. In contrast to the Received View, Sense 2 internal and external validity tend to be in unison.

Let us now move to the level of statistical assumptions. We have already seen, using the threat-and-prejudice example, that most researchers assume normality and consequently focus on means, when they could assume skew normality, and focus on locations. If the difference in means and the difference in locations are in the same direction, this is not so large a problem. But if the difference in means and the difference in locations are in opposing direction, there is a large problem because the two types of differences indicate opposing substantive stories. In the threat-and-prejudice example, we saw that a difference in means could support that threat causes prejudice while a simultaneous difference in locations supports that threat decreases prejudice. However, that discussion did not consider Sense 1 internal or external validity nor Sense 2 internal or external validity. So, let us now have that discussion.

From a Sense 1 internal validity perspective, that the difference in means and the difference in locations are in opposite directions need not be a problem. Either way, and even if the differences support opposite substantive stories, there is little doubt that the differences are due to the manipulation. Thus, we have good Sense 1 internal validity. From a Sense 2 internal validity perspective, of course, there is a large problem. And it is worth taking our time to understand the problem in its entirety.

It is useful to again consider the empirical hypothesis that the threatening essay is supposed to increase prejudice against the outgroup. But what does that mean exactly? For most researchers, at the statistical level, the idea would be that the threatening essay causes the distribution in the essay condition to shift in the positive direction relative to the distribution in the no essay condition. Well, then, if the shapes of the two distributions are different, as the skewness difference (skewness equals -0.1 versus 0.1 in the essay and no essay conditions) indicates, an alternative explanation is that the threat manipulation works by inducing a change in distribution shape, not by inducing change in distribution location. Thus, there is a serious Sense 2 internal validity problem. Moreover, the location data (0.77 versus 2.23 in the essay and no essay conditions) also suggest a plausible alternative explanation, that the threat manipulation decreases prejudice rather than increases prejudice.

Suppose we replicate the study in another culture. Even if the replication attempt succeeds, although that would support Sense 1 external validity, it would not support Sense 2 external validity because of the lack of clarity that the effect occurs—in either culture—for the theoretically correct reason (threat causes prejudice). As an alternative scenario, suppose that the researcher is sufficiently sophisticated to realize that she ought to use locations, rather than, or in addition to, means. And suppose the difference in locations is in the hypothesized direction. This would support Sense 2 internal validity, and it would also provide a good reason to be hopeful that the theory might generalize to another culture. In turn, if the location difference successfully replicates in the other culture, that would support Sense 2 external validity. In fact, even if the replication attempt fails in the other culture, due to a culturally inappropriate threatening essay, the failure can be turned into a Sense 2 external validity win by showing that a culturally appropriate threatening essay does influence the difference in locations in the predicted direction. Again, we see that Sense 2 internal and external validity go well together.

Finally, let us consider the inferential level and inferential assumptions. To set up the surprising conclusion to which we will come, imagine that Laplace's demon, who knows everything and always tells the truth, appears to give us a dire warning. The demon tells us that all our sample statistics have nothing, whatsoever, to do with corresponding population parameters. Thus, sample means say nothing about corresponding population means, sample correlation coefficients say nothing about corresponding population coefficients, and so on. In that case, several unpleasant items would follow. One of these is that there would be no reason to expect our studies to replicate. Another is that we would be able to make zero sound statements about populations based on our samples. A third, and this will be the present focus, is that we would not be able trust our data as providing sound tests of hypotheses. Once this is acknowledged, Sense 2 internal or external validity would be out of the question. Now, consider conventional wisdom that internal validity is a prerequisite for external validity because if the effect cannot be attributed to the alleged cause (Sense 1 internal validity), it does not matter whether the effect generalizes (Sense 1 external validity). However, Laplace's demon reverses this conventional wisdom. It is precisely our inability to generalize to the population that renders tests of hypotheses impossible. And without tests of hypotheses, little progress can be made for confirming or disconfirming theories. Stated again, the ability to generalize to populations is a necessity for testing hypotheses and drawing conclusions about theories. We will revisit this point multiple times in future chapters.

Fortunately for us, Laplace's demon does not exist. We often do have reason to believe that our sample statistics have something to do with corresponding population parameters, and so we are sometimes justified in generalizing to populations. This issue will be discussed more in later chapters and will feature strongly in Chapter 6. If we can generalize to populations, then we have some reason to believe that our data provide reasonable tests of hypotheses and, by implication, there is some reason to draw conclusions about theories. The ability to generalize to the population provides better reason to believe that the sample effect we get is due to the manipulation and is for the correct theoretical reason. In turn, better reason to believe that the sample effect is for the correct theoretical reason promotes optimism that the theory would work in other contexts too.

The necessity to be able to generalize from sample statistics to corresponding population parameters reverses a truism that internal validity is a prerequisite for external validity. We now see that it is possible to argue in the reverse direction too, that external validity—generalizing to populations—is a prerequisite for internal validity—soundly attributing findings to theoretically correct reasons.

Conclusion

In summary, the Received View is that the factors that promote internal validity militate against external validity, and the factors that promote external validity militate against internal validity. It follows that internal and external validity are in tradeoff; maximizing either occurs at the cost of the other. However, the present position is that the Received View is only correct if we limit ourselves to Sense 1 internal and external validity. If we emphasize Sense 2 internal and external validity, as we ought to do because the point of basic social science research is to draw conclusions about theories, then internal and external validity are in unison. Increasing either increases the other, too. Thus, from a Sense 2 perspective, the Received View is dead wrong.

In turn, the wrongness of the Received View is problematic for conventional advice to social science researchers. According to conventional advice, social science researchers should perform some studies to maximize internal validity, knowing that these studies will have poor external validity, and perform other studies to maximize external validity, knowing that these studies will have poor internal validity. The hope is that the internal validity studies will support internal validity, the external validity studies will support external validity, and so the multiple studies will support both internal validity and external validity. However, all of this assumes a Sense 1 validity perspective. From a Sense 2 validity perspective, where we care about the theory, explicitly, a fatal problem for conventional advice is that none of the studies will provide strong support for the theory. This is because, as we have seen, Sense 2 internal and external validity act in unison. Doing well with respect to Sense 2 internal validity bolsters Sense 2 external validity and doing well with respect to Sense 2 external validity bolsters Sense 2 internal validity. Or, doing poorly with respect to Sense 2 internal or external validity weakens the other as well, an objectionable state-of-affairs that the standard advice promotes. From a Sense 2 validity perspective, following conventional wisdom will merely result in the researcher having invested enormous effort and resources to conduct multiple studies, with the collection of studies nevertheless failing to provide a strong case for Sense 2 internal and external validity.

This is not to say that researchers should not perform multiple studies. They should perform multiple studies, but not to have separate tests of internal and external validity. Rather multiple studies provide opportunities to try out different auxiliary, statistical, or inferential assumptions, that is, to try out different ways to negotiate the TASI taxonomy. If different constellations of assumptions across the TASI taxonomy all support the theory, then the theory is on stronger ground. These would be auspicious constellations of assumptions. However, it might turn out that the various constellations of assumptions across the TASI taxonomy militate against the theory, which would provide good reasons to question it. Yet again, it might be that some constellations of assumptions across the TASI taxonomy will support the theory whereas other constellations of assumptions across the TASI taxonomy will disconfirm the theory. Such mixed findings should stimulate the researcher to carefully question the theory, the auxiliary assumptions, the statistical assumptions, and the inferential assumptions. This likely will require the researcher to perform much mental toggling across levels of the TASI taxonomy.

Finally, to end on a positive note, another advantage of mentally toggling across the TASI taxonomy is the possibility of increasing creativity. Standard views tend to focus on researchers starting with a theory, and then making deductions about expected findings. Although this sometimes happens, there is the obvious issue of how one comes up with a theory in the first place. Although there are many roads to theory, one of them is to consider many possible auxiliary, statistical, or inferential assumptions, and see if these imply anything about what material to include in the theory.

Chapter Summary

Chapter 1 explained that predictions come not only from theories, but from auxiliary assumptions too. However, the present chapter illustrated that, even with auxiliary assumptions, there is insufficient specificity for testing social science theories. To gain the required specificity, it is necessary to include statistical assumptions and inferential assumptions too. Thus, with categories of Theoretical, Auxiliary, Statistical, and Inferential assumptions, we have the TASI taxonomy.

Although the TASI taxonomy can be useful in many ways, one of these is to shed light on the crucial issue of internal and external validity. The Received View is that internal and external validity are in tradeoff, but the Received View depends on a Sense 1 conceptualization of internal and external validity. In contrast, if we switch to a Sense 2 conceptualization of internal and external validity, then not only is the Received View dead wrong, but internal and external validity function in unison. In turn, once we are no longer encumbered by the Received View, it becomes clear that the standard advice, to perform separate internal and external validity studies, is bad advice. A better research strategy is to perform multiple studies to explore different ways of negotiating the TASI taxonomy. The pattern of successes and failures can be used to correct not just the theory, but problems at all levels of assumptions. By continual mental toggling across the levels of the TASI taxonomy, researchers should be better able to discover auspicious constellations of assumptions.

4 Why We Should Not Engage Null Hypothesis Significance Testing

Null hypothesis significance testing (hereafter, NHST) has dominated the social sciences. And there are seemingly good reasons. As we discussed in Chapter 3, researchers wish to test hypotheses en route to drawing conclusions about theories and they wish to reduce the plausibility of "getting lucky" as an alternative explanation. The typical belief has been that if a researcher obtains a small P-value, that is, a P-value below threshold (usually set at 0.05), then getting lucky can be ruled out as a plausible alternative explanation. Therefore, it seemingly makes sense to perform NHST. Who would not want to rule out getting lucky as an alternative explanation?

Although our focus has been on basic research with the goal of testing theories, we can take an applied research perspective too. Although some applied research is closely tied to theory, some applied research is not. An interesting philosophical argument could be had about whether ostensibly atheoretical research is nevertheless tied to an implicit theory, so that there really is no such thing as truly atheoretical research. There will be no attempt to address that issue here. For present purposes, let us go ahead and assume there really is atheoretical research. However, even here, researchers would like to eliminate getting lucky as a plausible alternative explanation and so, again, NHST has dominated.

Despite NHST dominance for perhaps a century, there has been a recent movement against it. Interestingly, there have been arguments against it for about a century too, but these arguments have failed to seriously dent NHST. This includes an argument of mine that I had published in 2003, that failed just as miserably to cause change as all the previous attempts (Trafimow, 2003). Now, however, change is in the air. A recent editorial of mine (with Michael Marks) in 2015 kickstarted the change by banning significance testing from a social psychology journal I edited (and still edit), *Basic and Applied Social Psychology*. With the NHST ban as official journal policy, the problems with NHST could no longer be ignored and now there is an extremely lively debate about it. What's more, there is a scattering of journals in various areas of science that have changed their statistical policies since the ban in 2015. So, the obvious question is: "Why is NHST, that seems so obviously useful, so bad?" The answer is complex because different researchers have different, and sometimes contradictory, arguments about NHST.

The *Modus Tollens* Error

As Nickerson (2000) suggested in his careful review (also see Cohen, 1994), a typical belief is that a small P-value indicates the null hypothesis is unlikely to be true. As researchers wish to reject null hypotheses in favor of touted alternative hypotheses, no wonder NHST has been so fashionable! But is the belief true? Let us take our time and go through the logic carefully.

Let us commence with describing typical reasoning about P-values. You may recall computing test statistics (such as t, F, etc.) in your introductory statistics course, en route to obtaining a P-value. The hope was that the test statistic would be large, so that your corresponding P-value would be small and hopefully below threshold (the magic 0.05 level). The typical argument was that the probability of obtaining a P-value below 0.05 just by getting lucky is only 5% or less, this is unlikely, and so it is very likely that the null hypothesis is false. In turn, because the null hypothesis and alternative hypothesis are mutually exclusive, it is highly probable that the alternative hypothesis is true.

There are multiple problems here. One problem is that I have mischaracterized P-values, though I have not mischaracterized how many researchers characterize P-values, but we will save that issue for later in this chapter. A second problem is the logical issue, which we will address now.

Let us suppose, and we will un-suppose it later, that a P-value really does provide the probability of obtaining whatever you got in your study (or a value more extreme than that), given that the null hypothesis is true. As a shorthand, we are assuming, for now, that a P-value provides the probability of the finding, given the null hypothesis. To return to the threat-and-prejudice study that featured in Chapter 3, remember that we had imagined an experiment where participants are randomly assigned to read a threatening essay or not, with the hope of obtaining a difference on a subsequent prejudice scale. In this experiment, the null hypothesis might be that the population means in the essay and no essay conditions are the same: $\mu_{essay} = \mu_{no\ essay}$. An alternative hypothesis might be that they are different: $\mu_{essay} \neq \mu_{no\ essay}$, and yet another alternative hypothesis might be that they are different in the anticipated direction: $\mu_{essay} > \mu_{no\ essay}$. If we remain with $\mu_{essay} \neq \mu_{no\ essay}$ as the alternative hypothesis, then it should be clear that the null hypothesis and alternative hypothesis are mutually exclusive and exhaustive. That is, it cannot be true that the population means are both the same and different, and that they are the same or different covers all the possibilities.

Well, then, suppose that in our single threat-and-prejudice study, our specific P-value, p, equals 0.05. A typical conclusion would be that the null hypothesis only has a 5% chance of being true, and so the alternative hypothesis has a 95% chance of being true. This may seem valid based on the logic of *modus tollens*, of which we saw an example in Chapter 1. For another example, consider the following valid syllogism.

If the null hypothesis is true, the finding cannot happen.	{Premise 1}
The finding happens.	{Premise 2}
Therefore, the null hypothesis is not true.	{Conclusion}

This syllogism is logically valid by the logic of *modus tollens*. That is the good news: the occurrence of a finding that cannot happen under the null hypothesis validly disproves the null hypothesis. But unfortunately, this good news is not generally applicable. The more usual case is that the finding is considered unlikely under the null hypothesis, which renders a quite different syllogism than the previous one.

If the null hypothesis is true, the finding is unlikely to happen.	{Premise 1}
The finding happens.	{Premise 2}
Therefore, the null hypothesis is unlikely to be true.	{Conclusion}

This syllogism may appear valid because it seems to follow the same *modus tollens* form that the earlier syllogism followed. But appearances are deceiving; the syllogism does not follow the modus tollens form, but rather follows something we might call the *modus tollens type* form. Unfortunately, the *modus tollens type* form, that features probabilities, does not work. To render this obvious, consider another syllogism in the *modus tollens type* form.

If someone is American, it is unlikely that he or she is president.	{Premise 1}
Joe Biden is president.	{Premise 2}
Therefore, it is unlikely that Joe Biden is American.	{Conclusion}

The problem with this last syllogism is obvious and renders inescapable that a *modus tollens type* form, featuring probabilities, is not valid. This is the *modus tollens* error that researchers in the social sciences routinely commit.

In summary, the way researchers typically use NHST involves blatantly poor logic. It is indefensible. Consequently, you might wonder why anybody would defend NHST, especially sophisticated mathematicians and statisticians who are experts on logic. The answer is that

50   *General Methodological Issues*

NHST apologists agree researchers typically misuse NHST. However, saying that NHST is bad as typically (mis)used, is not equivalent to saying that NHST is bad when used properly. NHST apologists argue that the solution is not to ban NHST, but rather to educate social science researchers so they use it properly and avoid misuse. However, such a defense takes for granted that a proper use of NHST exists. Let us see if that is true.

The Necessity to Make Decisions

The usual sophisticated apology for NHST revolves around an assumed necessity to make decisions. From a decision-making perspective, it is unnecessary to know the probability that the null hypothesis is true. Rather, what is needed is a decision-making framework that will be correct most of the time. Thus, such researchers distinguish between making the error of rejecting the null hypothesis when it is true versus making the error of failing to reject the null hypothesis when it is false. If one makes enough assumptions (and this is a good time to put your hand in your pocket to see if your wallet is still there), it is possible to set thresholds for both types of errors and calculate whether any single study finding meets them. A conventional threshold is that the probability of rejecting the null hypothesis when it is true should be under 0.05, as we have already seen. Sophisticated NHST apologists caution researchers that if a P-value fails to come in under threshold, this does not mean one can accept the null hypothesis. There is wide agreement that this is a fallacy, though substantive social scientists routinely commit the fallacy, and such researchers are guilty of NHST misuse. You can avoid the sin by not drawing any conclusion if the P-value fails to come in under threshold; you can fail to reject the null hypothesis, which is different from accepting it. The insistence that failing to reject the null hypothesis is different from accepting the null hypothesis is very important for sophisticated apologists as the latter is considered misuse whereas the former is not.

Or consider P-values that come in under threshold so that researchers reject their null hypotheses in favor of alternative ones. Sophisticated apologists do not hold that when a P-value comes in under threshold, the researcher knows the probability that the null hypothesis is true, and so they differ from most researchers who do believe that. Instead, the argument is that by setting a decision threshold such as 0.05, the researcher can be assured of wrongly rejecting the null hypothesis only 5% (or whatever the threshold specifies) of the time in the long run. The tacit and often forgotten point is that there should be an added phrase, "under the many assumptions that need to be made." Then, too, in the typical context of a single or limited number of studies, it need not be clear how to specify the reference class to which a long run frequency pertains. Although I will not go into this complex issue further, the specification is not straightforward.

The point to focus on now is that this argument provides a clever way around the fact that there is no way to know the probability of the null hypothesis. Common sense would suggest that it does not make sense to reject a hypothesis when you have no idea about the probability it is true. However, by focusing on the long run probability of making an error—what some term 'error control'—NHST apologists can finesse common sense and are able to draw a conclusion despite not having any idea about the probability that the null hypothesis is true. As we saw in Chapter 2, sometimes scientific creativity beats common sense, but is this one of those cases?

Unfortunately, not, and for multiple reasons. A few of these are listed below.

In the interest of simplicity and clarity, I thus far have glossed over a huge problem, and this is where I stop glossing. Specifically, I had earlier characterized P-values as conditioned on null hypotheses (or test hypotheses). This is not quite true. The truth is that P-values are conditioned on both null hypotheses and additional assumptions. For example, we had mentioned in

Chapter 2 the ubiquitous assumption that the researcher has sampled randomly from the population. Greenland (2019) clarified that there are always added assumptions and Bradley and Brand (2016) and I (Trafimow, 2019a) both suggested taxonomies of assumptions because there are so many of them (also, see Chapter 3). Statisticians term the combination of a null hypothesis and additional assumptions a *model*. Thus, the model M is the null hypothesis H and the additional assumptions A. In mathematical notation, $M = H + A$. However, and this is crucial, there are so many assumptions that compose A, that it is tantamount to impossible that all of them are true. Even the most enthusiastic of NHST aficionados will admit, when pressed, that not all the assumptions are true, but retort that they are close enough to true to make NHST useful. We will address that soon. But for right now, it is sufficient that nobody defends that all the assumptions are true, and so everyone admits that the A in $M = H + A$ is false. However, if the A in $M = H + A$ is false, it means that $H + A$ is false too. And if $H + A$ is false, then M must be false too. The bottom line, then, is that the model is false. Because the hypothesis is embedded in a model known to be false before we even start the process of NHST, it follows that researchers cannot draw any sound conclusions. To illustrate via analogy, that an art museum has an ugly exterior does not justify concluding that a particular painting in that art museum is ugly too.

This argument may seem too strict. After all, it is often necessary to use a false model and that is often okay if the model is close enough to true, though false. For example, when researchers make estimates of mosquito populations from mosquito samples they use inferential models that are false. But the models are good enough to render estimation useful. Given the mosquito example, why be so hard on NHST apologists for using false models?

The answer is that the mosquito example concerns estimation and NHST concerns making dichotomous decisions. For dichotomous decisions, there is no such thing as close, there is only right or wrong. A woman is pregnant or not; there is no option in between. Put more generally, when close counts, as in estimation contexts, it is fine if the model is wrong if it is not too wrong. But when there is a dichotomous decision, that is either right or wrong, and there is no such thing as close, then slight wrongness is still wrong. Therefore, we see that the excuse that the model might be close to right, though still wrong, is insufficient. To nail this down, let us again consider the threat-and-prejudice experiment, and suppose that the finding is statistically significant. Exactly what are we justified in concluding? The problem is that we are justified in concluding very little. We cannot conclude that the null hypothesis is likely false because statistical significance could be due to one of the additional assumptions—the A in $M = H + A$ —being false. The thing to remember is that P-values do not index the closeness of the model to truth, as even NHST apologists will admit when pressed. If P-values did fulfill this function, they would be useful, but they do not, and that is that. The wrong-model problem is fatal for NHST even without considering any other problems. Yet, there are more.

Recall that the present apology for NHST rests upon a foundational assumption that it is necessary to decide. But why is this so? In the case of theory-testing research, which is the concern of almost everyone who conducts basic social science research, there may be no need for a decision at all. For reasons we investigated in Chapter 1, a single study rarely (if ever) provides decisive proof or disproof for a theory. The general rule is that scientists converge on their degree of acceptance or rejection of theories based on considering findings obtained from many studies, with different studies employing different auxiliary, statistical, or inferential assumptions as the TASI taxonomy presented in Chapter 3 indicates. No reputable scientist would countenance making decisions about theories based on single findings; this would constitute blatant bad scientific practice. And if one is not going to decide, where then is the justification for NHST, even if we ignore the wrong-model problem?

To be sure, an NHST apologist could argue that it is at least necessary to make decisions in applied social science. It is necessary to decide whether to employ an intervention on a large scale, promote a policy change, and so on. But if one reads the vast applied social science literature, it becomes immediately obvious that although that literature is replete with statistically significant findings, it rarely occurs that any of the statistically significant findings are ever applied by anyone to better the human condition. This is a point I and Magda Osman made in a recent editorial (Trafimow & Osman, 2022). That ostensibly applied research almost never betters the human condition is a problem, but the present point is that even in applied research in the social sciences, hardly anyone is making any decisions. So, if hardly anyone is making any decisions, we must again ask, where is the justification for NHST?

Even in the very rare case where a decision needs to be made, there is still a problem, in addition to the inevitable wrong-model problem. Let us consider a hypothetical example. Suppose someone performs an intervention to reduce prejudice and let us suppose the finding supports that the intervention really does reduce prejudice. Further, let us suppose that the finding is statistically significant. As we have seen, the wrong-model problem is immediately fatal for using the fact of statistical significance to conclude anything about the effectiveness of the intervention but let us ignore that for now. Suppose that politicians in multiple geographical areas wish to decide whether to invest money to put the intervention into practice to reduce prejudice. There is an obvious generalizability issue, as we discussed in Chapter 3, as we are attempting to generalize the findings to different geographical areas. But let us generously ignore that. The issue of present focus is whether it makes sense for politicians in different geographical areas to use the same decision rule and this requires a very brief discussion about rational decision-making.

When making decisions, there are at least two factors to consider. There are consequences of various courses of action, and these may be positive or negative or both. Secondly, there are probabilities of various consequences. Researchers who specialize in decision-making have suggested various ways of combining information about potential consequences and their estimated probabilities to enhance the effectiveness with which people can make decisions. How does this pertain to using NHST to make decisions? Well, the obvious problem is that NHST is strictly about probabilities and does not consider consequences at all. Thus, at face value, only a very poor decision-maker would use NHST. A potential counterargument might be that researchers could consider consequences in deciding where to set the threshold for statistical significance and so consequences would be considered, after all. There are immediately obvious problems with the counterargument, such as that NHST fails to provide a way for researchers to use potential consequences to set the bar. Such vagueness renders the counterargument feckless. And there is a worse problem.

When one performs an experiment, such as our intervention to decrease prejudice, there is no way for the researcher to know the consequences that pertain to the various potential consumers of the research. There may be more people who suffer from prejudice in one geographical area than in another, there may be more pressing problems than prejudice in one geographical location than in another geographical location, and so on. To believe that a single decision rule will be optimal for the different consumers of research would be the height of gullibility. Therefore, even ignoring the wrong-model problem, that decisions rarely need to be made, and that NHST fails to adequately consider potential consequences—which is ignoring a heck of a lot—there remains yet another fatal problem that different consumers of research need different decision rules. Thus, significance tests are again contraindicated. A much better strategy—if the goal really were to help people as opposed to exploiting a scientific ritual to publish papers to further one's career—would be to provide detailed information about the probabilities of various degrees of good or bad consequences so people in different circumstances could make their own decisions that are informed by their own circumstances. This will be the topic of Chapter 7.

We have seen that all the justifications for NHST fail and fail miserably. But there is yet worse. Specifically, NHST guarantees misleading scientific literatures. This is a very strong statement, and you might be questioning, how so? The answer lies in the statistical phenomenon of regression to the mean or simply statistical regression. Here is the idea. Any sort of score, and this includes P-values, has a random component. The hope is that there is a systematic component too but even if this is so, some randomness will nevertheless remain. There will be formal definitions in Chapters 9 and 10, but for now a division into systematicity and randomness is sufficient. Given that scores have systematic and random components, suppose someone performs particularly well on an occasion. For example, suppose a baseball player gets four hits in four times at bat in the most recent game. We might query why the baseball player did so well and there are two answers. First, the baseball player is a good hitter. Second, the baseball player got lucky. And both might be true. Well, then, if the performance was importantly influenced by luck, we would not expect the baseball player to get a hit at every time at bat in the future; we would expect less than that. In fact, our best prediction would be that the baseball player would score a batting average, across a future run of games, that is like the batting average he has achieved in the past run of games. In short, we would expect the baseball player to regress to his mean batting average in a future run of games.

Now that you know how statistical regression works, let us consider P-values and ask, "How does one obtain a statistically significant P-value?" There are two ways, and both are important simultaneously. The first way is by obtaining a large effect size. There are many effect size indices, with details forthcoming in Chapter 5. For now, it is sufficient that in our prejudice intervention, if participants who receive the intervention score much lower on prejudice than do participants in the control condition, then the effect size is large. But notice that this is a sample effect size and not a population effect size. And because effect sizes vary from sample to sample, simply as a matter of randomness, it should be obvious immediately that one reason for obtaining a large effect size is that the researcher got lucky, though it is possible that the intervention really works too.

Secondly, the sample size matters. If we imagine keeping the effect size constant across experiments with different sample sizes, studies with larger sample sizes would have smaller P-values than studies with smaller sample sizes. However, we can go the other way too. We can imagine keeping the sample size constant across experiments with different sample effect sizes. The studies with the larger sample effect sizes will have smaller P-values than the studies with smaller sample effect sizes. In turn, recognizing that sample effect sizes are, in part, a matter of luck, forces a crucial consequence: the P-values researchers obtain are, in important part, a matter of luck.

Recognizing that the P-values researchers obtain are, in important part, a matter of luck, necessitates that P-values are every bit as subject to statistical regression as are baseball players' batting averages, but to worse effect. Here is why. An unofficial rule that most journal editors and reviewers use for accepting manuscripts is that main findings must be statistically significant, so that P-values are under threshold (usually 0.05). But the P-values that perform exceptionally well in this respect do so in large part because of lucky sample effect sizes. If replication attempts are made, a topic to be discussed fully in Chapter 5, the expectation would be one of statistical regression—sample effect sizes should decrease, and associated P-values should increase. Not only is this mathematically inevitable, but the statistical regression of sample effect sizes has been supported empirically too. The Open Science Collaboration (2015) involved the replication of a large sample of studies published in top psychology journals. One result was that over 60% of the studies failed to replicate with respect to statistical significance. A second result was that the average effect size in the replication cohort of studies was less than half that in the original cohort of studies. Thus, the routine use of NHST has forced the social science literature to be replete with effects that dramatically overestimate true effect sizes. This is an undeniable and crucial NHST harm that is as inevitable as death and taxes.

Finally, it is easy to show that NHST prescriptions and alleged proper use of NHST are self-contradictory. Consider again that sophisticated NHST supporters agree that a nonsignificant P-value cannot be interpreted as supporting the null hypothesis; such a lack of significance merely indicates that one has failed to reject the null hypothesis, that is, no conclusion can be drawn. That is on the one hand. However, on the other hand, let us consider an applied experiment where the findings are to be used to decide whether to implement a policy. If a decision is to be forced upon us, the alleged proper use of NHST is as follows. If the finding is statistically significant, then engage the policy; if the finding is not statistically significant, do not engage the policy. Think about this again: if the finding is not statistically significant, we do not engage the policy. But not engaging the policy is, in essence, acting as though we accept the null hypothesis that the population parameters of interest in the two conditions are the same. In turn, such accepting of the null hypothesis in behavior, even if not in words, violates what was said earlier about statistical significance not justifying accepting the null hypothesis. It is contradictory not to accept the null hypothesis in words (only to fail to reject it), but then go ahead and accept the null hypothesis with respect to the behavior of not engaging the policy. If it sounds like NHST supporters are pulling something on you, it is because they are. Is your wallet still in your pocket?

P-Values without NHST

Many mathematically sophisticated researchers recognize that NHST is difficult to defend. They favor an alternative argument that researchers should use P-values without any significance threshold. These researchers understand that P-values do not give probabilities of hypotheses or provide good decision criteria but argue that P-values nevertheless provide something of value; P-values index the extent to which the data are incompatible with the statistical model. Knowing the extent to which data are incompatible with a statistical model, in turn, can be considered a useful cue in evaluating the model. Therefore, P-values are good, but only if the researcher avoids using them for NHST.

Let us evaluate this argument from two perspectives. One perspective involves accepting that P-values—or at least some kind of transformation of them—indexes the extent to which data are incompatible with statistical models. The other perspective involves not accepting the premise. We will see that both perspectives lead to problems.

To try out the first direction, Greenland (2019) provides a nice place to start. Not only does Greenland argue that P-values index incompatibility of data with models, but that there is a transformation that is even better than P-values for indexing incompatibility of data with models. Greenland's idea is to use a logarithmic transformation to convert P-values into bits of information against the model that he terms S-values: $s = \log_2(p)(-1)$. For example, P-values at the 0.05 level would transform to 4.32 or approximately four bits of information against the model. By using Greenland's log transformation, it is possible to avoid the baggage associated with P-values and move directly to thinking in terms of bits of information against models.

However, even assuming Greenland is correct on all counts, there remains a crucial problem. Consider again $M = H + A$. As explained earlier, A is tantamount to certainly false and so M is too. Therefore, it remains unclear how to draw conclusions about hypotheses that are embedded in wrong models. As we have already seen, knowing that the data are incompatible with the model tells us nothing about whether the data are incompatible with the hypothesis, embedded in the model, that we really care about. To repeat an illustrative analogy used earlier, knowing that an art museum has an ugly exterior provides no sound grounds to conclude that a single painting in the museum is ugly too.

Worse yet, it is far from clear that Greenland was correct in asserting that P-values or S-values index incompatibility with models (for full disclosure, I used to think this part correct). To see the problem, recall a foregoing comment that these depend on two things: sample effect sizes and sample sizes. Hence, it is inevitable that P-values or S-values confound sample effect sizes and sample sizes. If a researcher obtains a small P-value or large S-value, it is not clear whether this is because of a large sample effect size, a large sample size, or both. Or, if a researcher obtains a large P-value or small S-value it is not clear whether this is because of a small sample effect size, a small sample size, or both. These ambiguities force that P-values or S-values need not soundly index the incompatibility of data with statistical models, as can be exemplified with two extreme scenarios (Trafimow, in press).

In Scenario 1, suppose we again perform the threat-and-prejudice experiment, but twice, with an original and replication experiment. In the original experiment, we obtain means in the threat and no threat conditions equal to .1 and 0, respectively, and with standard deviations equal to 1 in both conditions. In addition, the sample size is $n = 100{,}000$ in each condition, so $p = 1.3 \times 10^{-110}$ and $s = 365$. Now, suppose a replication experiment, where the means and standard deviations are the same and $n = 250{,}000$ in each condition, so $p = 1.8 \times 10^{-273}$ and $s = 906$. Thus, the evidence against the hypothesis in the replication experiment, according to S-values, well exceeds twofold that from the original experiment. But is this reasonable given that (a) the means and standard deviations are precisely the same and (b) the immense sample sizes render extreme sampling precision in both experiments?

Well, it depends. There is an unfortunate tendency for many academics to assert that they are correct by definitional fiat. If we resort to that strategy here, we could insist that S-values index incompatibility of evidence against the model by definitional fiat. In that case, the discussion ends immediately as there is no arguing with definitional fiat. However, one of my goals in writing this book is to educate people into thinking for themselves, which includes learning to think outside of definitional fiat. Going the open-minded route indicates that (a) the effect sizes are precisely the same in both experiments and (b) the sample sizes are so immense in both the original and replication experiments to render obvious that the sample statistics are exceedingly good estimates of corresponding population parameters in both experiments (as will be discussed more precisely in Chapter 6). Therefore, it would be silly to believe that the replication experiment provides more than twice the evidence against the model as the original experiment. The scenario illustrates that it is problematic to confound sample effect sizes and sample sizes, and to believe that P-values or S-values index the extent to which data are incompatible with models.

Let us now consider Scenario 2, that might be even more extreme. In this scenario, we again consider an original and replication threat-and-prejudice experiment. In the original experiment, the means in the threat and not threat conditions are 0.1 and 0, respectively, and the standard deviations equal 1. The sample size is $n = 100{,}000$ in each condition, so $p = 1.3 \times 10^{-110}$ and $s = 365$. In contrast, in the replication experiment, the means are 0.3 and 0, respectively, keeping the

56 General Methodological Issues

standard deviations equal to 1. But now $n = 11{,}000$ in each condition so that $p = 1.8 \times 10^{-108}$ and $s = 358$. Going by P-values or S-values, the conclusion is that the original experiment provides better evidence against the model than does the replication experiment. But as it is obvious that the sample sizes in both experiments are more than sufficient for the sample statistics to provide excellent estimates of corresponding population parameters (see Chapter 6 for an exhaustive discussion), and that the effect size is thrice that in the replication experiment than in the original experiment, the indication is to the contrary, that the replication experiment provides stronger evidence against the model than does the original experiment. As in Scenario 1, we obtain a more accurate perspective keeping the sample effect size and the sample size distinct, as opposed to confounding them via P-values or S-values.

The scenarios point to an important conceptual question not addressed by P-value and S-value aficionados: "What is meant by *incompatibility with the model*?" Outside of definitional fiat, we might consider P-values or S-values to be incompatible with a model to the extent they provide a sound reason for assigning a low probability to the model; but our previous discussion of the *modus tollens* error shows that P-values (and S-values by extension) are insufficient for valid inverse inferences about the probabilities of models. In addition, many would argue that models are either true or false, so their probabilities equal 1.00 or 0.00, only we do not know which. From this perspective, it does not even make sense to talk about probabilities of models. Either way, there is no sound way to move from P-values or S-values to probabilities of models.

Or we might argue that evidence is incompatible with a model to the extent that descriptive statistics of interest (e.g., effect sizes) deviate from what they should be according to the model. This argument would be reasonable, provided sufficiently large samples to engender confidence that the descriptive statistics accurately estimate corresponding population parameters. However, Scenario 2 illustrates how P-values and S-values can be made to go against that; in this scenario, the larger effect size was associated with a smaller S-value.

There is no way, short of definitional fiat, to save P-values or S-values as indicating the incompatibility of data with models. Thus, although P-values or S-values without NHST are less bad than with NHST, they remain problematic and contraindicated for drawing conclusions about hypotheses.

Traditional Confidence Intervals Do Not Solve the Problem

Many have touted confidence intervals as a better alternative than NHST or P-values without NHST. To use confidence intervals the traditional way, the research computes a confidence interval, usually a 95% confidence interval, around the sample summary statistic (usually the sample mean). The idea is that the population parameter, usually the population mean, is likely to be in that interval. To foreshadow, this sentence is much less clear than it seems on the surface but let us accept it at face value for the moment. If the value specified by the null hypothesis, usually 0 if one is interested in the difference in means between experimental and control conditions, is outside the confidence interval, that is equivalent to saying that the finding is statistically significant. So, you see, confidence intervals are typically used as an alternative way to perform NHST and consequently are plagued with all the problems mentioned in the foregoing pages.

Remaining with fashionable usages, a typical—though incorrect—interpretation of confidence intervals is that they give the probability that the population parameter of interest is within the interval. For example, if a researcher computes a 95% confidence interval around the sample mean, the population mean has a 95% chance of being within that interval. If this interpretation were true, I would love confidence intervals. It would be wonderful to have a way to know the probabilities that parameters are within intervals. The fly-in-the-ointment, however, is that confidence intervals do not soundly fulfill this function. The truth is that a 95% confidence interval fails to tell us the probability that the population mean is within the computed interval.

Well, then, if a 95% confidence interval does not signify that the population mean has a 95% chance of being within the computed interval, why do statisticians call it a 95% confidence interval? Here is why. Imagine performing an experiment repeatedly until you have indefinite replications and that you compute a 95% confidence interval around the sample mean for each of them. If all assumptions are true (and they will not be!), then 95% of the confidence intervals computed will surround the population mean. That is the good news. Does this mean that in any single case, you have a 95% probability of surrounding the population mean? The unfortunate answer—and this may take some thinking to see—is that it does not. If you think about it, you will see that this inference is merely a disguised version of the *modus tollens* error described previously. The fact that 95% of 95% confidence intervals surround the population mean does not justify that the probability that the population parameter is within a single computed 95% confidence interval is 95%. The blunt fact of the matter is that there is no way to know that probability.

Although typical researchers either believe, or act as if they believe, that computing a 95% confidence interval around the sample mean ensures a 95% probability of surrounding the population mean, it might have occurred to you that sophisticated statisticians know better than that. And if so, you are right! They do know better. Which brings up the issue of alternative reasons for supporting traditional confidence intervals.

An alternative argument in favor of confidence intervals concerns the issue of precision. In brief, narrow confidence intervals show that the data are precise whereas wide confidence intervals show that the data are not precise. However, there are two problems with this argument. One problem is that very few substantive researchers in the social sciences use confidence intervals to index precision, and so the argument fails to reflect sociology-of-science reality. Secondly, the precision argument itself is flawed, as I hope to clarify now.

Let us ask, what do we mean by 'precision'? One potential meaning concerns sampling precision. Under the ubiquitous assumption of random selection from a population, the larger the sample size, the better the sample statistics will estimate corresponding population parameters. We will revisit this point in Chapter 6, but for now it is sufficient merely to note that this is only one kind of precision. A second potential meaning concerns measurement precision: the more the measuring instrument in a study is subject to random measurement error, the less the precision; the less the measuring instrument in a study is subject to random measurement error, the more the measurement precision. It is worth repeating that measurement precision is a function of the measuring instrument, which differs from sampling precision that depends on the size of the sample.

A third potential meaning concerns precision of homogeneity: the more similar the scores are to each other, the easier it is to see the effect of the manipulation on the dependent measure. Imagining that there is no random error, let us return to the threat-and-prejudice experiment and suppose there are ten participants in each condition, with the following scores in Experiment 1. In the essay condition, the scores are 2, 2, 2, 2, 2, 2, 2, 2, 2, 2 and in the no essay condition, the scores are 1, 1, 1, 1, 1, 1, 1, 1, 1, 1. The mean equals 2 in the essay condition and 1 in the no essay condition and the difference is immediately obvious. In contrast, moving to Experiment 2, suppose the scores in the essay condition are 0, 3, 3, 3, –1, 0, 3, 3, 3, 3 and the scores in the no essay condition are –3, –3, 3, 3, 3, –3, 2, 2, 3, 3. In Experiment 2, the means in the essay and no

58 General Methodological Issues

essay conditions are 2 and 1, just as in Experiment 1. However, in Experiment 2, the difference between conditions is difficult to perceive whereas it is immediately obvious in Experiment 1. The reason is that the people are homogeneous in both conditions of Experiment 1 with respect to their prejudice scores but are heterogeneous in Experiment 2. In terms of variance defined in Chapter 3, there is much more variance within conditions in Experiment 2 than in Experiment 1. Hence, we have our three types of precision. Sampling precision depends on sample size, the larger the sample the more precision. Measurement precision depends on characteristics of the measuring device, the less the random error, the more the measurement precision. And precision of homogeneity depends on differences between people with respect to the dependent variable of interest, the less the variance between people, the more the precision of homogeneity.

Why take the trouble in the previous paragraphs to detail the three types of precision? To answer this question, let us consider again the sophisticated confidence interval argument that confidence intervals are useful for indexing the precision of the data. But here is the rub. It is not clear what kind of precision we are talking about. In fact, if one delves into the mathematics of confidence intervals, it becomes clear that all three types of precision figure into confidence interval widths. I have shown elsewhere that confidence intervals narrow as (a) sampling precision increases, (b) measurement precision increases, and (c) precision of homogeneity increases (Trafimow, 2018a). Clearly, then, if confidence intervals are wide, as they usually are in psychology, it could be due to deficits with respect to any, or more than one, of the three types of precision. Thus, confidence intervals, used as precision indices, are triply confounded!

Perhaps a statement could be made for a very limited confidence interval type of utility, that if confidence intervals are wide, there is a precision problem somewhere, but the vagueness of this statement renders it not very useful. In addition, as we will see in Chapter 13, it is possible to estimate each of the three types of precision separately. This fact leads to a fatal dilemma for the precision justification for confidence intervals. That is, if a researcher honestly cares about precision, she should assess each type of precision separately instead of settling for a triply confounded precision index. Alternatively, if a researcher does not care about precision, then the precision justification for confidence intervals is immediately irrelevant. Either way, the precision justification for confidence intervals fails.

Worse yet, I and a former graduate student performed computer simulations with user-defined confidence intervals, where we set the population parameters ahead of time, to determine how closely sample confidence intervals approximate the truth (Trafimow & Uhalt, 2020). At typical sample sizes, sample confidence intervals perform very poorly, though they improve as sample sizes increase. Thus, we again see that confidence intervals are inadequate to address researchers' inferential needs.

Bayes Factors

A completely different approach involves Bayesian thinking that depends, not surprisingly, on Bayes theorem. There are so many ways to use Bayes theorem to address inferential issues that it would require a very large book to do so, and there will be no attempt to be complete here. However, it is reasonably convenient to consider the most popular Bayesian prescription, which is to use Bayes factors to draw conclusions about hypotheses.

Bayes factors come out of a version of Bayes theorem expressed below as Equation 1:

$$\frac{P(H_1)|D}{P(H_2)|D} = \frac{P(H_1)}{P(H_2)} \frac{P(D|H_1)}{P(D|H_2)}. \tag{4.1}$$

Let us start with what Bayes factor enthusiasts wish to achieve, which is to determine the relative probability of two competing hypotheses, H_1 and H_2, given the data. This is often called the posterior odds. To connect this discussion to our earlier discussion about NHST, one hypothesis might be the null hypothesis and another hypothesis might be the alternative hypothesis. The straight line (|) is usually read as 'given,' so that $P(H_1)|D$ is read as the probability of Hypothesis 1 given the data. Likewise, $P(H_2)|D$ is read as the probability of Hypothesis 2 given the data. Bayesians consider the posterior odds as indicating the relative probability of the two competing hypotheses, given the data. A value exceeding 1 indicates that the data support H_1 as a better bet than H_2 whereas a value less than 1 indicates that the data support H_2 as a better bet than H_1.

To achieve the goal, that is, to find posterior odds, there are two other fractions. The first, and the most troubling, is $\frac{P(H_1)}{P(H_2)}$, which can be broken down by numerator and denominator. $P(H_1)$ is considered the prior probability of Hypothesis 1; that is, the probability of Hypothesis 1 before the researcher considers the data. Likewise, $P(H_2)$ is considered the prior probability of Hypothesis 2; that is, the probability of Hypothesis 2 before the researcher considers the data. The total quantity, $\frac{P(H_1)}{P(H_2)}$, can be considered the prior odds of the hypotheses, and it is philosophically problematic. How would one know the prior probability of either hypothesis, or the prior odds? One solution is to simply make a guess. Another solution is to set the prior odds at 1 to provide a level playing field for the two hypotheses. Neither is satisfactory. About the former solution, one might ask: What right do you have to make guesses and then draw conclusions from them? About the latter solution, one might ask: What right do you have to set the prior probabilities of the hypotheses equal when it is practically certain that they are not? Thus, many Bayes factor enthusiasts favor simply reporting the Bayes factor and not worrying about the prior odds, an issue we consider now. For full disclosure, there was a time when I supported thinking along this line, though I am more pessimistic now (Trafimow, 2003; 2005). An important reason for my previous positivity was the appeal of considering two competing hypotheses simultaneously, rather than only one hypothesis. I still favor competing predictions, but no longer feel that Bayes factors are the way to implement them inferentially.

The last fraction in Equation 1, $\frac{P(D|H_1)}{P(D|H_2)}$, is called the Bayes factor. Bayesians interpret $P(D|H_1)$ as indicating the probability of the data given Hypothesis 1 and $P(D|H_2)$ as indicating the probability of the data given Hypothesis 2. In turn, the Bayes factor is interpreted as indicating the extent to which the data are more likely given one hypothesis than given the other. If the Bayes factor exceeds 1, the data are more likely given Hypothesis 1 than Hypothesis 2; if the Bayes factor is less than 1, the data are more likely given Hypothesis 2 than Hypothesis 1. A more conceptual interpretation might be that the Bayes factor provides the extent to which the data support one hypothesis over the other hypothesis. Some Bayes factor enthusiasts argue that researchers can simply report the Bayes factor and let each reader of the article insert whatever prior odds they like to compute their own posterior odds of the two hypotheses.

Using Bayes factors is less objectionable than NHST, and yet, there are still important problems and perhaps even fatal ones. To commence, there is the issue of how strong the Bayes factor must be to draw a solid conclusion. Some Bayesians insist that the Bayes factor equal or exceed 10, though other Bayesians have suggested different values. Whatever value is used, there is the risk of being every bit as arbitrary as researchers who use NHST with its insistence on a threshold level (such as 0.05).

Another problem, and a more serious one in my opinion, is that my foregoing presentation, though presenting the typical Bayes factor position, is extremely misleading. To see why, consider the two elements that go into Bayes factors, $P(D|H_1)$ and $P(D|H_2)$. I presented them earlier as symbolizing the probability of the data given Hypothesis 1 and the probability of the data given Hypothesis 2, respectively. However, just as we saw with NHST, there is more that goes into these conditional probabilities than just the hypotheses and the data. In calculating the probability of the data given Hypothesis 1 or Hypothesis 2, it is necessary, as always, to make additional assumptions. Consequently, the symbolism does not accurately reflect what scientists are forced to do. Rather, scientists must use inferential models, with the hypothesis being one of many assumptions embedded in them. Therefore, a more accurate symbolic depiction would be to replace H_1 with M_1 and to replace H_2 with M_2. The new and more accurate Bayes factor, then, would be: $\dfrac{P(D|M_1)}{P(D|M_2)}$. In English, we would have the probability of the data given Model 1 divided by the probability of the data given Model 2.

Why does replacing hypotheses with models matter? Consider again the usual interpretation of a Bayes factor, as giving the relative degree to which the data support one hypothesis at the expense of the other hypothesis. In contrast, replacing hypotheses with models changes the interpretation: Bayes factors give the relative degree to which the data support one model at the expense of the other model. However, we have already seen that all models contain at least one wrong assumption, which means it is tantamount to certain that any model we wish to consider is wrong. Once we acknowledge this, it follows naturally that there is little point in saying that the data are more likely given one wrong model than given another wrong model. There is no way for us to know whether this is because of the relative worth of the hypotheses, the relative worth of the other assumptions in the two models, or an interaction between these. In summary, although Bayes factors are not as deleterious to science as is NHST, I no longer support them. As Chapters 6 and 7 show, we can do a lot better.

We have seen that none of the usual inferential prescriptions, NHST, P-values without NHST, traditional confidence intervals, nor Bayes factors, work well. Of course, it is possible to misuse these procedures, and aficionados rightly point out that the fact that procedures can be misused, to the harm of the social sciences, need not indicate that procedures must be misused. If the procedures are used properly, then they are helpful. The solution, then, is education into proper use as opposed to telling people not to use the procedures. However, there are important problems with the proper education argument.

Before discussing these problems, you might consider a preliminary point that various people who consider themselves statistical authorities have been preaching about better statistical education for many decades. It has not worked. Of course, it might work in the future, but the fact that it has not worked so consistently suggests that it might be well to look elsewhere. As the famous saying goes: "It is the height of madness to keep doing the same thing and expect different results."

A more telling problem is that misuse is so tempting that even the best statisticians have fallen into it, as Richard Morey explained in his blog about Jerzy Neyman, one of the greatest statisticians who ever lived. As the blog clarifies, Neyman committed the very NHST misuses he warned people not to commit in his weather research in the 1960s (*BayesFactor: Software for Bayesian inference: Neyman does science, part 1*). The problem was not that Neyman was unaware of the ways to misuse NHST, but rather that NHST fails to provide sound reason for believing or disbelieving hypotheses. Because the goal is to support or disconfirm hypotheses, it is not surprising that even Neyman committed misuse. The Neyman case exemplifies a serious dilemma that NHST apologists still refuse to acknowledge. Put simply, researchers can either (a) draw conclusions about hypotheses from NHST or (b) not draw conclusions about hypotheses from NHST. If they draw conclusions, they are automatically committing misuse because NHST does not soundly permit that, as we have seen. But if researchers do not draw conclusions about hypotheses, then there is only an empty ritual. Either way, the researcher is sunk, and better education, though generally desirable, has no chance of resolving the dilemma.

Then, too, the assumption underlying the education argument is that there actually is a sound use for NHST and it is possible to educate researchers about that. However, we have seen that this assumption is wrong. There is no sound way to use NHST to draw conclusions about hypotheses. Therefore, there is no proper use for NHST, and pretending that there is constitutes not education, but rather a distortion of education—an indoctrination into a harmful religion.

Chapter Summary

In the present discussion of NHST, we discussed the *modus tollens* error, as well as the usual way out of it, which is to focus on error control. However, once we distinguish between null hypotheses and the models in which they are embedded, the error control argument fails too. We then moved to an argument that rather than using P-values to make dichotomous decisions, we can use them to evaluate the incompatibility between data and null hypotheses. However, it is possible to provide examples to demonstrate that P-values do not soundly indicate the incompatibility of data with null hypotheses.

We subsequently switched to traditional confidence intervals as an alternative. But that was problematic too. For one thing, confidence intervals do not provide the probability that the parameter of interest is within the interval. In addition, a defense based on the notion that confidence intervals index precision was shown not to work either. Worse yet, computer simulations further argue against confidence intervals being useful.

Finally, we attempted Bayes factors, that ostensibly inform about the relative fit of the data with two competing hypotheses. However, this is a misstatement because the calculations are based on hypotheses plus additional assumptions—that is, models rather than hypotheses. Because we know the models are wrong, all we are left with is the relative fit of data with wrong models, which fails to provide much information about the hypotheses embedded therein.

Thus, none of the popular inferential procedures work well. And the usual NHST apology, that the undeniable harm caused to social science literatures is due to misuse rather than proper use, is not convincing due to the inability to make the case for that which would constitute proper use. As I will explain in Chapters 6 and 7, we can do better.

5 How to Think about Replicating Findings

Imagine a chemistry theory that, in conjunction with widely accepted auxiliary assumptions, predicts that when you mix the contents of Test Tube A with the contents of Test Tube B, the solution should turn green. However, the solution does not turn green. Is the empirical defeat

DOI: 10.4324/9781003365167-6

fatal for the theory? Not necessarily. Perhaps one of the test tubes was mislabeled, which would suggest that the empirical defeat was a problem at the auxiliary assumption level rather than at the theoretical level. But let us suppose 20 attempts by different researchers, with careful checks on the contents of the test tubes, with an empirical defeat every time. Although it remains possible that the auxiliary assumptions are problematic across all 20 replication attempts, this argument becomes increasingly more difficult to swallow as replication failures mount. Or suppose that in some of the experiments, the solution does not turn green but in some of the experiments, the solution does turn green. It is difficult to know what to conclude here and one might wonder what is going on across the different experiments. The moral of the story is that empirical defeats must replicate if they are to seriously militate against the theory. Or, in the case of empirical victories, they must replicate too to seriously militate for the theory. A caveat, as we learned in Chapter 1, is that empirical defeats can be blamed on theory or auxiliary assumptions and empirical victories can be credited to theory or auxiliary assumptions.

Matters get murkier when we move to psychology. In the case of the chemistry experiment, where the empirical hypothesis is that the solution turns green, we only have the theory and auxiliary assumptions to worry about. Thus, we need not worry about statistical or inferential assumptions, as we did in Chapter 3, because the solution either turns green or not. Statistical and inferential assumptions are unnecessary, thereby leaving only theoretical and auxiliary assumptions from the TASI taxonomy. In contrast, consider that multiple attitude theories, for approximately a century, have agreed that attitudes cause behaviors, though there might be other causes of behaviors too and the effect might not be direct. There exists an ambiguity that does not exist with respect to the chemistry experiment, concerning the strength of connection between attitudes and behaviors that we deem 'good enough.'

As a test, suppose a researcher measures attitudes and behaviors towards using seatbelts and predicts a correlation between them. However, suppose the correlation coefficient is near zero. In that case, the study could hardly be said to provide impressive support for the theory and might, indeed, be interpreted as evidence against the theory. There is ambiguity here due to the lack of specification of how large a correlation coefficient needs to be to count as evidence in favor of the theory. Another difficulty is that if we performed multiple studies, random variations across them would result in some manifesting larger correlation coefficients, some manifesting smaller ones, and some perhaps even manifesting negative correlation coefficients. The inferential hypothesis is no clearer than the statistical hypothesis. And, unfortunately, these are relevant in the attitude study in a way they are not in the chemistry study.

Before continuing, let us remember that correlation coefficients can be –1.00 at one extreme, which indicates a perfect negative relationship so that as attitudes towards using seatbelts improve, actual seatbelt usage decreases. At the other extreme, a correlation coefficient equal to +1.00 (or simply 1.00) indicates a perfect positive relationship so that attitudes towards using seatbelts and actual seatbelt usage increase or decrease together. Finally, in the middle, a correlation coefficient equal to 0 indicates no statistical relationship at all. Thus, attitudes towards using seatbelts have no statistical relationship whatsoever with actual seatbelt usage. Suppose that a researcher obtains a statistically significant correlation coefficient equal to 0.20, which would be quite representative of much research in the social sciences.

Given that the correlation coefficient in the original study equals 0.20, what would count as a successful replication in the new study? There are many potential answers.

1. The most common answer would be based on a statistical significance test. The idea would be to propose a null hypothesis, for the new study, that the correlation coefficient equals 0.

The researcher would then hope to obtain a small P-value (usually less than 0.05) to disconfirm the null hypothesis that the population correlation coefficient equals 0 in favor of the alternative hypothesis that the population correlation coefficient is greater than zero. In this case, if the new correlation coefficient is statistically significant (that is, the P-value the researcher calculates is less than 0.05), the study counts as having successfully replicated the original one. The original correlation coefficient was significantly greater than 0 and now the replication correlation coefficient is significantly greater than 0 too. And life is good!

Or is it? The first thing to do is review Chapter 4, where I had explained carefully why significance testing is an unsound procedure. Based on Chapter 4, you should be very suspicious of the present answer. In addition, we have said nothing yet about the actual value of the correlation coefficient in the replication study. Let us remedy that here and imagine it is 0.83. There are at least two ways to look at it. One way is to say that they are both statistically significant in the theoretically correct direction, so life remains good. However, aside from the basic unsoundness of significance testing, consider that the new correlation coefficient equal to 0.83 is extremely different from the original correlation coefficient equal to 0.20. The original value of 0.20 suggests that although the correlation coefficient is there (again ignoring the basic unsoundness of significance testing), it is rather trivial. Yes, attitudes predict actual seatbelt usage, but only poorly. Thus, the evidence is (a) not impressively supportive of the theory and (b) not impressively supportive of an intervention designed to manipulate attitudes to increase seatbelt usage. In contrast, the replication value of 0.83 suggests a very nontrivial effect. To be sure, the effect is not foolproof as one cannot be sure whether attitudes cause behavior, behavior causes attitudes, or something else causes both. That is a general problem with correlation coefficients. And yet, if we generously assume that the correlation coefficient is for the right theoretical reason—attitudes towards seatbelts cause seatbelt usage—the large correlation coefficient in the replication experiment impressively supports the theory whereas even under generosity, the original correlation coefficient does not. Furthermore, the replication correlation coefficient provides good reason to at least suspect that an intervention based on attitudes might be impressively effective whereas the original correlation coefficient does not. Thus, even ignoring Chapter 4, basing judgments of whether a replication attempt is successful on significance tests is contraindicated.

And to nail this point home, imagine that the correlation coefficient in the replication study is 0.19, and not statistically significant, whereas the original correlation coefficient is 0.20, and statistically significant. How silly would it be to say that the second study constitutes an unsuccessful replication attempt, when the two studies produce extremely similar correlation coefficients?

2. A second answer ignores significance tests and focuses just on the sample statistic of interest. In this case, returning to the two correlation coefficients being 0.20 and 0.83 for the original and replication studies, respectively, focusing on the actual values of the statistic of interest suggests that the second study is not a successful replication of the first study. The implications of a correlation coefficient equal to 0.83 differ wildly from the implications of a correlation coefficient equal to 0.20. And going to the other case, where the two correlations are 0.20 versus 0.19, rather than concluding the replication attempt is unsuccessful because of lack of statistical significance, it would be better to conclude that the replication attempt is successful because of obtaining almost the same correlation coefficient as in the original study.

Nevertheless, although this second answer is much superior to the first answer, it is not without difficulties. To see this, suppose that the original and replication correlations are

0.20 and 0.35, respectively. The two numbers differ, but they are not extremely different. Do they differ sufficiently to justify a conclusion that the replication attempt is unsuccessful? The usual way to address the question would be to perform a significance test, but we have already seen that this procedure is unsound. A better answer would be to consider how well the sample statistics estimate the corresponding population parameter, but you do not know how to do that yet. Happily, you will find out in Chapter 6. For now, let us tolerate the ambiguity and internalize the take-home message that focusing on the similarity or difference of the correlation coefficient across the two studies is better than focusing on significance tests.

Exact, Quasi-Exact, or Conceptual Replications

Suppose you wish to perform an exact replication of the original seatbelt study. So, you use the same materials, in the same order, using a sample as like the original as you can get, and so on. Unfortunately, no matter how hard you try, you will not perform an exact replication. In the first place, there is no way for you to perform your study at the same time as the original; your study will be after the original, which constitutes a difference. In addition, even if your sample is like the original sample, it will inevitably not be the same. Nor will the lighting conditions be the same, the height of the experimenter the same, and so on. Thus, whenever someone claims to have performed an exact replication, this is simply not true. A better interpretation is that they attempted to do that, but nevertheless suffered differences. We might say that an attempt to perform an exact replication is really a quasi-exact replication. The good thought was there, but it could only be approximated. It is *quasi*.

Although so-called exact replications are quasi-exact replications, they can nonetheless be convincing, especially if they fail spectacularly. A startling example comes out of "money-priming" studies. Vohs, Mead, and Goode (2006) published a highly cited article in the prestigious journal, *Science*. They primed participants in the experimental condition with the concept of money (they made the concept of money accessible to these participants) but not participants in the control condition and obtained seemingly impressive effects on subsequent behaviors not obviously connected to money, including persistence at a task, volunteering, and others. Hence, Vohs et al. seemed to have demonstrated far-reaching and surprising effects of money-priming. However, Rohrer, Pashler, and Harris (2019) performed two replication studies and published their findings in *Basic and Applied Social Psychology*. Although these were not exact replications, they were quite close; they were quasi-exact. However, an important improvement was that the Rohrer et al. studies were performed with many more participants than the original. Nevertheless, where Vohs et al. succeeded spectacularly, Rohrer et al. obtained effects so near to null that they can be considered null. One lesson that Rohrer et al. teach us is that when researchers report spectacular findings, it is best to consider that the findings might not hold up. This is not to say that Vohs et al. took liberties with the data or cheated in some other way; it is quite possible that this was simply a matter of the luck of the draw (see Chapter 4). It is even possible that it was Rohrer et al. who got it wrong, though that is much less likely due to their much larger sample sizes. Caveats aside, when researchers report findings that seem too good to be true, they might really be too good to be true!

In contrast to so-called exact replications, which are quasi-exact rather than exact, researchers sometimes wish to replicate previous empirical work *conceptually*. Here the idea is to purposely deviate from the original study in ways that should not matter from the perspective of the theory. Successful replications across studies that differ in a wide variety of ways support that the empirical victories replicate, and that the theory generalizes well across a variety of experimental paradigms. I will relate a perhaps too-long story about that because there is a lesson to be conveyed not just about replication, but also about the benefits of being open-minded and free-wheeling in one's thinking.

A Perhaps Too-Long Story

During graduate school, I had an interesting conversation with Sharon Goto, a very nice and intelligent graduate student in the same psychology program. She was telling me of her interests, which were extremely different from mine, but I listened to her anyhow partly to be polite and partly because I have always been interested in listening to smart people no matter the topic. She informed me about research using the 20 statements test (Kuhn & McPartland, 1954), where participants are presented with lines commencing with "I am" and then they complete the rest. The typical finding was that participants from individualist cultures write down more of their traits (e.g., "I am smart") and states (e.g., "I am hungry") than do people from collectivist cultures. Let us call these *private self-cognitions*. In contrast, people from collectivist cultures tend to write down more group memberships (e.g., "I am Chinese"). Let us call these *collective self-cognitions*. It occurred to me that there are at least two ways of accounting for the data. One way is what I called the one-basket theory, which assumes that people from individualist and collectivist cultures differ in the relative frequency with which the two types of self-cognitions are represented in memory. In contrast, the two-baskets theory assumes that there is a separate 'private self' where private self-cognitions are stored, and 'collective self' where collective self-cognitions are stored, and the crucial factor is the relative accessibility of the two selves. Specifically, the private self is more accessible for members of individualist than collectivist cultures whereas the collective self is more accessible for members of collectivist than individualist cultures. According to the two-baskets theory, but not the one-basket theory, it should be possible to prime either of the two self-concepts and influence the retrieval of self-cognitions. Priming the private self should increase the retrieval of private self-cognitions whereas priming the collective self should increase the retrieval of collective self-cognitions.

There was also a secondary prediction involving the order in which people should write down their self-cognitions. If self-cognitions are randomly thrown into a single self-structure as the one-basket theory asserts, and so the only factor is the relative frequency of private versus collective self-cognitions represented therein, the order of retrieval should be random. In contrast, according to the two-baskets theory, retrieving, say, a private self-cognition implies that the private self is activated, and so the next item should be another private self-cognition. Or, if a collective self-cognition is retrieved, that implies that the collective self is activated, and so the next item should be another collective self-cognition. In a word, the retrieval of self-cognitions should be clustered (non-random).

Seeing these possibilities made me happy, but I would have forgotten about them, had I not accidentally met Harry Triandis—a world famous researcher and advisor of Sharon Goto—while getting a drink at the drinking fountain. I exclaimed, "What a coincidence, I was just thinking about you!" He asked, "What were you thinking?" I replied by explaining the foregoing reasoning. He then excitedly expostulated, "I have been looking for this for twenty years, and you just happen to have it!" The result of my fortuitous conversation with Sharon, and my equally fortuitous drink at the drinking fountain, was a paper that we published together in *Journal of Personality and Social Psychology* (Trafimow, Triandis, & Goto, 1991). It has been cited thousands of times and established a new area within social psychology. For students, there are lessons here that go beyond the replication issue that I will take up again shortly.

- Listen to other people.
- Care about work outside your own area.
- Do not assume that your lack of expertise in an area precludes you from making an important contribution to that area.
- Give your imagination free play.

But what happened in the experiments? There were two experiments, each of which involved priming the private self or the collective self but using very different priming methods. Thus, Experiment 2 was a conceptual replication of Experiment 1, but within the same article. In both experiments, the predictions of the two-baskets theory were upheld whereas the predictions of the one-basket theory were disconfirmed. Thus, there was a winning theory—the two-baskets theory—and a losing theory—the one-basket theory. As we know from Chapter 1, this does not necessarily mean that the two-baskets theory is true or that the one-basket theory is false, however, the experiments certainly placed the two-baskets theory in a much better position than the one-basket theory. And the fact that it was possible to conceptually replicate, using different priming methods, importantly contributed to the superior position of the two-baskets theory over the one basket-theory. To put the icing on the cake, there have been many successful conceptual replications with a very wide range of different methods, reviewed by Oyserman and Lee (2008).

Replications Need Not Be Definitive: Falling Objects

The victory of the two-baskets theory over the one-basket theory, with many conceptual as well as quasi-exact replications, may seem to indicate that successful replications are definitive. And they often are considered so in the limited world of the social sciences, but this might not be a good thing. To see why, let us consider again a topic in Chapter 2, falling objects.

In Chapter 2, we discussed falling objects and Aristotle's trait theory that objects have a nature to fall with heavier objects having more of this nature than light objects. Although the ancient Greeks were not empiricists, let us use our imaginations and pretend that they were. Consider four heavy objects: iron skillet, large stone, heavy brick, iron sword. And consider four light objects: feather, small scrap of papyrus, lint, and small leaf. It is possible to imagine dropping any of the four heavy objects at the same time as dropping any of the four light objects, from the same height. There are 16 ways to do this, with the result that the heavy object always contacts the ground before the light object does, consistent with Aristotle's theory. We might also imagine the ancient Greeks performed each of these 16 experiments but using 10 different heights (e.g., 4 feet, 5 feet, etc.), so there are now 160 experiments. And then, we could imagine doing these 160 experiments in 10 different locations (e.g., Athens, Sparta, and so on), so there are now 1600 experiments. All of these would replicate: the heavy object contacts the ground before the light object does. How impressively have our imagined 1600 replications supported Aristotle's trait theory of falling objects?

There is more than one answer. Going the positive route, although the ancient Greeks did not usually perform formal experiments, we might consider everyday experience as roughly in the ballpark of having unofficially performed many experiments, with heavy objects always falling quickly and light objects always falling slowly. Hence, our imagined 1600 successful replications might not be considered all that far off from experiences of ancient Greeks supporting Aristotle's theory. But as is explained in Chapter 2, Aristotle was nevertheless wrong. When the interaction of object characteristics with the Earth's atmosphere is considered—where the lack of such consideration by the ancient Greeks is a blatant auxiliary assumption failure by omission—then light objects fall as fast as do heavy objects, as Galileo demonstrated almost two millennia later. Thus, successful replications—whether quasi-exact or conceptual—need not be definitive. It is worth remembering this when researchers, including myself, tout how wonderful their research is because of the many successful quasi-exact and conceptual replications.

Is There a Crisis Where Successful Replications Are the Exception Rather than the Rule?

For decades, psychology researchers have suspected that most findings in the literature do not replicate. When I was in graduate school, more than one professor told me of an easy way to quickly obtain a nice publication record. "All you need do," I was told, "is attempt to replicate something already published in a good journal. When the replication attempt fails, perform more studies to find out why, and then publish the set of studies!" Note the basic premise, which is that the attempt to replicate will almost certainly fail. This basic premise was considered so obvious, that it was taken as a given.

What everyone suspected, anecdotally, was formalized by the Open Science Collaboration (2015) replication project, as we saw in Chapter 4. To review, their replication failure rate exceeded 60% (going by statistical significance) and the average effect size in the replication cohort of studies was less than half that in the original cohort of studies. Other replication studies in both the social sciences and other sciences have not overturned the conclusion, though many have argued that replication failures are not surprising, not important, or otherwise not as worrisome as it seems at face value. Let us briefly consider these issues.

Are replication failures surprising? From the point of view that we are allegedly 'doing science,' and science findings are supposed to replicate, our replication failure record is, indeed, surprising. However, from a statistical point of view, that recognizes that there is variance across samples, it is not very surprising, as we saw in Chapter 4. The unsoundness of significance testing renders replication failures even less surprising; it might be considered a no-brainer that if we use an unsound method to decide if findings replicate, we are likely to be in trouble. Once we acknowledge that replication failures are not surprising, it is a short step to then conclude that they are unimportant. We see this in politics constantly, where some new fact comes out that is unfavorable to one party or the other, with the almost automatic riposte: "There is nothing new here. We already knew that!" The inference we are supposed to make is that because "we already knew that" the new fact is unimportant.

There are at least three problems with the "we already knew that" argument. The first problem is that it is overused. It is often the case that we did not already know that. We saw this earlier with the Rohrer et al. (2019) spectacular failures to replicate the money priming studies of Vohs et al. (2006). Although many suspected the original money priming findings too good to be true, many did not, and the Rohrer et al. replication failures were consequential demonstrations. Even those who suspected that something was wrong lacked the ability to make the much more definitive negative case that Rohrer et al. provided. Secondly, it is far from unheard of in science—especially in psychology—for a fact or argument to be published that deserves attention but fails to get it. It may require several iterations of the argument, by different authors, presented in different ways, for the item to get the attention it deserves. On the one hand, it is possible to argue that the latter authors have not contributed anything novel, and so their manuscripts should not have been published. On the other hand, a perhaps better argument is that if the latter authors better the field by ensuring that the potentially important item fulfills that potential, then publication is justified, after all. And so, we have another reason to reject the "we already knew that" argument.

Finally, and crucially, there is the issue of whether something we already knew is applied in an enlightening way. And to make this point, let us return to the money priming example. In setting up their replication failures, Rohrer et al. (2019) stated the following to demonstrate the importance of the Vohs et al. (2006) money priming findings (p. 263):

> Nobel Prize winner Daniel Kahneman (2011) wrote in his best-selling book *Thinking, Fast and Slow* that the research is "remarkable" and that the experiments are "profound" (p. 56). The findings also inspired a large literature of money-priming studies using a variety of manipulations and measures. To date, Google Scholar lists more than 1,300 citations of the article—the majority in the past 5 years.

The Rohrer et al. quotation renders indisputable that the money priming findings were of great consequence. Did we already know that many findings fail to replicate? Yes, sophisticated researchers already knew that. But somehow it was not until over two decades after the original work that it occurred to anyone to apply our knowledge of the difficulty of replicating findings to the specific money priming case at hand. I will summarize with the three bullet points below.

- Did we already know that replications are problematic before the Open Science Foundation (2015) article? Some did and some did not, but the case was less compelling without hard data.
- Did previous arguments that replications are problematic need making again, and in a different way? Surely, and the Open Science Collaboration (2015) article did that.
- Even given the previous two bullet points, did researchers understand to apply the notion of replication failures to the money priming work? The answer is in the negative, until Rohrer et al. (2019).

Thus, we see that, even though it is not surprising that replication failures are prevalent, prevalence is nevertheless important. The lack of surprisingness in no way reduces importance.

To finish off this point, consider again where we started, that empirical failures, even if we generously assume the auxiliary assumptions true, cannot falsify theories unless they are replicable. Likewise, empirical successes, as important as they otherwise might seem, cannot provide strong support for theories unless they are replicable. Knowing that replication failures are prevalent, and thus unsurprising, in no way reduces these critical points.

The Elephant-in-the-Room: Auxiliary Assumptions

Chapters 1–3 showed how theories have nonobservational terms and so auxiliary assumptions are necessary to traverse the distances between these terms and the observational terms in empirical hypotheses. Statistical and inferential assumptions matter too, but at present, let us focus on auxiliary assumptions. A friend and colleague named Brian Earp and I attempted to apply the necessity to have auxiliary assumptions to the replication issue (Earp & Trafimow, 2015). The application is straightforward.

Consider again the theoretical connection between attitudes and behaviors, but with an explicit recognition that attitudes cannot be observed. Thus, to measure attitudes towards wearing seatbelts, or towards anything whatsoever, it is necessary to make auxiliary assumptions to traverse the distance between unobservable attitudes and observable check marks on an attitude measure. Why should we believe that these check marks soundly indicate people's attitudes? Or we might consider the theoretical connection between threat and prejudice. We cannot observe threat or prejudice, and so it is necessary to make auxiliary assumptions to traverse the distance between unobservable threat feelings and a manipulation designed to influence them. Why should we believe that the manipulation influences threat? Or even if we grant that, why should we believe that the manipulation does not influence anything else that might affect prejudice? The answer to these questions, of course, is that we hope that our auxiliary assumptions are true, though hope is no guarantee of reality.

To connect to the replication issue, consider that researchers who perform conceptual replications need to make many auxiliary assumptions. They not only need to make the typical ones connecting their nonobservational theoretical terms to their observational empirical terms, but they need additional ones too. For example, if I replicate a study finding a correlation between attitudes and behaviors, but with a different attitude measure, a different behavior measure, or both, I need to find reasons why these differences should not matter. I need to make more auxiliary assumptions. The theory itself does not explain why these differences should not matter, it is up to the researchers who perform conceptual replications to make those arguments. And those arguments, with their implicit or explicit auxiliary assumptions, might be wrong!

The upshot is that there is not only the problem of random differences across samples that hinder replication attempts from succeeding, but there is an additional problem of extra auxiliary assumptions. Even if it were somehow possible to magic away the problem of random differences across samples, the problem of extra auxiliary assumptions would nevertheless remain. Although the issue of auxiliary assumptions is obviously essential for understanding replication failures, it still gets insufficient attention in replication discussions. My earnest hope is that you will not commit that sin of omission.

Imaginary Universes and Their Application to the Issue of Replicability

It should be obvious by now that the issue of replicability in the social sciences is difficult and complex. Consider some questions with no clear answers, bullet-listed below.

- How close does a second study have to be to an original study to be considered a replication attempt as opposed to being a different study?
- How does one specify the auxiliary assumptions in sufficient detail to know whether a second study should be considered a replication attempt as opposed to being a different study?
- Are studies performed with the purpose of generalizing to other contexts, cultures, and so on replication attempts or generalizability studies?
- How does one distinguish between a replication attempt versus a generalizability study?

It is possible to continue, but the bullet-listed questions should be sufficient to dramatize that the replication issue is difficult. Is there a way to simplify and avoid the bullet-listed questions?

I will now argue, as I have done previously (Trafimow, 2018b), that there is a way to simplify and thereby avoid many difficult questions. To approach the simplification, suppose it were possible to perform an original experiment the same way again. In other words, suppose it were possible to perform an exact replication without resorting to performing a quasi-exact replication. Even here, there are two possible meanings of an exact replication. One meaning is that everything, even random influences, are the same. In that case, the finding would replicate perfectly, by definition, and so there is little to gain by using this meaning. Secondly, we could mean that all systematic factors are the same, but that randomness could still influence the findings. Under the second meaning, it is not guaranteed that the finding would replicate because random factors might cause a replication failure. Let us see how far the second meaning can take us.

We might imagine two universes. One universe is the present universe, where both systematic and random factors influence research findings, and it is impossible to render all systematic factors the same across studies. Let us term this the 'real universe.' But stretching the idea in the previous paragraph implies a second universe, where it is possible to render all systematic factors the same across studies. Let us term this the 'ideal universe.' In thinking about the replication issue, there are two types of factors in the real universe that can cause replications to fail: systematic and random. In contrast, only randomness can be a problem in the ideal universe. If we restrict ourselves to the ideal universe for now, it should be possible to calculate the probability of successfully replicating even if we never actually perform the replication attempt. How so?

To complete the argument, we need two pieces. The first piece is that we need to agree on what we mean by a successful replication. The second piece is that we need to assume it is possible to mathematize the first piece. Both are possible, and even reasonably easy, as will be explained in the following subsections.

What Is a Successful Replication?

We have already discussed why it is a poor idea to conceptualize a successful replication in terms of significance tests. Instead, we saw that a much better way to go is consider a replication attempt successful if the statistic of interest is similar in both the original and replication study. For example, if it is a correlational study, we would hope that the correlation coefficient would be approximately the same in the two studies. If it is an experimental study, we would hope that the effect size is approximately the same in the two studies. But it is possible to do even better.

In Chapter 4, we contrasted samples against the populations from which they are drawn, and we saw that what we really want is to obtain sample statistics that are good estimates of corresponding population parameters. Thus, we hope that our sample correlation coefficient is a good estimate of the corresponding population correlation coefficient, that our sample difference between means is a good estimate of the population difference between means, and so on. Once we recognize that what really matters is the unknown population parameter of interest, we can see both an original and replication attempt as serving in the interest of estimating that unknown population parameter. In turn, then, it follows that if the sample statistics from both studies are close to the corresponding population parameter we want them to estimate, then we have a successful replication. Of course, this reasoning implies a question: How close do we want our sample statistic to be to the corresponding population parameter?

At this point, it is necessary to be arbitrary. For example, we might insist that our sample statistic is within one-tenth of a standard deviation of the corresponding population parameter. There is nothing magical about one-tenth. If it suits our purposes, we could use two-tenths, or any other fraction. Given an arbitrary closeness interval (say, one-tenth), if we know the sample size—and we should if the study has already been performed—it is possible to calculate the probability of obtaining a sample statistic within that interval provided we have a reasonable approximation of the relevant distribution (normal, skew normal, uniform, and so on). The issue of distributions will be discussed at length in Chapter 6. For now, we will take it as given that we know a distribution that provides a reasonable approximation of the population.

Let us suppose that the sample size of an experiment is 385, and that we have good reasons for assuming a normal distribution. We can do much better than this, as will be explained in

72   General Methodological Issues

Chapter 6, but let us go ahead anyhow with the almost certainly false assumption that the population is normally distributed. We wish to calculate a sample mean to estimate the population mean. What is the probability that the sample mean is within one-tenth of a standard deviation of the population mean? That probability is 0.95. In Chapter 6, you will see exactly how to make the calculation, and there will be links to free and user-friendly programs that will aid you in making the calculation under different sorts of assumptions, but that complexity is unnecessary at present.

Using the 0.95 value, let us now consider the probability of replication in our ideal universe. To warm you up to this, let us commence by imagining two flips of a fair coin and calculate the probability that both are heads. If the coin is fair, then the probability of heads on one coin flip is 0.5, so that the probability of getting heads on two flips is $0.5 \cdot 0.5 = 0.5^2 = 0.25$. Or, if we imagine a fair die with six sides, the probability of getting a '6' on two rolls is $\frac{1}{6} \cdot \frac{1}{6} = \left(\frac{1}{6}\right)^2 = \frac{1}{36}$.

Moving now to the probability of replication, if the probability of obtaining a sample statistic close to the corresponding population parameter in one experiment is 0.95, then the probability of obtaining a sample statistic close to the corresponding population parameter in two experiments is $0.95 \cdot 0.95 = 0.95^2 = 0.9025 \approx 0.90$. In other words, there is an approximately 90% chance of successfully replicating.

It is important to be upfront about the switch here from the usual way of conceptualizing what a successful replication means. To reiterate, the usual idea is that there is a successful replication if both studies result in a statistically significant P-value. We saw that a better way is to imagine a replication attempt as successful if the sample statistics are similar in the two studies. But now we have an even better way to think, which hearkens back to our goal to have sample statistics that are good estimates of corresponding population parameters. If the sample statistics from the original study, and from the replication attempt, are both close to the population parameter we wish to estimate, then we have a successful replication.

In general, then, the probability of replication in our ideal universe is the probability of obtaining a sample statistic within the specified distance of the corresponding population parameter (e.g., one-tenth) in a single study, squared. Or to use symbols: $P_{replication} = \left(P_{being\ close\ in\ one\ experiment}\right)^2$.

There is one small fly in the proverbial ointment. To arrive at our elegant way to calculate the probability of replication, it was necessary to assume an ideal universe where all differences between the two studies are due to randomness, with no systematic differences. But you might well wonder whether the ideal universe provides any basis, whatsoever, for drawing conclusions in the real universe that we are forced to inhabit. Happily, there is a simple way to address this issue. Consider again that in the ideal universe, the only thing that can go wrong is randomness whereas in the real universe systematic factors can go wrong too. Thus, there is more that can go wrong in the real universe than in the ideal universe, which is why we invented the ideal universe. Well, then, recall the example where the probability of replication, in the ideal universe, is approximately 0.90. Because there is more that can go wrong in the real universe than in the ideal universe, the probability of replication in the real universe must be some value less than 0.90. Our ideal value of 0.90 is an upper limit on the probability of replication in the real universe.

But what is the value in having an upper limit? The value is this. In most studies, sample sizes are a good deal less than 385 as we had set it in the example. As will become clear in Chapter 6, the larger the sample size, the better the probability of obtaining a sample statistic that is within the interval defined as close to the population parameter. Therefore, because the probability of replication is simply that probability squared, it follows that the probability of replication depends crucially upon the sample size of the study. For example, had we used 273 participants instead of 385 in the example, the probability of obtaining a sample mean within one-tenth of the population mean would only be 0.90, so that the probability of replication would be $0.90 \cdot 0.90 = 0.90^2 = 0.81$. However, even this would be a very high value for psychology. Because most psychology experiments use considerably fewer participants, even the ideal probability of replication is usually quite low, thereby rendering the real probability of replication even lower.

A way for you to use the notion of an ideal probability of replication is as follows. When you read an article, you can note the sample size. Given the sample size, and the type of distribution the authors assume for whatever statistics they compute (usually normal), it is easy to calculate the idealized probability of replication. You can use the programs to be presented in Chapter 6 to calculate the probability of obtaining a sample statistic within the distance of the corresponding population parameter you specify. In turn, merely square that value, and you have the idealized probability of replication. If that idealized probability of replication is small, you know that the real probability of replication is even smaller, and so you will know not to trust that finding. Having a way to know what not to trust is a big deal. In addition, in the few cases where the idealized probability of replication is not small, then you can have at least some reason to believe the finding can be trusted.

Chapter Summary

The ability to replicate matters. Findings that fail to replicate fail to convincingly support or disconfirm theories. That replication failures seem to be the rule, rather than the exception in psychology, has worried many. However, an important problem is that most researchers use a significance testing way of thinking to assess whether findings replicate, and this is unsound. A better way is to look at the actual descriptive statistics across studies to see how similar or different they are. However, an even better way is to imagine an idealized universe where it is possible to perform an exact replication and the only thing that can go wrong is randomness. In the idealized universe, it is easy to calculate the probability of replication. In turn, because systematic differences exist in the real world, as well as differences attributable to randomness, there is more that can go wrong in the real universe than in the idealized universe. Hence, the idealized probability of replication sets an upper limit on the real probability of replication. If the idealized probability of replication is unimpressive, and it usually is, then the probability of replication in the real world must be even less impressive, and the work should not be trusted. In the few cases where the idealized probability of replication is impressive, this does not prove that the real probability of replication is impressive too, but it is at least a reasonable hope.

6 The A Priori Procedure (APP)

In Chapter 4 we saw that much is wrong with the null hypothesis significance testing procedure. In Chapter 5 we saw that there are important problems pertaining to psychology researchers being able to replicate findings and that there is a connection between significance testing and what many consider to be a replication crisis. However, an important limitation of these chapters is that I have not yet proposed any alternatives to significance testing other than not to do it. The present chapter and the following chapter present positive alternatives.

To set up the current direction for progress, let us consider a basic problem with significance testing which is that it promises to do that which cannot be done soundly by any inferential statistical procedure. Specifically, no such procedure can soundly tell researchers what hypothesis they should believe. Like it or not, what to believe requires subjective judgment and hopefully expert judgment too. This is because there are many factors that ought to influence what you believe, with inferential statistical factors only composing a subset of them. To ask such a procedure to tell you what hypothesis to believe is an exercise in idiocy, though such thinking has pervaded the social sciences for the last century.

Well, then, if inferential statistical procedures cannot soundly answer the question, "What should we believe?" Is there a different question that such procedures can answer? There is. Inferential statistics can answer the question: "How likely are my sample statistics to be within particular distances of corresponding population parameters?" Or, prior to data collection: "What sample size do I need to be confident that my sample statistics are close to their corresponding population parameters?" Or, to ask this in a general way: "What sample size do I need to be able to trust my sample statistics as good estimators of their corresponding population parameters?" In essence, the idea is to move from using an inferential statistical procedure to tell us what to believe—which it cannot do soundly—to using an inferential statistical procedure to help us obtain sample sizes that ensure sample statistics that are good estimates of corresponding population parameters. But why should you care about population parameters?

Well, I have already given you the answer in Chapter 3, and I'll repeat and summarize here. In Chapter 3, we imagined Laplace's omniscient demon who warns us that our sample statistics have nothing to do with corresponding population parameters. And we saw that this would be a disaster: there would be no reason to believe that our findings would replicate and no way to draw conclusions about hypotheses. Thus, having confidence that sample statistics are good estimates of corresponding population parameters is a prerequisite for drawing conclusions about hypotheses. Just as the American colonists insisted, "No taxation without representation," it should be obvious that in social science experiments that depend on sample statistics, "There is no hypothesis testing without estimation." In turn, under the assumption of random selection from the population (which is usually false, but we will address that later), the trustworthiness of sample statistics to estimate corresponding population parameters depends on sample sizes. So, let us talk about sample sizes.

As the simplest case, let us unrealistically assume that participants are randomly selected from a normally distributed population with known variance. Our goal is to compute the sample mean and hope it is a good estimate of the population mean. Commonsense suggests that the larger the sample, the better the sample mean will estimate the population mean. But there remain two questions we need to ask ourselves, bullet-listed below.

- The precision question: How close do we want our sample mean to be to the population mean?
- The confidence question: What probability do we want to have of meeting our precision specification?

Once we have answered both bullet-listed questions, it is possible to estimate the sample size necessary to meet our specifications.

76 *General Methodological Issues*

For instance, suppose that we want our sample mean to be within one-tenth of a standard deviation of the population mean, and we wish to have a probability of 0.95 of meeting that goal. In a priori procedure (APP) language, we desire to have precision at the 0.10 level and confidence at the 95% level. In my paper to introduce this topic (Trafimow, 2017b), I proved Equation 1 below:

$$n = \left(\frac{z_{(1-c)/2}}{f}\right)^2, \qquad (6.1)$$

where,

- n is the sample size the researcher needs to collect,
- f is the desired level of precision,
- and $z_{(1-c)/2}$ is the z-score that corresponds to the level of confidence desired.

Let us continue the example where the researcher wishes to have precision at the 0.10 level and confidence at the 95% level. The Z-score that corresponds to 95% confidence is approximately 1.96 and indexes the tail value under the normal distribution that corresponds with a given probability. Put another way, if you imagine splitting the 0.05 that is left over after subtracting 0.95 from 1.00 into two parts, each equal to 0.025, the Z-score gives the value that corresponds with having the 0.025 left over in the right tail of the normal distribution. If you have not had enough statistics to understand what this means, do not worry because help is on the way after finishing the example. Instantiating 0.01 and 1.96 into Equation 1 renders the following:

$n = \left(\dfrac{1.96}{0.01}\right)^2 = 364.16 \approx 385$. It is an APP convention to always round up to the nearest whole

number because participants do not come in fractions. Thus, if the researcher wishes to have a probability of 0.95 of obtaining a sample mean within one-tenth of a standard deviation of the population mean, it is necessary to collect 385 participants or more.

Well, then, suppose the researcher collects 385 participants. In that case, within the limits of the specifications, the researcher can trust that the sample mean is a good estimate of the population mean. There is no need for a significance test because the researcher already knows that the sample mean can be trusted. The inferential work is performed before data collection; hence, the name, a priori procedure (APP).

If you found Equation 1 or the part about Z-scores tough going, do not worry. There is an easier way, which is to use the following link to a free and user-friendly program (Li et al., 2020): https://app-normal.shinyapps.io/N_SingleSample_EstimateMean_KnownVariance. After activating the link, enter the desired precision and confidence in the boxes provided (e.g., 0.10 and 0.95), and the program will return the necessary sample size. It is that easy!

If the population variance is unknown (the usual case), use the following link instead: https://app-normal.shinyapps.io/N_SingleSample_EstimateMean_UnknownVariance. There is only a very slight difference, so if you accidentally use the wrong link, the damage will be minimal.

Comparing Means or Locations

Researchers are often interested in comparing means, such as the experimental condition mean versus the control condition mean. Furthermore, the design might be within-participants, which means that the same participants are involved in both conditions. This is sometimes termed a matched samples or matched groups design. Alternatively, the design might be between-participants, which means that there are different participants in each condition. This is sometimes termed an independent samples or independent groups design. In addition, it is possible to assume that participants are randomly selected from normally distributed populations, but there are other possibilities too such as skew normal populations. In the latter case, the mathematics can get quite complex, but as there are computer programs available to do the heavy mathematical lifting, there is no need to delve into the mathematics. Citations will be provided in case the reader wishes to delve into the mathematical derivations.

Assume Normal Distributions

In a recent paper, I and two colleagues showed how to apply APP thinking to cases where researchers wish to compare two means under normality (Trafimow, Wang, & Wang, 2020). Whether you have matched or independent samples, you can use the following link: https://app-normal.shinyapps.io/N_TwoSamples_EstimateMean. Either way, enter your specifications for precision and confidence in the boxes provided, and the program will return the minimum sample size necessary to meet your specifications. There is a slight complication in reading the output because there are two minimum sample sizes, not one. The smaller of the two values is for matched samples and is marked thusly. The larger of the two values is for independent samples and is also marked appropriately. Note that when the samples are matched, the sample size in each group also equals the total sample size, whereas when the samples are independent, the total sample size is the sum of the sample sizes in each group. Thus, the total sample size is much larger for independent samples than for matched samples.

Assume Skew Normal Distributions

Although psychology researchers usually assume their data are normally distributed, this is rarely a true assumption. Distributions are usually skewed (Blanca et al., 2013; Ho & Yu, 2015; Micceri, 1989). In Chapter 3, we discussed that whereas normal distributions have two parameters, mean and standard deviation, skew normal distributions have three parameters, location, scale, and shape. When the shape parameter is zero, the distribution is normal; the location equals the mean, and the scale equals the standard deviation. But when the shape parameter does not equal zero, the distribution is not normal; the location does not equal the mean, and the scale does not equal the standard deviation. In Chapter 3 we saw how differences in means and locations can go in opposite directions and so it crucial to get right whether one is dealing with normal or skew normal distributions.

It is worth stressing that because the family of normal distributions is a subset of the larger family of skew normal distributions, the family of skew normal distributions is more widely applicable than the family of normal distributions. This relation gives rise to an interesting asymmetry. If a distribution is skew normal, and you assume it is normal, then you are plain wrong. However, if a distribution is normal, and you assume it is skew normal, then there is still no problem because the family of normal distributions is included in the family of skew normal distributions. Therefore, it is generally better to assume skew normality than to assume normality.

The advice in the previous paragraph goes counter to typical social science advice. Most social scientists consider normal distributions 'good' and skew normal distributions 'bad.' When a distribution is not normal, social science researchers often perform data transformations to render the data near normal, and this is understandable from a null hypothesis significance testing standpoint, where the significance tests are much easier to perform under the assumption of normality. Moreover, social scientists often cite the Central Limit Theorem as indicating that it is okay to assume normality even when it is not true. According to the Central Limit Theorem, the distribution of sample means tends towards normality even if the parent distributions are not normal, and the larger the sample size, the closer the trend in the direction of normality. Therefore, the argument goes, it does not matter if the assumption of normality is violated. The Central Limit Theorem is a good theorem, but it need not indicate that researchers should ignore skewness, as we shall see presently.

Skew normal distributions are taller and narrower than normal distributions, which implies that a higher percentage of the points are within the bulk of the distribution than out in the tails of the distribution. A positive consequence is that estimates pertaining to skew normal distributions should be more accurate than estimates pertaining to normal distributions. To view skew normal distributions, you can go to the following website: https://en.wikipedia.org/wiki/Skew_normal_distribution. Increasing skewness, in either the positive or negative direction, causes skew normal distributions to become increasingly taller and narrower.

Let us commence with a single sample, but assuming a skew normal distribution (Trafimow, Wang, & Wang, 2019). The goal is not to estimate the mean, but rather to estimate the location, as it is the location that is a parameter of skew normal distributions. To compute the necessary sample size, use the following link: https://appforsn.shinyapps.io/nonesample/. Instead of the usual two boxes, there are now three boxes. Two of them pertain to precision and confidence, as usual. And there is a box that pertains to the shape parameter. If you have previous data, you might have a reasonable indication of the shape of the distribution. If not, you might have no idea about the shape of the distribution. In the latter case, a conservative strategy would be to assume normality and set the shape parameter at zero. A slightly less conservative strategy would be to set the shape parameter at 0.10. It is a very rare distribution that would not have at least this much skewness and setting the shape parameter at 0.10 nevertheless provides substantial participants savings. In addition, once the data are collected, you can see for yourself whether there is at least a very slight amount of skewness, as a check on whether you were justified to use the 0.10 value for the shape parameter. As an alert, all programs pertaining to skew normal distributions may take a minute to produce the desired output.

It is instructive to use the computer program to enter values for shape, precision, and confidence to see what happens. Figure 6.1 illustrates the results based on entering 0.10 for precision, 0.95 for confidence, and letting the shape parameter vary between 0 and 0.5.

Figure 6.1 illustrates how the necessary sample size to meet specifications decreases as the shape parameter increases (more skewness). The necessary sample size is 385, 231, 75, 36, 22, and 14, when the shape parameter is 0, 0.1, 0.2, 0.3, 0.4, and 0.5, respectively. In contrast to the usual characterization that skewness is bad, Figure 6.1 demonstrates the opposite; skewness is good! The more skewed the distribution, the greater the sample size savings. Consider the extremes. When there is no skewness, 385 participants are needed to meet specifications whereas when the shape parameter is 0.5, only 14 participants are needed, for a savings of 385 − 14 = 371. Even very slight skewness, that would be difficult to see in a graph, such as when the shape parameter equals 0.10, nevertheless results in impressive participants savings: 385 − 231 = 154. Contrary to the usual pronouncements, skewness is your friend and not your enemy!

Or suppose there are two matched samples, and the goal is to estimate the difference in locations (not means) between the two groups (Wang, Wang, Trafimow, & Myüz, 2019). To carry out the APP, use the following link: https://appforsn.shinyapps.io/nmatch/. As in the one-sample

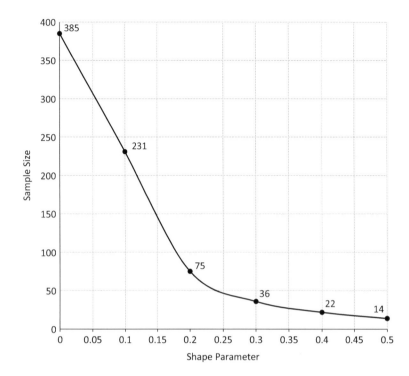

Figure 6.1 The minimum sample size necessary for precision at the 0.10 level and confidence at the 95% level ranges along the vertical axis as a function of the shape parameter along the horizontal axis.

case, there is a box for you to enter the shape parameter, the desired level of precision, and the desired level of confidence. The output does not look very different from the one-sample case, so I did not include a figure.

A more complex case is if there are two independent samples, and the goal is to estimate the population difference in locations (Wang, Wang, Trafimow, & Chen, 2019). In that case, you should use the following link: https://one-location.shinyapps.io/ninddiffloctn/. Using this program is more difficult than using the others discussed so far, but it is still reasonably easy. In this case, there are six boxes, with two of them being the familiar ones for precision and confidence. The other four boxes pertain to the two conditions: there are two shape parameter boxes and two scale boxes. We saw in the one-sample and matched samples cases that it is necessary to enter a value for the shape of the distribution. The present case is no exception, except that there are two conditions and so it is necessary to enter two shape parameters, one for each condition. Then, too, there are two scale boxes. As explained earlier, the scale in skew normal distributions is roughly analogous to the standard deviation in normal distributions, and the two are the same when the shape parameter equals 0, so there is normality.

Although the shape is more important than the scale for determining sample sizes, the scale nevertheless matters. Figure 6.2 illustrates the case where the precision was set at 0.10, the confidence at 95%, and both the shape parameters varied together (both set at 0, 0.10, 0.20, 0.30, 0.40, and 0.50) and the scale parameters were set at 1.00 (bottom curve) or 2.00 (top curve).

80 *General Methodological Issues*

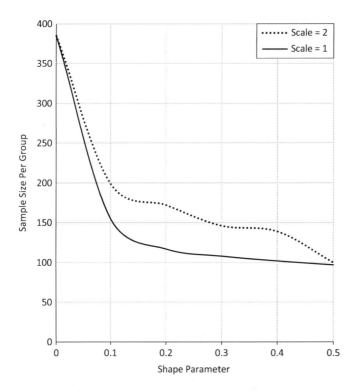

Figure 6.2 The sample size per group ranges along the vertical axis as a function of the shape parameter for both groups along the horizontal axis (shape of both groups = 0, 0.10, 0.20, 0.30, 0.40, and 0.50). The scale is set at 1.00 (bottom curve) or 2.00 (top curve).

Figure 6.2 shows two interesting effects. Consistent with Figure 6.1, skewness produces sample size savings. Secondly, the smaller the scale value, the fewer the participants needed to meet specifications for precision and confidence. This is not surprising as variability in the data is generally deleterious for estimation. The skewness effect is more important. Again, skewness is your friend and not your enemy. Thus, ignoring skewness constitutes a sizable opportunity cost.

There are additional APP applications to skew normal distributions. Suppose you have a single sample but in contrast to being interested in the location, you are rather interested in the scale (Wang, Wang, Trafimow, & Zhang, 2019). You wish to determine the minimum sample size needed so that your sample scale statistic is a good estimate of the population scale parameter. The procedure is like that which we have seen already. You decide upon specifications for precision and confidence and use a convenient computer program to obtain the minimum sample size necessary to meet your specifications. You can use the following link: https://appforsn.shinyapps.io/nscale/. As we have seen with the program concerning sample sizes for estimating a sample location parameter, this program also has three boxes: the shape parameter, the precision specification, and the confidence specification. If you wish to assume normality and are concerned with the standard deviation (which is the same as the scale under this condition), simply set the shape parameter at 0.

Or you might be interested in estimating the shape parameter (Wang, Wang, Trafimow, Xu, 2021). In that case, use the following link: https://appforsn.shinyapps.io/nskewness/. There are only two boxes: precision and confidence.

Correlational Research

Much research in the social sciences is correlational rather than experimental. Thus, there is only one sample of participants, and the goal is to determine the correlation coefficient between two variables. The hope, of course, is that the sample correlation coefficient is a good estimate of the population correlation coefficient. What sample size is needed to meet specifications for precision and confidence such that the sample correlation coefficient can be trusted to be a good estimate of the population correlation coefficient? My colleagues and I derived the answer (Wang et al., 2021). To make the calculation easily, use the following link: https://appforsn.shinyapps.io/ncorr/. There are only two boxes: precision and confidence. Furthermore, this program works regardless of whether the distribution is bivariate normal or bivariate skew normal.

Sometimes researchers are interested in predicting a criterion variable from multiple predictor variables. The usual procedure is multiple regression analysis, which results in regression coefficients for each of the predictor variables. What sample size is necessary to justify trust that all the sample regression coefficients are good estimates of their corresponding population regression coefficients? My colleagues and I derived the answer (Tong et al., 2022a), and it can be obtained by activating the following link: https://probab.shinyapps.io/linearregressionweights/. There are four boxes. Two of them refer to precision and confidence, as usual. A third box refers to the number of predictor variables. And there is a fourth box that refers to a noncentral parameter. The idea is that distribution means sometimes deviate from zero, so they are noncentral. When there is a lack of previous data on which to base a guess, you can use 4.0 as a conservative default value.

Common sense suggests that as the number of predictor variables increases, the minimum sample size necessary to meet precision and confidence specifications for all of them should increase too. However, in this case, common sense is wrong. In fact, as the number of predictor variables increases, the minimum sample size necessary to meet precision and confidence specifications for all of them decreases!

To see how this works, let us set precision at 0.10 and confidence at 95%, and use a default value of 4.0 for the noncentral parameter. What happens when we vary the number of predictor variables? Figure 6.3 illustrates the answer.

As Figure 6.3 illustrates, adding predictor variables decreases, rather than increases the minimum sample size necessary to meet specifications for precision and confidence. The effect is dramatic when the number of predictor variables is small. For example, when there is only a single predictor variable, the necessary sample size is 1013 but decreases dramatically with the inclusion of more predictor variables. When there are few predictor variables, adding another predictor variable can result in impressive sample size savings. However, when there are many predictor variables, the benefit of adding another one is less impressive.

A caveat is that this program assumes multivariate normality. We are currently developing an APP application where this assumption is not necessary.

Proportions

Sometimes researchers are interested in proportions. For example, a marketing firm might be interested in determining the proportion of participants who intend to buy their product. I and some colleagues addressed this issue (Trafimow et al., 2020). As there are only two choices, such as the intention to buy or not buy a product, the relevant distribution is binomial, and can be approximated by a normal distribution. It is easy to obtain the sample size necessary to trust that the sample proportion to be obtained meets specifications for precision and confidence for

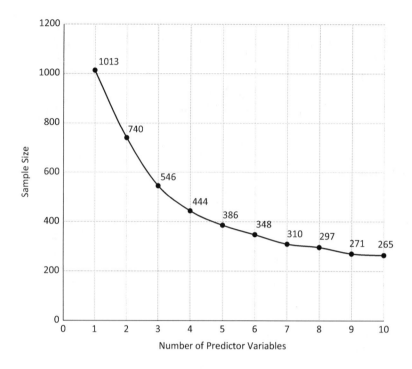

Figure 6.3 The minimum sample size necessary to meet specifications for precision and confidence ranges along the vertical axis as a function of the number of predictor variables along the horizontal axis. The ten values along the curve are exact sample size values.

estimating the population proportion. Merely activate the following link: https://app-normal.shinyapps.io/EstimateProp_OneSample.

Upon activating the link, you will see three boxes. One of them is for precision, but it works slightly differently than in the other programs. In the case, for example, when one is interested in a mean, the precision refers to obtaining a sample mean within some distance of the population mean, say, one-tenth of a standard deviation. In contrast, for proportions, precision refers to an absolute value. For example, if precision is set at 0.03, with 95% confidence, the meaning is that the sample proportion has a 95% chance of being within 0.03 of the population proportion. The precision value is absolute and not tied to the standard deviation as previously. Of course, there is a box for confidence too, that works in the usual way. Finally, there is a box for entering the expected proportion based on previous data. Alternatively, if there are no prior expectations, you can enter a default value of 0.50, which is the most conservative option.

Alternatively, researchers are sometimes interested not in proportions, but rather in the difference between proportions in two groups. For example, marketing researchers might be interested in the difference between the proportion of males versus females who are interested in their product, so they can target the more favorable population. I and my colleagues addressed this too (Trafimow et al., 2020). To make the calculation easily, activate the following link: https://app-normal.shinyapps.io/EstimateProp_TwoSamples.

Upon activating the link, four boxes will appear. Two of them pertain to precision and confidence. The other two boxes pertain to the estimated proportions for both groups. In the absence of prior data or some other reason to have expectations, you can enter 0.50 in both boxes, which is the most conservative option.

For most research involving proportions, the foregoing link using the normal approximation to the binomial distribution is fine. However, for extreme proportions, such as those near 0.01 or 0.99, a more accurate estimate can be obtained by using a skew normal, rather than normal, approximation to the binomial distribution. Thus, we have mathematics and a computer program that is useful in such extreme cases (Cao et al., 2021). Here is the link to the computer program: https://one-location.shinyapps.io/nproportionmean/. There are three boxes. One box is for the estimated proportion. If you suspect that the proportion will be an extreme value, such as 0.01, then enter that in the box provided. Remember that you can check this guess against the data when you obtain it. And there are boxes for precision and confidence just as when we use a normal approximation to the binomial distribution.

Cohen's d

Sometimes researchers are less interested in differences in means, and more interested in standardized differences in means. That is, they are interested in how much larger the mean is in one than the other condition, but in standard deviation units. An underlying assumption is that the population standard deviations in both groups are the same. Based on this assumption, Cohen's d is the most popular effect size index (Cohen, 1988), and it is easy to calculate: Cohen's $d = \dfrac{M_1 - M_2}{s}$, where M_1 is the mean of the first group, M_2 is the mean of the second group, and s is the standard deviation.[1]

Under the assumption of normally distributed populations, my colleagues and I have derived a way to estimate the minimum sample size, per group, necessary to obtain a sample effect size (Cohen's d), that is within specifications for precision and confidence (Chen et al., 2021). Furthermore, this can be done for either matched or independent samples. To make the calculation easily for matched samples, activate the following link: https://appcohensd.shinyapps.io/matched/. Using the program is a bit tricky and may take a few minutes to understand because there are unfamiliar places in which to make entries.

The first entry is your guess about what Cohen's d will be, based on previous data. Larger entries imply larger minimum samples sizes to meet specifications for precision and confidence. Therefore, entering large values is more conservative than entering smaller values. If no previous data are available, a reasonably conservative entry would be 0.5 which is Cohen's cutoff for a medium effect size. If you wish to be extremely (perhaps unreasonably) conservative, you can enter a value of 0.8, which is Cohen's cutoff for a large effect size.

The second entry is your guess about the shape of the distribution formed by subtracting scores in one distribution from scores in the other. In the absence of relevant previous data, the most conservative option is to assume that this distribution is normal, in which case you should enter 0 in this box. As we have seen in Figure 6.2 and Figure 6.3, entering a value different from zero will return a smaller minimum sample size necessary to meet specifications for precision and confidence. This is the reason entering 0 is the most conservative option. If you have a strong suspicion that the shape will not equal zero, you could enter a less conservative value and later check that value against the data when you acquire it.

The third entry is the correlation between your two matched samples. If you have previous relevant data, you can use that to help decide what you enter. If not, which is more likely, then you can use 0.50 as a reasonable entry. Happily, entries in this box have very little effect in making your sample size estimate.

84 *General Methodological Issues*

Finally, the fourth and fifth entries pertain to the familiar precision and confidence specifications. As an alert, it may take a minute or so for the program to return your sample size estimate.

For independent samples, there is a different link: https://appcohensd.shinyapps.io/independent/. This program is easier to use than the program for matched samples, and there are only three entries. The first entry is your guess about what Cohen's *d* will be. As is true for matched samples, when the samples are independent, a larger entry will return a larger estimate for the minimum sample size needed to meet specifications for precision and confidence. Therefore, in the absence of prior data, a reasonably conservative value would be 0.50, and an extremely conservative value would be 0.80. The second and third entries pertain to precision and confidence, respectively. Like the matched samples program, it may take a minute for this program to return the desired output.

There is one last point. When the samples are independent, remember that the total sample size is the sum of the sample sizes of the two groups. The value that the program returns is the value for one group, and you will have to double this to obtain the total sample size that includes both groups.

What If You Make the Wrong Distributional Assumption?

As a preliminary to answering the question, consider again the large conceptual difference between using an inferential statistical procedure to use sample statistics to estimate corresponding population parameters, versus using an inferential procedure to give a dichotomous answer to whether a hypothesis is true. In the latter case, there are only two possibilities, you can be correct or incorrect. There is no such thing as close, and we saw in Chapter 4 that this is a fatal problem for the null hypothesis significance testing procedure. That is the bad news. But in the present estimation context, we are no longer forcing dichotomania on ourselves. For estimation, the expectation is that the researcher will be wrong, but if the researcher is reasonably close to being right, the estimate may nevertheless be useful. If a pollen researcher estimates the concentration of pollen in the atmosphere based on samples, that estimate will not be exactly right, but it may be close enough to be useful. This is the good news.

Let us apply this thinking to the APP. Suppose that due to model wrongness, an APP program overestimates the sample size necessary to meet specifications for precision and confidence. How bad is this? The answer is that it may not be that bad. For example, returning to Figure 6.2, suppose that you assume normality and you are wrong, and the shape parameter is 0.10. The penalty for being wrong, as we have seen, is that you collect 154 participants more than you needed to collect to meet specifications of 0.10 for precision and 95% for confidence. This might be inconvenient or cost you more money. On the other hand, a positive consequence is that you have even better precision or confidence than you had desired to obtain. Thus, overestimating the minimum sample size necessary to meet specifications for precision and confidence may not be a bad thing, and could even be a good thing.

Or suppose that you overestimate the size of the shape parameter, so you collect fewer participants than you need to meet specifications for precision and confidence. In that case, your precision or confidence will be less than you had desired to obtain. If you are only slightly wrong, this need not be fatal. For example, if you desired precision at the 0.10 level, and instead you have it at the 0.11 level, although this is undesirable, the estimate may nevertheless remain useful. And remember that once you have the data, you can check the accuracy of your guesses. Of course, if you are very wrong, such as ending up with precision at the 0.40 level when you wished to have it at the 0.10 level, this would be a serious problem. Because, in most cases, underestimating is worse than overestimating, I recommended conservative entries in those places where guesses had to be made, such as guesses about distribution shapes. However, if you are in a research area where obtaining participants is extremely costly, such as if you need to use highly trained personnel as participants, you might opt for more liberal options.

We are now ready to talk about using the wrong distribution. We have already seen that if distributions are skewed, and you assume normality, the cost in participants can be high. If participants are expensive to obtain, this cost may be prohibitive. But for most research conducted with introductory psychology students or online participants, the cost of obtaining participants is low, and overestimating the minimum sample size necessary to meet specifications for precision and confidence may not be much of a problem. It may even be a positive because of better sampling precision.

Sometimes, however, assuming the wrong distribution has very little in the way of consequences for estimating the minimum sample size necessary to meet specifications for precision and confidence. My colleagues and I tested gamma distributions versus lognormal distributions for using the sample mean to estimate the population mean (Cao et al., 2022). To estimate the minimum sample size necessary to meet specifications for precision and confidence under lognormality, you can use the following link: https://probdiffgamma.shinyapps.io/lognormal/. There are three entries. There is a guess to be made about the standard deviation to be entered in the first box. And then there are the familiar entries for precision and confidence.

For gamma distributions, you can use the following link: https://probdiffgamma.shinyapps.io/app-gamma/. Again, there are three entries. The first entry is a guess to be made about shape and the latter two entries again pertain to precision and confidence.

The reason for mentioning lognormal and gamma distributions is that we performed computer simulations to test whether wrongly assuming a lognormal distribution, when it is really a gamma distribution, or the reverse, is strongly deleterious for estimating the minimum sample size needed to meet expectations for precision and confidence. In contrast to the issue of normality versus skew normality, here being wrong makes very little difference. For example, the necessary sample size to meet specifications of 0.10 for precision and 95% for confidence is 391 for a lognormal distribution and 392 for a normal distribution (see Cao et al., 2022, Table 1 and Table 2). The larger lesson is that being wrong can matter more, or matter less, for estimation goals, and each type of wrongness must be evaluated separately.

The APP Is Not Power Analysis

As we have seen, the APP goal is to determine minimum sample sizes to meet specifications for precision and confidence, so that the sample statistics to be obtained will be good estimates of corresponding population parameters. There is a surface similarity to traditional power analysis, that also has the goal of determining minimum sample sizes researchers need to collect. Consequently, it is easy to confuse the APP and power analysis as both seem to have the same goals.

However, there is a crucial difference. For the APP, the end goal is to have good estimates of population parameters. For power analysis, the end goal is to 'detect effects,' which ultimately translates to obtaining statistical significance. In power analysis, one assumes a population effect size one wishes to detect, typically Cohen's $d = 0.50$ (a so-called medium effect size). One also must be concerned with power, which informally is the ability to avoid the error of accepting the null hypothesis when it is false and is typically set at 80%. These values can be instantiated into a power analysis equation to determine the minimum sample sizes needed to meet these specifications. It is worth reiterating, however, the contrast in goals: to obtain good estimates of population parameters (APP goal) or obtain statistical significance (power analysis goal).

The difference in goals should remind us of what we learned in Chapter 4, that null hypothesis significance testing is an unsound procedure. This is a fatal problem for power analysis because the goal of power analysis is to aid with null hypothesis significance testing, which researchers should not be doing anyhow!

In addition to the main conceptual problem, that the power analysis goal is a poor one, there are also concrete problems at the level of actual answers provided. For example, suppose that you have a typical experimental design involving an experimental and control group and you have a continuous dependent variable. How many participants do you need to collect? Let's answer the question using power analysis and then using the APP.

According to power analysis, using the typical values of 0.05 for statistical significance, 80% for power, and 0.50 for Cohen's d, a power analysis calculator (https://www.gigacalculator.com/calculators/power-sample-size-calculator.php) renders the minimum sample size to meet specifications equal to 63 per group for a total of 126. The APP is too new for there to be much in the way of conventions, other than to round fractional sample sizes upward to the nearest whole number and setting confidence at 95%. Therefore, we will try multiple possible entries and see what happens under the typical assumption of normality, using the following link: https://app-normal.shinyapps.io/N_TwoSamples_EstimateMean. To commence, let us try specifications we have been using throughout: precision equals 0.10 and confidence equals 95%. Entering these specifications into the APP program yields a minimum sample size, per group, of 770 so that the total sample size is 1540. Obviously, these values are very different from the values obtained via power analysis.

Let us now keep confidence at 95% but settle for worse precision at the level of 0.20. Now the APP program yields 194 per group, for a total of 388, which is still much larger than the sample sizes yielded by power analysis.

It is interesting to ponder the precision that would be obtained using the sample size of 63 obtained from the power analysis website. Using the APP program yields a precision level of .248, keeping confidence at the traditional 95% level. Of course, this is only an example, but the example suggests the possibility that sample sizes in the social sciences are often too small to obtain sample statistics that are good estimates of corresponding population parameters. This possibility is supported by formal analyses of published research that I and my colleagues have performed in five different areas of psychology: social, clinical, developmental, cognitive, and neuro. Interestingly, although sample sizes are too small in all five areas to render good estimates of corresponding population parameters, the problem is worse in cognitive psychology and neuro psychology than in social psychology or developmental psychology (Trafimow & Myüz, 2019). And what's more, a similar problem manifests in the field of marketing (Trafimow, Hyman, & Kostyk, 2020).

It is ironic that an often-touted advantage of power analysis is to ensure that studies are not underpowered so that, among other things, the ability of researchers to replicate their findings is maximized. But now we see that using power analysis, as it is typically used, renders sample sizes that practically guarantee that researchers obtain sample statistics that are poor estimates of corresponding population parameters. Given this, as we saw in Chapter 5, the consequence is poor replicability. If researchers wish to obtain replicable findings, they would be better off using the APP than using power analysis to obtain the minimum sample sizes they need to collect.

Summary

We commenced by considering that an important problem with the null hypothesis significance procedure is that there is no sound way for an inferential statistical procedure to tell researchers which hypotheses to believe or disbelieve. There is inevitable subjectivity here, and expert substantive knowledge is beneficial. However, it is possible to ask a different question that inferential statistics can address reasonably. And that question pertains to using sample statistics to estimate corresponding population parameters: What is the minimum sample size needed to obtain sample statistics that are good estimators of corresponding population parameters? I have proposed the APP to answer this question.

To obtain this answer, it is necessary to ask two questions bullet-listed below.

- Precision: How close do I want my sample statistic to be to its corresponding population parameter?
- Confidence: What probability do I want to have of meeting the precision specification?

Given specifications for precision and confidence, it is possible to use the APP to determine the minimum sample size needed to meet the specifications.

Of course, there remains the matter of deciding what parameter you care about and what distributional assumptions you want to make. As we have seen, you might be interested in means, differences in means, locations, differences in locations, scales or standard deviations, distribution shapes, correlation coefficients, regression weights, proportions, or standardized effect sizes (e.g., Cohen's d). Then, too, you might wish to assume normal, skew normal, lognormal, or gamma distributions. Fortunately, the mathematics for various combinations of these issues have been developed, with appropriate computer programs for which links were provided. Although APP applications have been developed for many types of parameters and distributional assumptions of interest to researchers, many more APP applications remain to be developed. For example, my colleagues and I have performed some APP work pertaining to multiple means or multiple locations (Wang, Wang, Trafimow, & Talordphop, 2020), though there are no computer programs yet. In addition, my colleagues and I have performed some preliminary work to derive Bayesian APP versions (Cao et al., 2022; Wei, Wang, Trafimow, & Talordphop, 2020). An advantage of going Bayesian is that it is possible to use prior information to reduce the minimum sample size necessary to meet specifications for precision and confidence. A disadvantage is the necessity to make stronger assumptions.

Finally, we discussed the issue of making wrong assumptions. We saw that if wrong assumptions cause the researcher to collect a larger sample size than necessary to meet specifications for precision and confidence, the consequence is that the researcher has more precision or confidence than desired, which can be considered positive. In contrast, if wrong assumptions cause the researcher to collect a smaller sample size than necessary to meet specifications for precision or confidence, then the researcher may overestimate the justifiable precision or confidence. If this overestimation is small, it may not be much of a problem. But if the overestimation is large, it could be an important problem. Therefore, in those cases where choices need to be made to use the programs, we have seen that it is better to make conservative than liberal choices because overestimation is not deleterious whereas underestimation may be. A potential exception is if the researcher is working in a substantive area where obtaining participants is expensive or otherwise difficult.

Happily, once data are collected, it is possible to check the assumptions against the actual data. Suppose it turns out that there is more skewness than anticipated. In this case, the researcher will have overestimated the sample size and will have better precision or confidence than expected. Or suppose there is less skewness than anticipated. In this case, the researcher will have underestimated the sample size and will have worse precision or confidence than expected. How much better or worse? This is easy to determine simply by activating the appropriate APP program again, post data collection, using the actual data to obtain a better estimate of the parameter in question (e.g., the shape parameter). In turn, instantiating that better estimate into the program will return a different minimum sample size to meet specifications for precision and confidence than formerly. The old and new calculated sample sizes can be compared so that the researcher can determine the direction of being off, and by how much. If the newly calculated sample size exceeds the old one, the researcher has better precision or confidence than originally desired, and all is well. If the newly calculated sample size is less than the old one, the researcher can look at the size of the difference and thereby gain an idea of how much to worry about it. If there is reason for worry, one possible solution is to simply collect more data until the actual sample size meets or exceeds the newly calculated one.

Finally, we contrasted the APP against power analysis and saw that the APP is far superior. In general terms, the APP goal of obtaining sample sizes that will yield sample statistics that are good estimates of corresponding population parameters is better than the power analysis goal of obtaining statistical significance. Specifically, power analysis, as it is typically performed, yields sample sizes that are too small according to the APP. Thus, power analyses are problematic not only for estimating population parameters but may contribute to replication difficulties too.

In conclusion, the APP is far superior to null hypothesis significance testing. And it is easy to use too, with a wide variety of user-friendly computer programs that you now know how to use. My earnest hope is that you try some of them out and see for yourself the ease with which you can perform the APP to determine the sample sizes you need for your research.

Note

[1] As sample standard deviations are likely to be different, it is customary to compute a pooled standard deviation. If the sample standard deviations are extremely different, that might provide a reason to question the assumption that the population standard deviations are the same.

7 Gain-Probability Diagrams

Imagine that you are a doctor who specializes in heart issues, and a research team invents a new treatment for patients suffering from bradycardia, a heart rate that is too low. Should you prescribe the new medicine to your patients who suffer from bradycardia? An important

DOI: 10.4324/9781003365167-8

90 General Methodological Issues

impediment to your making a good decision is that you likely will gain insufficient data from the published study, even if it is a randomized control trial with sample sizes in the thousands, such as a typical publication in the prestigious *New England Journal of Medicine*. If you read the article, you likely will learn the means and standard deviations in the treatment and control conditions, and either a P-value or confidence interval. Unfortunately, knowledge of means, standard deviations, P-values, and confidence intervals is insufficient for you to make a good decision. Although it is nice to know that the mean heart rate in the treatment condition is larger than in the control condition, that may not be a sufficient reason to prescribe the medicine to your patients. Even leaving out the issue of potential side effects, it is not clear how confident you can be that the medicine will increase your patients' heart rates to enough of an extent to make a noticeable difference in their health. What you really need to know, but have no way of knowing, are the probabilities that patients who take the medicine will be better off by varying degrees, or worse off by varying degrees.

According to the Mayo Clinic website (https://www.mayoclinic.org/healthy-lifestyle/,fitness/expert-answers/heart-rate/faq-20057979), the normal resting heartbeat level for adults is between 60 and 100 beats per minute or 60–100 bpm. Suppose a team of researchers has performed a large-scale randomized control trial with 5000 patients suffering from bradycardia in the treatment condition and 5000 similar participants in the control condition. The mean heart rate is 2 bpm greater in the treatment condition than in the control condition, the standard deviation is 30 in both conditions, and the populations in the two conditions are normally distributed. Consequently, the researcher performs a *t*-test to determine statistical significance: $t(9998) = 3.333333$, $p = 0.000861$. As the P-value is well below the conventional 0.05 threshold, this finding is highly statistically significant and the seemingly obvious thing to do is recommend the medicine to your patients who have bradycardia.

However, suppose that we ignore the statistical ritual and instead use our brains. Recall and consider that the mean difference is 2 bpm, an obviously small amount going by common sense. And we can make this formal and compute Cohen's *d*, which is 0.06667. Conventionally speaking, this effect size would be considered small, and the implication might seem to go against the significance test as the effect might be considered too small to be worthwhile. On the other hand, as Cohen (1988) had warned, even a small effect size can matter in some circumstances, such as when the disease is very serious, the prevalence is high, and others. Thus, although it is helpful to compute Cohen's *d*, the information we have thus far acquired is not sufficiently helpful for you to know whether to prescribe the medicine to your patients who suffer from bradycardia.

Suppose that it were possible to estimate the probability that the heart rate medicine would increase people's heart rates by varying amounts. Of course, it is possible that the medicine might decrease some people's heart rates by varying amounts too. We could, for example, compute the probabilities of increasing or decreasing heart rates by 1, 2, 3, … bpm. Or, this might be too fine-grained, and we might instead compute the probabilities of increasing or decreasing heart rates by 5, 10, 15, … bpm. It is obvious that having such information would put you in a much better position to decide whether to prescribe the medicine to your patients. This chapter explains how to do just that, but there is one more matter that needs attention first.

In Chapter 6, we discussed the a priori procedure (APP), and how researchers can use it to obtain sample sizes that ensure that the sample statistics to be obtained—such as sample means and standard deviations in the foregoing example—will be good estimates of corresponding population parameters. Unlike social science research, where we saw in Chapter 6 that sample sizes are often too small, this is rarely a problem in the top medical journals, where sample sizes tend to be in the thousands per condition (Trafimow et al., 2019). And the example exemplifies the lack of an estimation problem, as there are 5000 patients in each condition. However, even so, there remains the issue of how to obtain a better grade of information from the sample statistics that researchers report. And this returns us to the issue of estimating the probability of being better off or worse off by varying degrees.

Using Skew Normal Distributions to Construct Gain-Probability Diagrams

Because the ideas to be presented in this chapter are new, there is only one relevant journal article: Trafimow et al. (2022). And there is a book chapter too (Tong et al., 2022b).

The most crucial point to understand is that the type of estimations of current concern cannot be carried through unless one knows—at least approximately—the appropriate distribution to use. In turn, the easiest way of knowing is to visually display your data. Possibly the easiest and most basic way is to have the computer draw histograms of your data. However, there are other methods too, and these are reviewed in an interesting article by Valentine, Aloe, and Lau (2015) in *Basic and Applied Social Psychology*. The journal had banned null hypothesis significance testing that year and Valentine et al. proposed a variety of valuable methods for researchers to visually represent their data and not depend on P-values.

After a close inspection of the data, it should be possible to propose a distribution that fits it reasonably well. Because research in this area is in its infancy, the requisite mathematics have only been worked out for skew normal (including normal) and lognormal distributions. Therefore, these will feature in the ensuing discussion. We have seen in Chapter 3 and Chapter 6 that skew normal distributions have three parameters: location, scale, and shape. If the shape parameter equals 0, then the distribution is normal. In this special case, the location equals the mean, and the scale equals the standard deviation. If the shape parameter does not equal zero, the location does not equal the mean and the scale does not equal the standard deviation.

Because researchers rarely have population sized data sets, it is unlikely the data fit either a skew normal or lognormal distribution perfectly. However, if there is a reasonably good fit, the estimates will not be far off and consequently will be useful.

Back to the Example

In the example, we assumed normally distributed data. We also imagined 5000 bradycardia patients in the treatment condition and 5000 similar patients in the control condition, which is more than enough to trust that the sample statistics are good estimates of corresponding population parameters. We imagined that the treatment mean was 2 bpm greater than the control group mean (let's say that the mean in the treatment group equals 51 and the mean in the control group equals 49). Finally, we assumed that the standard deviation equals 30 in both conditions. Our goal is to convert all this information into probabilities of being better off (higher heart rate) or worse off (lower heart rate) if one takes the medicine than if one does not.

The mathematics are complex and described in detail in the chapter that my colleagues and I published (Tong et al., 2022b). In the present chapter, we will avoid complex mathematical derivations and focus on how to use computer programs for which I will provide links. In the present case, where we assume normality, it is important to remember that the family of normal distributions is a subset of the family of skew normal distributions, so we can use the program that pertains to skew normal distributions. The link is as follows: https://probab.shinyapps.io/inde_prob/.

Using the links in the present chapter is more difficult than in Chapter 6, so let us proceed systematically. Upon activating the link, you will see eight places for you to make entries. The first place is where you enter the location of one of the groups. Under the assumption of normality, the location equals the mean, so you can enter the mean. Because we are pretending the mean equals 51 in the treatment group, we could enter that.

The second place for entering a value refers to the scale, squared. Because we are assuming normality, the standard deviation equals the scale and so we merely square the standard deviation to know what to enter. We are imagining that the standard deviation equals 30, so the variance equals $30^2 = 900$, and so we enter 900.

The third place for entering a value is the shape parameter (alpha in the program). Because we are assuming normality, enter 0.

The fourth place for entering a value is the location parameter of the other group. In this case, enter 49 for the same reason as you entered 51 in the first place for entering a value.

The fifth place for entering a value is the scale, squared, of the other group. As we imagined that the scale equals the standard deviation equals 30 (as in the second place for entering a value), squaring that value renders 900.

The sixth place for entering a value is the shape parameter of the other group. As we saw when discussing entering a value in the third place, we are assuming normality and so the value to be entered is 0.

The seventh and eighth places for entering values are difficult to explain but hopefully you can bear with me. These depend on an equation: $Z = X + aY + b$. To understand the equation and how it applies to our goal, let us start by forcing $b = 0$. In that case, if $a = -1$, X and Y would cancel out so that $Z = 0$ if the two distributions are the same. In that case, we would expect the probability to be 0.50 of being better off by taking the medicine than by not taking it. Or, going the other way, we would expect the probability to be 0.50 of being worse off by taking the medicine than by not taking it. In contrast, if the distributions are not the same, and they are not for the present example because the means differ, then we would expect the probability of being better off with the medicine than without the medicine to be some number larger than 0.50. To uncover that probability, let us enter -1 for the entry point labeled a and 0 for the entry point labeled b.

With all eight entry points filled with appropriate values, we are now ready to discuss the returned output. There are two output tabs, 'Table' and 'Plot.' The latter provides a picture of the difference between the two distributions, but it is the former that is more important and will be our focus. The Table is marked by $P(Z > 0)$ and has a value too. In the present example, that value is 0.518799 but we can round it to 0.52. The meaning is that the probability of being better off with the medicine than without it is 0.52, so that the probability of being worse off with the medicine than without it is 0.48. Thus, we see that the medicine has a slight effect, but is it enough to make it worth taking? To find out, let us try some more values.

Let us consider 4 bpm increments. This is an arbitrary decision, and you could consider smaller or larger increments. But staying with 4 bpm increments, suppose we consider the probability of being better off with the medicine than without, but by at least 4 bpm. In that case, all the foregoing entries remain the same, except for the last one. Instead of entering 0, we would now enter -4. The reason for entering the negative value is that we want to put ourselves at a disadvantage, rather than at an advantage, with respect to the equation: $Z = X + aY + b$. Or to put this another way, the probability of concern has to do with having Z exceed 0, and so the value for b must be negative when we are considering being better off, and positive when we are considering being worse off. We will see the latter case in reasonably short order. Moving to the output, the probability of being better off by at least 4 bpm is 0.481201 which we can round to 0.48.

Gain-Probability Diagrams 93

Moving to being better off by at least 8 bpm, we enter −8 for b, and the program returns a value of 0.443769 which we can round to 0.44. Moving on, for being better off by at least 12, 16, 20, 24, 28, and 32 bpm, we have 0.406832 (0.41), 0.370706 (0.37), 0.335687 (0.34), 0.302039 (0.30), 0.269996 (0.27), and 0.23975 (0.24), respectively. And we could go on, but I'll trust this is sufficient to make the point.

Now what about the probability of being worse off by 4 bpm or being better off than that? Or to expand, what if we use 8, 12, 16, 20, 24, 28, or 32 bpm? Now we enter positive values for these in the last place for entering a value (that is, for b). These values are as follows, respectively: 0.556231 (0.56), 0.593168 (0.59), 0.629294 (0.63), 0.664313 (0.66), 0.697961 (0.70), 0.730004 (0.73), 0.76025 (0.76), and 0.788546 (0.79).

Once we have used the program to obtain the values, the next step is to organize them into an easy-to-read figure. There are two types of gain-probability diagrams, Type A and Type B. In those cases where what matters is being over threshold amounts, Type A is best. In those cases where what matters is comprehending where people tend to fall on a distribution, Type B is best. Probably Type B is best for most purposes, but I will demonstrate both. The easiest way is to use your favorite spreadsheet, and mine is EXCEL so I will use that.

To start with a Type A diagram, simply make a column of increments −32, −28 …, 0, 4, 8, …, 32 and make a second column using the numbers obtained from the program. Make sure each of these numbers is aligned with the appropriate increment. For example, being worse off by 32 bpm, or being better off than that, corresponds to 0.788546 if you want to be exact, or 0.79 if you want to round to two decimal places. Once this is done, you can use the graphing capabilities of EXCEL to obtain Table 7.1. The actual gain-probability diagram, based on the values in Table 7.1, is Figure 7.1.

To interpret Figure 7.1, let us consider the value of 0 along the horizontal axis, where the corresponding probability is 0.52 (rounded to two decimal places). This means that the probability of being better off with the medicine than without is 0.52. Conversely, the probability of being worse off with the medicine than without is 0.48. Moving to your right, the probability of being better off by at least 4 bpm is 0.48, and so on. Or, moving to your left from the zero point, the

Table 7.1 How your Excel spreadsheet should look, with the first column representing increments of 4 bpm and the second column representing the probabilities of being better off than the cutoff points represented in the first column

−32	0.79
−28	0.76
−24	0.73
−20	0.70
−16	0.66
−12	0.63
−8	0.59
−4	0.56
0	0.52
4	0.48
8	0.44
12	0.41
16	0.37
20	0.34
24	0.30
28	0.27
32	0.24

94   *General Methodological Issues*

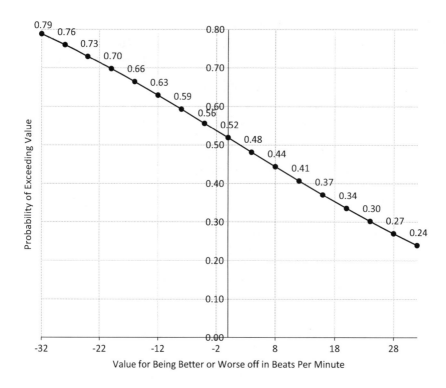

Figure 7.1 Type A gain-probability diagram where the probability of exceeding various values for being better or worse off by taking the heart rate medicine ranges along the vertical axis as a function of the actual values along the horizontal axis.

0.56 value indicates that the probability of being worse off by 4 bpm, or better than that, with the medicine than without the medicine is 0.56, and so on as you move to your left. The big advantage of this Type A diagram is if you are interested in exceeding certain criterion points. For example, let us say you insist on an improvement of at least 12 bpm to render the treatment worthwhile. A quick look at Figure 7.1 shows that the probability of meeting that criterion is 0.41. Based on everything you know about your patient, you and he or she can decide whether the probability is sufficiently impressive to justify prescribing the medicine.

Alternatively, you might not have any single criterion in mind, but wish to gain an overall perspective of the probabilities of being better or worse off by varying degrees. In this case, it is best to move to a Type B gain-probability diagram that makes use of the same values as the Type A diagram. But there is a twist. Specifically, to make a Type B gain-probability diagram, it is necessary to determine the probability of being worse off than your lowest point. In the present case, we stopped at being better off or worse off by 32 bpm, and so the lowest value is –32 bpm. Because the probability associated with that value is 0.79, it means that the probability of being worse off than that is 1.00 – 0.79 = 0.21.

To get the other values, simply keep subtracting. For example, the next value in the spreadsheet is 0.76, and subtracting this from 0.79 yields 0.03. So, the probability of being between 32 bpm worse off and 28 bpm worse off is 0.03. Similar subtracting all the way down the line yields a new set of two EXCEL columns, exhibited in Table 7.2.

Table 7.2 How your Excel spreadsheet should look, with the first column representing the ranges and the second column indicating the probabilities of being within the ranges

Worse than –32	0.211454
Between –32 and –28	0.028296
Between –28 and –24	0.030246
Between –24 and –20	0.032043
Between –20 and –16	0.033648
Between –16 and –12	0.035019
Between –12 and –8	0.036126
Between –8 and –4	0.036937
Between –4 and 0	0.037432
Between 0 and 4	0.037598
Between 4 and 8	0.037432
Between 8 and 12	0.036937
Between 12 and 16	0.036126
Between 16 and 20	0.035019
Between 20 and 24	0.033648
Between 24 and 28	0.032043
Between 28 and 32	0.030246
Better than 32	0.23975

Interpreting Figure 7.2 is easy. Each bar to the right of the zero point is slightly, but only very slightly, larger than the corresponding bar to the left of the zero point. Thus, the figure is almost, but not quite, symmetric. Thus, it is easy to see that the medicine works, but not very well. If it is expensive, has important side effects, and so on, you likely would not prescribe it for your patients. And so, we see an important advantage of gain-probability diagrams over effect sizes and significance tests.

Thus far, we have always kept the seventh entry in the program, labeled a, constant at the value of –1. This is because beats-per-minute has a very clear meaning and so it made sense to look at increments. However, for many social science measures, a scale point need not have an obvious meaning. For example, it is not clear what a one-point difference on an attitude scale means. Thus, there may be cases where it is more informative not to think in terms of increments as in Figures 7.1 and 7.2, but rather in terms of a multiplier. For example, we might be interested in the probability of being 1.1, 1.2, 1.3, ... times better off with the treatment than without the treatment. To obtain such probabilities, it is best to keep the eighth entry in the program, labeled b, at 0 and vary a. For example, we could set a at –1.1, –1.2, ... to obtain the desired probabilities of being 1.1 times better off, 1.2 times better off, and so on. For being 1.1 times better off or better, the probability equals 0.474077; for being 1.2 times better off or better, the probability equals 0.433902; and you can obtain as many such probabilities as you wish. You can graph these with a Type A or Type B diagram, just as when we kept a constant at –1 and varied b.

A Real Example: Hyman et al. (2002) and Willingness to Try New Brands

In a marketing study, Hyman et al. (2002) tested, among other things, male versus female willingness to try new brands. When my colleagues and I (Trafimow et al., 2022) graphed the data via histograms, it was obvious that a skew normal distribution fit well. As Hyman provided access to the raw data, we were able to estimate the locations, scales, and shapes for both males and females. For males, these were: location = 4.04, squared scale = 0.96, and shape = –0.50.

96 *General Methodological Issues*

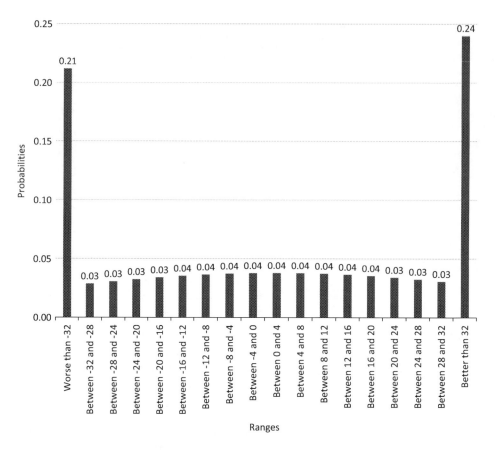

Figure 7.2 Type B gain-probability diagram giving the probabilities of being within each of the ranges.

For females, these were: location = 3.85, squared scale = 0.70, and shape = –0.52. Cohen's d = 0.19, which is under the 0.20 threshold for a small effect, thereby suggesting that males and females differ only trivially. However, we can gain more information from a gain-probability diagram.

The foregoing values can be converted into a Type B gain-probability diagram. Because it is not clear what a scale point in willingness to try new brands means, it might be that scale increments are less informative than using multipliers. Therefore, it is illustrative to use multipliers, which implies setting b at 0 and letting a vary. Let us consider the probabilities that a randomly selected male is 1.3, 1.6, or 1.9 times more willing than a randomly selected female to be willing to try new brands. And we can go the other way too and consider the probabilities that a randomly selected female is 1.3, 1.6, 1.9 times more willing than a randomly selected male to be willing to try new brands. As a starting point, if we set a at –1 and b at 0, the program tells us that the probability of a randomly selected male being more willing than a randomly selected female to try new brands is 0.546223 (0.55) and the probability of a randomly selected female being more willing to try new brands than a randomly selected male is 0.453777 (0.45). Note that these add to 1.00, as they should.

Anyway, after repeatedly using the program, it is easy to construct an EXCEL file as Table 7.3 shows. And from that, to draw a Type B gain-probability diagram as Figure 7.3 illustrates.

Table 7.3 This is how your Excel spreadsheet should look, with the first column representing ranges and the second column indicating the probabilities of being within the ranges

Females 1.9 times or more	0.04
Females between 1.9 and 1.6	0.08
Females between 1.6 and 1.3	0.19
Females between 1.3 and 1.0	0.45
Males between 1.3 and 1.0	0.55
Males between 1.6 and 1.3	0.25
Males between 1.9 and 1.6	0.10
Males 1.9 times or more	0.04

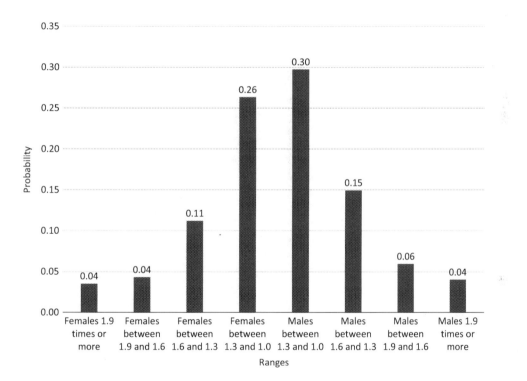

Figure 7.3 Type B gain-probability diagram giving the probabilities of being within each of the ranges, which refer to females being varying degrees more willing than males to try new brands or males being varying degrees more willing than females to try new brands.

Unlike Figure 7.2, there is more asymmetry in Figure 7.3. The greater asymmetry makes a strong case that males and females really are different with respect to willingness to try new brands, and perhaps the small Cohen's d of 0.19 implies an understatement of this effect. Consider the two middle bars of Figure 7.3, where there is a 10% probability difference between a randomly selected male being more willing than a randomly selected female to try new brands or the reverse (0.55 − 0.45 = 0.10). Or going to the next set of bars, the probability of a randomly selected male being 1.3 times more willing than a randomly selected female to try new brands is 0.25 compared to only 0.19 for the reverse. Not surprisingly, the difference in pairs of bars decreases out in the extreme tails of Figure 7.3.

Before continuing to lognormal distributions, it is worth reminding the reader of the following. Firstly, although I used increments of 1, 1.3, 1.6, and 1.9 for Figure 7.3, I could have used practically anything. For example, I could have used 1.1, 1.2, 1.3, ... Secondly, I could have used increments in scale points rather than using multipliers, analogous to Figure 7.2. For your own data, it is worthwhile to carefully consider whether to use increments or multipliers. The meaningfulness of the scale units is one factor that perhaps may figure into your decision. Another factor might be the goal of the research.

How to Obtain Location, Scale-Squared, and Shape Parameter Estimates

I have thus far assumed that you know how to estimate location, scale-squared, and shape parameters. In case you do not, I will explain that now. The first step is to use your statistics program or spreadsheet to obtain the sample mean, variance, and skewness in each condition or group. All statistics programs of which I am aware will do this easily and many spreadsheets, such as EXCEL, will do it too.

The next thing to do is obtain something called delta δ. We will use 'hat' symbolism to remind ourselves that we do not have access to population parameters, so we are using estimates. Thus, δ is estimated by $\hat{\delta}$. To get to $\hat{\delta}$, it is necessary to use the sample skewness, that we will symbolize here as $\hat{\gamma}_1$ and that you can obtain directly from your statistical package or spreadsheet. In EXCEL, you can look for the 'Skew' command under 'Statistics' but make sure to use the sample skewness, and not the population skewness (do not use Skew.P unless you have population data).

At this point, you can estimate delta using the following equation: $|\hat{\delta}| = \sqrt{\dfrac{\pi}{2} \dfrac{\hat{\gamma}_1^{2/3}}{\hat{\gamma}_1^{2/3} + \left(\dfrac{4-\pi}{2}\right)^{2/3}}}$.

Once you have $\hat{\delta}$, it is possible to move directly to estimating the shape parameter $\hat{\alpha}$: $\hat{\alpha} = \dfrac{\hat{\delta}}{\sqrt{1-\hat{\delta}^2}}$.

Your favorite statistical package or spreadsheet also should render the mean and variance (standard deviation squared) for each of your conditions or groups. The sample mean is often symbolized by M and the sample standard deviation by s, so that the sample variance is s^2. In contrast, the population mean is usually symbolized by μ and the population standard deviation by σ, so that the population variance is σ^2. In keeping with our 'hat' symbols to remind us that we are using sample statistics to estimate corresponding population parameters, the sample mean, and sample variance will be designated as follows, respectively: $\hat{\mu}$ and $\hat{\sigma}^2$. Using these symbols, the population scale-squared (ω^2) can be estimated as follows: $\hat{\omega}^2 = \dfrac{\hat{\sigma}^2}{1-\dfrac{2}{\pi}\hat{\delta}^2}$.

Of course, the best estimate of the population scale is obtained by taking the square root: $\hat{\omega} = \sqrt{\hat{\omega}^2} = \sqrt{\dfrac{\hat{\sigma}^2}{1 - \dfrac{2}{\pi}\hat{\delta}^2}}$.

There is only one skew normal parameter left to estimate and it is the population location (ξ), to be estimated as follows: $\hat{\xi} = \hat{\mu} - \sqrt{\dfrac{2}{\pi}}\hat{\delta}\hat{\omega}$. And so, we now have all the parameter estimates needed to use the program to construct gain-probability diagrams.

Delta Lognormal Distributions

Lognormal distributions only have two parameters: mean and standard deviation (Wang, Wang, Trafimow, & Xu, 2022). However, unlike normal distributions, these are not the mean and standard deviation of the observed data, but rather the mean and standard deviation of logarithmically transformed data. The transformation is: $Y = \ln(X)$. The key is to understand that although the original data are not normally distributed, they are normally distributed after transformation. To avoid confusion, I will refer to means and standard deviations of logarithmically transformed data as *ln means* or *ln standard deviations*, respectively, to keep them distinct from means or standard deviations of data that have not been logarithmically transformed.

Delta lognormal distributions are like lognormal distributions, but with the added flexibility of allowing values equal to 0. For example, one might be interested in rainfall on different days, but there might be some days where there is no rainfall at all, so there would be many entries of 0 in the data file.

To find the probability of people being better off or worse off by varying degrees, under the umbrella of delta lognormal distributions, it is useful to activate the following link to a computer program: https://dlnprobability.shinyapps.io/independent/. There are eight values to enter. The first value to enter is *a* and the second value to enter is *b*, and these work as they did when we used the skew normal program. The third value to enter is the probability of a 0 in the data pertaining to one of the groups and the fourth value is the probability of a 0 in the data pertaining to the other group. This probability is simply the number of 0 entries in your data for the group in question, divided by the total number of entries for that group. If there are no 0 entries, then the probability of a 0 entry equals 0. The fifth value to enter is the ln mean of the first group and the sixth value to enter is the ln mean of the second group. The seventh value to enter is the ln variance (squared ln standard deviation) of the first group and the eighth value to enter is the ln variance of the second group.

Hyman et al. (2002): Living Space

To construct a gain-probability diagram, consider again data from Hyman et al. (2002) concerning the living space, in square feet, for males and females. However, let us first consider a conventional analysis. The mean amount of living space for men is 2300 and the standard deviation is 705. The mean amount of living space for women is 2186 and the standard deviation is 671. The effect size is miniscule: Cohen's $d = 0.04$. Likewise, the effect is not statistically significant, $t(564) < 1$. Any conventional researcher would conclude that there is nothing there, despite the large sample size. But might a gain-probability diagram suggest something different?

100 *General Methodological Issues*

Table 7.4 This is how your Excel spreadsheet should look, with the first column representing ranges and the second column indicating the probabilities of being within the ranges

Females 2.12 times or more	0.04
Females between 2.12 and 1.9	0.06
Females between 1.9 and 1.6	0.12
Females between 1.6 and 1.3	0.24
Females between 1.3 and 1.0	0.46
Males between 1.3 and 1.0	0.54
Males between 1.6 and 1.3	0.32
Males between 1.9 and 1.6	0.17
Males between 2.12 and 1.6	0.09
Males 2.12 times or more	0.06

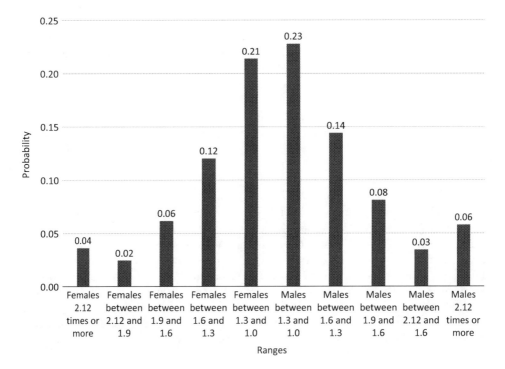

Figure 7.4 Type B gain-probability diagram giving the probabilities of being within each of the ranges, which refer to females having varying degrees more living space than males or males having varying degrees more living space than females

After performing the logarithmic transformation described by $Y = \ln(X)$, the ln mean for males is 7.69 and the ln standard deviation is 0.31. Squaring the latter value renders ln variance for males equal to 0.0961. The ln mean for females is 7.64 and the ln standard deviation is 0.32. Squaring the latter value renders ln variance for females equal to 0.1024. It is difficult to imagine differences in absolute square footage, but it is easy to comprehend what it would mean, say, for a male to have twice the living space as a female, or vice versa. Therefore, let us use multipliers, as in Figure 7.3.

Table 7.4 shows the EXCEL file and Figure 7.4 shows the gain-probability diagram, Type B.

Let us interpret Figure 7.4. The middle two bars give the probability of having 1 to 1.3 times the living space of the other sex. The probability of a male advantage in this category is 0.54 and the probability of a female advantage in this category is 0.46, a sizable advantage for males. Going to the next pair of bars giving the probability of having 1.3 to 1.6 times the living space of the other sex, we see another probabilistic advantage for males over females: the probabilities are 0.32 and 0.24, respectively. The advantage for males starts decreasing as we go to increasingly large advantages for one sex over the other because the probabilities decrease generally. The obvious asymmetry of Figure 7.4 clarifies that the lack of statistical significance and miniscule effect size we noted earlier are quite misleading and hide effects that the gain-probability diagram brings out.

Narita et al. (2020) and Systolic Blood Pressure

Narita et al. (2020) performed an impressive and large-scale experiment with thousands of participants examining at-home systolic blood pressure during summer, winter, spring, and fall seasons in a Japanese population. There were different participants for each season, so the experiment was an independent samples design. For present purposes, we can focus on the largest difference, which was between summer and winter. For summer participants the mean systolic blood pressure was 134.1 mm Hg, and the standard deviation was 15.6 mm Hg. For winter participants, the mean was 140.3 mm Hg, and the standard deviation was 15.5 mm Hg. Narita et al. reported that this difference was highly statistically significant, $p < 0.001$. Because it has been well established that blood pressure is lognormally distributed, this study fits well in the present section on lognormal distributions.

The ln mean and ln standard deviation for the summer participants are 2.125 and 1.329, respectively. For winter participants, these are 2.144 and 1.325, respectively. After squaring the ln standard deviations and entering the values in the appropriate places in the computer program, it is possible to construct Figure 7.5. Because blood pressure units, in mm Hg are meaningful, it seemed reasonable to construct a Type B gain-probability diagram using increments of 10 mm Hg.

A look at Figure 7.5 suggests that despite impressive statistical significance, there is very little difference between the systolic blood pressure of summer and winter participants. The figure is very close to being symmetric. There is very little difference between the two middle bars, and this perpetuates across the various pairs of bars. The data on living space showed us how lack of statistical significance could hide effects and the data on systolic blood pressure illustrate how statistical significance can be misleading the other way, by suggesting an impressive difference between two groups where there is none.

Seemingly Trivial Skewness May Not Be Trivial

Imagine an advertising program designed to increase seatbelt use. Two thousand participants are randomly assigned to get the ad (experimental condition) or not (control condition), and the dependent variable is average number of hours per week using seatbelts. Suppose that the data are as follows for the experimental condition: mean = 45, standard deviation = 3, skewness = –0.10. The data in the control condition are as follows: mean = 45, standard deviation = 3, skewness = +0.10. Thus, the two conditions are the same with respect to means and standard deviations, but there is a slight difference with respect to skewness. According to conventional thinking, the skewness is so slight in both conditions that it can be ignored; both conditions can be assumed normally

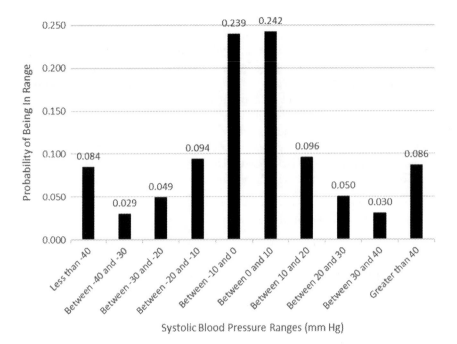

Figure 7.5 Type B gain-probability diagram giving the probabilities of being within each of the ranges, which refer to summer participants having higher or lower blood pressure, by varying degrees, than winter participants.

distributed. Further in accord with conventional thinking, because the means and standard deviations are the same in both conditions, it is obvious that the ad does not work.

But recall the equations presented earlier in this chapter for estimating skew normal parameters. If we instantiate the sample statistics in the previous paragraph into those equations, we end up with the following estimates of skew normal parameters. In the experimental condition, the location is 46.85, the scale is 3.52, and the shape is –0.87. In the control condition, the location is 43.15, the scale is 3.52, and the shape is 0.87. Of course, squaring the scale gives a scale-squared value of 12.41. Let us enter these values into the skew normal program, using the link provided earlier in this chapter and draw a gain-probability diagram, Type B.

Given what had seemed obvious, that the ad does not work, the truth is surprising and perhaps even shocking. To have an electrifying experience, check out Figure 7.6.

To interpret Figure 7.6, remember that the means and standard deviations were the same, and so it seemed that the ad does not work. However, the blatant asymmetry illustrated by the figure demonstrates that the ad works well, indeed, despite appearances based on means and standard deviations. And all this despite the means and standard deviations being the same in both conditions and based on skewness statistics that practically everyone would consider trivial!

What Size Increments Should You Use?

Based on the foregoing examples, you may have concluded that the size of increments along the horizontal axis is arbitrary. And your conclusion would be right! As gain-probability diagrams

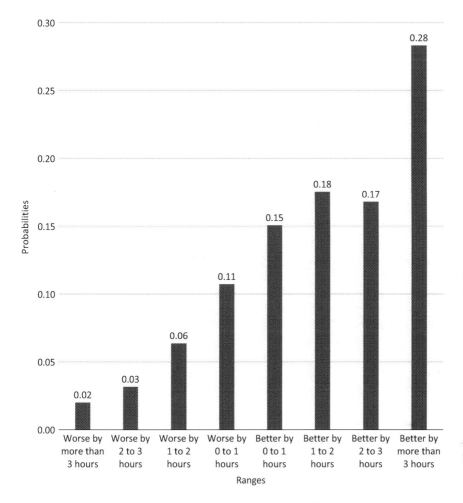

Figure 7.6 Type B gain-probability diagram giving the probabilities of being within each of the ranges, which refer to being better or worse off, to varying degrees, with respect to hours per week using seatbelts.

are still in their infancy, many conventions have yet to be established. However, the lack of relevant conventions need not prevent us from considering factors that might matter.

The most obvious factor is your own substantive knowledge about the topic. In the systolic blood pressure example, a heart specialist would have much substantive knowledge and could use that substantive knowledge to arrive at reasonable increments. One reason for emphasizing the arbitrariness of increment size is to give you permission to use your substantive knowledge to decide what is reasonable. What's more, you likely know more about your project than anyone except another expert in your area, so few people would be likely to be better than you at deciding what increments are reasonable.

Another factor is a tradeoff between ease of comprehension and being more fine-grained. The more fine-grained you wish to be, the more bars you will need in a Type B diagram, and the more difficult the diagram is to comprehend. However, that having been said, even many bars

104 *General Methodological Issues*

need not be all that difficult to comprehend. There are many bars in Figure 7.6, but the Figure remains reasonably comprehensible. Perhaps a good rule is that you are not sure, it is better to err on the side of being too fine-grained rather than on the side of not being fine-grained enough.

This is perhaps a good place to mention a point about publication. If your gain-probability diagram is too fine-grained, reviewers can suggest that you collapse bars to result in a simpler diagram, which should be no problem for you in a revision. In contrast, if your gain-probability diagram is not fine-grained enough, reviewers might argue that you have not sufficiently supported your conclusion, and then recommend rejection. Well, then, if being too fine-grained is likely to result in your being asked for a revision and not being fine-grained enough is likely to result in your being rejected outright, the publication-smart thing to do is err on the side of being too fine-grained. This should gain you the revision request and hopefully eventual publication in the journal.

Chapter Summary

Chapter 6 is useful because it aids in determining minimum samples sizes necessary to meet specifications for precision and confidence. Suppose a researcher collects a sample that is sufficiently large, according to specifications for precision and confidence, using the programs for which the chapter provided links. Two implications of the chapter are (a) it is possible to use the data to double check any assumptions that were made and (b) the sample statistics can be trusted as good estimates of corresponding population parameters, of course within the limits of the specifications. However, a shortcoming of the chapter is that it does not tell us what we really want to know, which is the probability of being better off, or worse off, by varying degrees, depending on whether one is in the experimental or control condition (e.g., whether people get the medicine, are exposed to the ad, and so on). Chapter 7, the present chapter, addresses the limitation.

Chapter 7 provides links to programs under the umbrella of skew normal distributions, that include normal distributions too, as a subset of skew normal distributions, and lognormal distributions. In those cases where there is a clear criterion, Type A gain-probability diagrams are useful, as illustrated by Figure 7.1. In most cases, where there is no clear criterion, Type B gain-probability diagrams are more useful, as illustrated by the other figures. Such figures have the advantage of providing researchers with a concise picture of the probabilities of being better off, or worse off, by varying degrees depending on whether one is in the experimental or control condition.

We have seen that it is possible to have nonsignificant findings or small effect sizes, but where a gain-probability diagram shows important asymmetries that otherwise would have remained invisible. Conversely, we have seen, too, that it is possible to have extremely statistically significant effects (e.g., P-values less than 0.001), but where a gain-probability diagram exposes that there is nothing but trivial differences.

Another insight reaped from gain-probability diagrams is the importance of skewness in the data, even if that skewness is trivial according to conventional thinking. Figure 7.6 illustrates how even when the means and standard deviations in two conditions are the same, a slight difference in skewness between two conditions can render important effects. Figure 7.6 is blatantly asymmetric, thereby showing that seemingly trivial skewness can be crucial. Nor is this the first time we have seen this. In Chapter 6, we learned that seemingly trivial skewness can have large effects on minimum sample sizes necessary to meet specifications for precision and confidence. In Chapter 7, we learned that seemingly trivial skewness can create large differences in the probabilities of being better off, or worse off, to varying degrees, even when the means and standard deviations of the two conditions are the same. Skewness—even seemingly trivial skewness—can be decisive. It is a shame that the strong tendency of the social sciences to focus on null hypothesis significance testing, with the almost automatic assumption of normality, has caused researchers not to understand that seemingly trivial skewness can generate vital effects.

Finally, although gain-probability diagrams can be amazingly useful and provide surprising insights, a limitation is that they are so new that conventions have yet to be established. Although the lack of conventions can be positive, in the sense of not limiting researchers to single perspectives, it can be a disadvantage too in the sense that some decisions have an arbitrary component. And the most obvious of these concerns the increments researchers should use in drawing gain-probability diagrams. There is a tradeoff between providing as much information as possible and making gain-probability diagrams easy to comprehend. I had suggested that it is better to err on the side of being too fine-grained than to err on the side of not being fine-grained enough.

In toto, gain-probability diagrams are much superior to effect sizes alone, P-values alone, or even the combination of effect sizes and P-values. The social sciences would benefit greatly if researchers would acquire the habit of constructing gain-probability diagrams rather than depending on significance tests and effect sizes. If we combine the implications of Chapters 6 and 7, we come to a prescription for a three-step inferential process that is much superior to what social science researchers do now. Step 1 is to use the APP to determine sample sizes. This occurs before data collection. Step 2 is to use the data to check the assumptions made in Step 1. Finally, Step 3 is to construct gain-probability diagrams to attain a much more extensive understanding of the full implications of the data.

8 The Unfortunate Dependence of Much Social Science on Mediation Analysis

Imagine a typical attitude study where the researcher measures attitudes, behavioral intentions, and behaviors towards using seatbelts. The researcher wishes to argue that attitudes cause behavioral intentions which, in turn, cause behaviors. An easy way to visualize the line of reasoning is to consider a set of three dominos, where tipping over the first domino tips over the second domino which, in turn, tips over the third domino. If the second domino were to be prevented from tipping over, perhaps by holding it upright with a firm grip so that the tipping over of the first domino has no effect, then the third domino would not tip over either. Returning to our imagined study, if behavioral intentions, analogous to the second domino, were somehow fixed at a particular level, regardless of attitudes, then the relationship between attitudes and behaviors should disappear.

Before continuing, this seems a good time to recall what everyone learns in introductory social science courses, which is that correlation need not necessitate causation. If attitudes and behavioral intentions are correlated, it could be that attitudes cause behavioral intentions, that behavioral intentions cause attitudes, or that some outside variable, or set of outside variables, causes both attitudes and behavioral intentions. There is no way to know which. It should be obvious, then, that the road for researchers to draw causal conclusions from correlational data is fraught with potholes. Therefore, when researchers draw causal conclusions from correlational data, it is unlikely the conclusions can be trusted. And so, there is a sense in which the present chapter could end right here.

However, no matter how unsound the reasoning, the fact of the matter is that researchers routinely draw causal conclusions from correlational data. The typical route is to perform a mediation analysis. Such an analysis commences with the correlation of each item with each other item. In our imagined study, there are three such correlation coefficients: there is the correlation between attitudes and behavioral intentions, between attitudes and behaviors, and between behavioral intentions and behaviors. You may have already intuited that if it is unsound to draw causal conclusions from one correlation coefficient, it is not sound to draw conclusions from three correlation coefficients either. And your intuition would be correct! Nevertheless, researchers do it anyway, under the rubric of mediation analysis.

To understand mediation analysis, let us start with regression coefficients. To keep matters simple, let us continue to imagine that there are three variables, such as attitudes, behavioral intentions, and behaviors. For the sake of briefer symbolism, let us designate the final variable—behaviors—as y. And let us designate attitudes as 1 and behavioral intentions as 2. Thus, there are three correlation coefficients: these are between attitudes and behaviors r_{y1}, attitudes and behavioral intentions r_{12}, and between behavioral intentions and behaviors r_{y2}.

There were few equations in the preceding chapters and so formal numbering was unnecessary, but there will be sufficient equations here to justify numbering them. Hence, Equations 8.1 and 8.2 indicate how to obtain attitude and behavioral intention regression coefficients based on the three bivariate correlation coefficients: r_{y1}, r_{12}, and r_{y2}. Most regression statistics books, such as Pedhazur (1997), provide the equations needed to obtain regression weights for each of the predictor variables (e.g., attitudes β_1 and behavioral intentions β_2) in predicting the criterion variable (e.g., behaviors).

$$\beta_1 = \frac{r_{y1} - r_{y2}r_{12}}{1 - r_{12}^2} \tag{8.1}$$

$$\beta_2 = \frac{r_{y2} - r_{y1}r_{12}}{1 - r_{12}^2}. \tag{8.2}$$

A quick look at Equations 8.1 and 8.2 suggests something interesting, which is the impressive interdependence of the equations on both predictor variables. Thus, if the measure of one of the variables is off, whether due to random sampling error or a systematic factor, both regression weights can be affected. Thus, regression weights are (in)famous for instability. There is even a name for the phenomenon, based on the use of the Greek letter beta β, and it is 'bouncing betas.'

Another point to consider is that all the entries in Equations 8.1 and 8.2 are correlation coefficients. Remembering, then, that correlation need not indicate causation, neither need regression weights, that are based on correlations, indicate causation.

Some argue that although regression coefficients need not indicate causation, a special kind of regression coefficient does indicate causation. The name for such special regression coefficients is path coefficients. To see why, consider the proposed causal pathway, that attitudes cause behavioral intentions which, in turn, cause behaviors. If we assume an arrow connecting attitudes to behavioral intentions, and another arrow connecting behavioral intentions to behaviors, then the assertion is that the path coefficient assigned to the first arrow gives the strength of the causal path by which attitudes cause behavioral intentions, and the path coefficient assigned to the second arrow gives the strength of the causal path by which behavioral intentions cause behaviors. Finally, it is possible to imagine a third arrow connecting attitudes directly with behaviors, not going through behavioral intentions, with a path coefficient indicating the strength of that causal connection. The combination of the first and second arrows is said to be the 'mediated' pathway from attitudes to behaviors, and the third arrow is the 'unmediated' or 'direct' pathway from attitudes to behaviors. Figure 8.1 provides an illustration.

Equations 8.1 and 8.2 show how regression weights depend on the bivariate correlation coefficients. Path coefficients, as a category of regression weights, are no different. And as I stated already, and will continue to reiterate, because correlation coefficients need not indicate causation, neither need the path coefficients based on them indicate causation. This is despite the typical pronouncement that path coefficients provide a convincing case for causation.

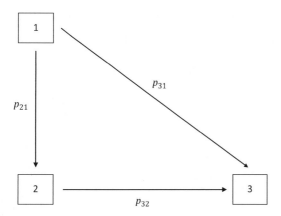

Figure 8.1 Path diagram showing how the variable labeled '2' mediates between the variable labeled '1' and the variable labeled '3,' with path coefficients along the arrows.

$$p_{21} = \beta_{21} = r_{21}, \tag{8.3}$$

$$p_{31} = \beta_{31.2} = \frac{r_{31} - r_{32}r_{12}}{1 - r_{12}^2}, \tag{8.4}$$

$$p_{32} = \beta_{32.1} = \frac{r_{32} - r_{31}r_{12}}{1 - r_{12}^2}. \tag{8.5}$$

The Special Issue of *Basic and Applied Social Psychology* in 2015 on Mediation

Consider a preliminary demonstration why you should be suspicious when researchers make causal claims based on mediation analysis. In 2015, I had commenced a special issue of *Basic and Applied Social Psychology* on mediation analysis, to bring out the problems. To introduce the topic, I thought it would be both dramatic and entertaining to perform a mediation analysis on the eight official planets of the solar system to demonstrate how horribly wrong researchers can be when they depend on mediation analysis (Trafimow, 2015a). In one of my demonstrations, I was concerned with the masses, velocities, and momenta of the planets. The masses and velocities of the planets are well-known, and momentum can be calculated just by multiplying mass and velocity, so that *momentum = mass* x *velocity*. There are three relevant correlation coefficients: between mass and velocity $r_{mass-velocity} = -0.361$, between mass and momentum $r_{mass-momentum} = 0.997$, and between velocity and momentum $r_{mass-velocity} = 0.-313$.

Based on these three underlying correlation coefficients, it is easy to test mediation models. One mediation model is that mass causes velocity causes momentum (mass → velocity → momentum) and the other mediation model is that velocity causes mass causes momentum (velocity → mass → momentum). It should be obvious that both mediation models are false as mass does not cause velocity nor does velocity cause mass. Nevertheless, let us temporarily set our knowledge aside to see what happens when we perform mediation analyses.

We can start with the following model: mass → velocity → momentum. It is merely necessary to instantiate the correlation coefficients from the previous paragraph into Equations 8.3 through 8.5, setting the following designations: $r_{21} = r_{mass-velocity} = -0.361$, $r_{31} = r_{mass-momentum} = 0.997$, and $r_{32} = r_{mass-velocity} = 0.-313$. The results are bullet-listed below:

- $p_{21} = \beta_{21} = r_{21} = -0.361$

- $p_{31} = \beta_{31.2} = \frac{r_{31} - r_{32}r_{12}}{1 - r_{12}^2} = 0.054$

- $p_{32} = \beta_{32.1} = \frac{r_{32} - r_{31}r_{12}}{1 - r_{12}^2} = 1.016$.

Under traditional mediation thinking, the bullet-pointed results would be taken not to support the mediation model: mass → velocity → momentum. To use mediation language, the reasonably good value for p_{21} would be described as an effect of mass on velocity even though there is little reason to believe in a direct causal linkage between mass and velocity. A perhaps

110 General Methodological Issues

more likely explanation is that if large planetary masses were too close to the sun, gravitational attraction would force them to fall into the sun, thereby rendering reasonable that the planets near the sun have less mass than planets far away from the sun. Anyway, however, this reasonably good value would be taken as supporting the model. In contrast, the near zero value for the effect of velocity on momentum would be taken as not supporting the model. Finally, the huge unmediated effect directly from mass to momentum also would be taken as not supporting the proposed mediation. Ideally, from a mediation perspective, the unmediated effect should be near zero.

However, let us now test the second model: velocity → mass → momentum. As we did with the first model, let us bullet-list the path findings, but remembering that it is now mass, rather than velocity, that is the mediating variable.

- $p_{21} = \beta_{21} = r_{21} = -0.361$

- $p_{31} = \beta_{31.2} = \dfrac{r_{31} - r_{32}r_{12}}{1 - r_{12}^2} = 1.016$

- $p_{32} = \beta_{32.1} = \dfrac{r_{32} - r_{31}r_{12}}{1 - r_{12}^2} = 0.054.$

There is an obvious effect of velocity on mass (–0.361), though I emphasize the idiocy in believing that velocity causes mass (except for a hypothetical case where a planet travels at a velocity near the speed of light, in which case Einstein's theory would kick in). In addition, there is a whopping effect of the mediating variable—mass—on momentum (1.016). Further supporting the model, when the mediating variable—mass—is statistically controlled, the direct path from velocity to momentum decreases almost to zero (0.054). Thus, all is right from a mediation analysis perspective.

The foregoing mediation analyses of two planetary models may seem an ideal case of the power of mediation analyses to test opposing models. The mediation analyses strongly support the second model, velocity → mass → momentum, over the first model, mass → velocity → momentum. And yet, the second model is spectacularly false! To repeat the refrain: correlation need not support causation, even when there is more than one correlation and even when mediation analysis is employed.

Now that you are properly suspicious, let us delve deeper into the matter. How is it that mediation analyses can go so horribly wrong?

The Complexity Problem

Imagine the case of a simple model where A causes B ($A \rightarrow B$). There is only one relevant correlation coefficient, which is between A and B. The symbol is r_{AB}. Suppose that this correlation coefficient is a respectably large value. The empirical success could be because A really does cause B, or for some other reason such as that B causes A or some other variable or set of variables causes both A and B. Nevertheless, let us momentarily be generous and assume that the probability that the respectable correlation coefficient is for the right theoretical reason (A causes B) a large value such as 0.70. Under our generosity, we conclude that although the respectable correlation coefficient might not be because of the hoped-for reason, there nevertheless is a good chance that it is because of the hoped-for reason. Of course, if we are not generous, then the correlation coefficient remains weak as evidence for a theorized causal connection. But let us continue to remain generous and see what happens.

We might become more complex and assume that A causes B causes C ($A \rightarrow B \rightarrow C$), though there are other possible models too involving these three variables. Whatever the model, there are three relevant correlation coefficients: r_{AB}, r_{AC}, and r_{BC}. In the spirit of generosity, let us assume that all three correlation coefficients come out in a way that supports the causal model. And let us continue to assume that the probability that each correlation coefficient for the correct theoretical reason is 0.70. Nevertheless, for the model to be correct, all three correlation coefficients must be for the right theoretical reason. If each correlation coefficient is independent of the others, the probability that all three are for the correct theoretical reason equals 0.70^3 = 0.343 or much lower than 0.50. It is also possible not to assume independence, but although the numbers change the general message does not (Trafimow, 2017a). Thus, even with a very simple mediation model, and under generosity, the probability that the model is true is already well below a coin toss.

Now suppose we add a variable, so there are six relevant correlation coefficients: r_{AB}, r_{AC}, r_{AD}, r_{BC}, r_{BD}, and r_{CD}. Remaining with generosity, the probability that all correlation coefficients are for the correct theoretical reason drops to 0.70^6 = 0.118 or near zero.

We can move to five variables, in which case there are ten relevant correlation coefficients. Now the probability that all are for the correct theoretical reason drops to 0.70^{10} = 0.028. If there are six variables, there are 15 relevant correlation coefficients, and the probability that all are for the correct theoretical reason drops to 0.70^{15} = 0.0047. And if there are seven variables, there are 21 relevant correlation coefficients, and the probability that all are for the correct theoretical reason drops to 0.70^{21} = 0.00056.

In summary, despite our generosity, there is a problem even when there are only three variables in the model, and the problems increase dramatically as more variables are added. For example, in a recent article in *Organizational Research Methods* that won an award for best quantitative article of 2021, Rohny Saylors and I showed that the average model in the management area features seven variables (Saylors & Trafimow, 2021)! Even if we are crazy generous and assume a base probability of 0.90 for each correlation coefficient being for the correct theoretical reason, the probability that all 21 are for the correct theoretical reason would be only 0.90^{21} = 0.11. And there is worse to come in the following sections.

The Efficient Cause Issue

James Grice and his colleagues provided one of the articles in the special issue on mediation in 2015 in *Basic and Applied Social Psychology* (Grice et al., 2015). They pointed out that there are many kinds of causes, such as Aristotle's traditional ones that include material, formal, efficient, and final causes. Then, too, philosophers in the Middle Ages added more causes, such as instrumental, accidental, and others. According to Grice et al., mediation analysis concerns efficient causes. An efficient cause is "that which by its activity or exercise of power produces existence or change in another" (Wuellner, 1956, p. 39).

For example, let us return to the example of three dominos, where tipping the first causes the second to fall over which, in turn, causes the third to fall over. The tipping of the first domino is the efficient cause of the second domino falling over. In turn, the second domino falling over is the efficient cause of the third domino falling over. And, so on if we had more dominos in the sequence. But let us move to a psychology example. Suppose we hypothesize that being extraverted causes people to go to parties and, in turn, that going to parties causes people to drink alcoholic beverages. Ideally, from the point of view of the hypothesis, we would want people who are extraverted to go to parties and drink, but for people who are not extraverted not to go to parties and drink. Suppose we had four participants with the following pattern:

- Joe is extraverted, goes to a party, and drinks.
- Sarah is extraverted, goes to a party, and drinks.
- Daniel is introverted, does not go to a party, and does not drink.
- Patricia is introverted, does not go to a party, and does not drink.

From the point of view of the hypothesis, the bullet-listed cases are perfect because everyone behaves consistently with the model.

But let us consider six more bullet-listed cases with zeroes or ones to indicate being extraverted, going to a party, and drinking (1 in all cases) or not (0 in all cases).

- Jeff is extraverted (1), goes to a party (1), and does not drink (0).
- Sally is extraverted (1), does not go to a party (0), and does not drink (0).
- Mike is introverted (0), goes to a party (1), and drinks (1).
- Jackie is introverted (0), does not go to a party (0), and drinks (1).
- Joseph is extraverted (1), goes to a party (1), and drinks (1).
- Amy is introverted (0), does not go to a party (0), and does not drink (0).

Note that in four of the six cases (67%), the hypothesis is false. Only two cases are consistent with the model (33%). In fact, the correlation between introversion–extraversion and going or not going to a party is 0.33, the correlation between going or not going to a party and drinking or not drinking is 0.33, and the correlation between introversion–extraversion and drinking is 0.33. Let us use Equations 8.3 to 8.5 to find the path coefficients. These are as follows: $p_{21} = 0.33$, $p_{31} = 0.25$, and $p_{32} = 0.25$, reasonably representative path coefficients in social science literatures. If we imagine sufficient participants (say, several hundred of them), with equal samples following each of the six bullet-listed patterns, all path coefficients would be highly significant. The typical researcher's conclusion would be that introversion–extraversion causes going or not going to parties, and that going or not going to parties causes drinking or not drinking. The typical researcher would conclude that there is also an unmediated path from introversion–extraversion to drinking or not drinking. Or, to use the magic mediation analysis word, there is *partial* mediation consistent with the model. In short, a typical mediation analysis would result in the conclusion that the model is supported.

And yet, remember that only 33% of the participants show a pattern of data that is consistent with the model. This means that 67% of the participants show a pattern of data that is inconsistent with the model. Thus, looking at individual responses renders obvious that the model is a very poor model, whereas a typical mediation analysis supports that the model is a good one. And it would be publishable too!

And this brings us back to the Grice et al. (2015) point about efficient causes. The better approach is to look at each participant, to see whether each exhibits a pattern of data that is consistent or inconsistent with the model. If most exhibit a pattern of data that goes against the model, this evidence against the model should take strong precedence over the seemingly supportive mediation analysis. Unfortunately, researchers in the social sciences depend on mediation analyses and fail to look at the participant-by-participant data patterns.

The Unhappy Marriage between Mediation and Null Hypothesis Significance Testing

In the special issue on mediation analysis, Rex B. Kline (2015) made a variety of criticisms, including that mediation analysis depends on significance tests to determine whether the path coefficients are there or not there. To see the issue, let us take an ostensible ideal case, where there is a statistically significant path coefficient linking A and B, a statistically significant path coefficient linking B and C, and a statistically insignificant path coefficient linking A and C when controlling for the mediating variable B. Put in more general language, most researchers hope for statistically significant path coefficients along the mediated pathway from the first variable in the chain to the last variable in the chain, and for the direct (unmediated) pathway to be statistically insignificant.

However, if you recall Chapter 4, null hypothesis significance testing is unsound, and researchers should not use it. I will not repeat the general arguments from Chapter 4 but will instead focus on specific arguments about null hypothesis significance testing in the context of mediation analysis.

The first thing is to remember that we are talking about correlational data. But as Meehl (1967) famously pointed out, everything is correlated with everything, though many correlations are weak. An empirical reason for Meehl's famous statement is that he and his colleagues had collected data on a large set of variables, many of which seemed unconnected, and yet when they correlated everything with everything else, their large sample caused the many seemingly unconnected variables to nevertheless be significantly correlated. To put this more dramatically, it is unlikely, in the extreme, that the correlation between two variables that a researcher chooses to study equals 0.0000000000000000000000000000000000000000. And if the correlation is not exactly 0, then it is there. Therefore, a significance test to see if an effect is there is the height of idiocy because of course it is there, though possibly very small.

To nail this point down, consider the following quotation from Meehl (1967, p. 109, emphasis in the original):

> Data ... derived from a huge sample of over 55,000 Minnesota high school seniors, reveal statistically significant relationships in 91% of pairwise associations among a congeries of 45 miscellaneous variables such as sex, birth order, religious preference, number of siblings, vocational choice, club membership, college choice, mother's education, dancing, interest in woodworking, liking for school, and the like. The 9% of non-significant associations are heavily concentrated among a small minority of variables having dubious reliability, or involving arbitrary groupings of non-homogeneous or non-monotonic subcategories. The majority of variables exhibited significant relationships *with all but three of the others*, often at a very high confidence level ($p < 10^{-6}$).

Thus, if the sample size is large enough, and the measures reliable, a statistically significant effect is tantamount to guaranteed.

And to compound matters, let us consider the direct path from the first to the last variable in the sequence. The researcher's hope, of course, is that this is not statistically significant, in which case the researcher claims complete mediation. But consider the extreme unlikelihood that if one knew the population path coefficient, it would be exactly zero. The truth is that whether any path coefficients come out statistically significant or statistically insignificant depends on (a) the size of the sample effect and (b) the sample size. If the sample size is too small, none of the path coefficients will be statistically significant. If the sample size is too large, all the path coefficients will be statistically significant, including the direct pathway that is not supposed to be statistically significant, to make the case for complete mediation. In those cases where researchers report complete mediation, it is simply a matter of having picked the optimal sample size so that the path coefficients along the mediated route are statistically significant and the path coefficient representing a direct effect is not.

And there is another problem with interpreting lack of significance of the path coefficient representing the direct effect as supporting complete mediation. That is, even according to null hypothesis significance testing orthodoxy, a lack of significance merely means that one cannot reject the null hypothesis of no effect, not that one can accept the null hypothesis. But when a researcher uses a statistically insignificant effect to declare complete mediation, the researcher is accepting the null hypothesis based on the statistically insignificant effect. Thus, significance testing in the context of mediation analysis, as it is typically used, is problematic even from an orthodox and pro significance testing standpoint.

Statistical Indistinguishability

One of the points that Kline made in his 2015 special issue article is that even with only three variables, there are many potential models that would be consistent with a statistical analysis. In fact, he drew pictures of 15 of them (also see Thoemmes, 2015). The problem with having many models consistent with a statistical analysis is that the statistical analysis cannot distinguish between them. In turn, if the statistical analysis cannot distinguish between alternative models, then that analysis fails to provide a strong case for any of them. This is the problem of statistical indistinguishability, and it hangs over mediation models like a veritable sword of Damocles.

A caveat is that mediation analyses are not the only place where this is so. Even in the case of a true experiment, with random assignment of participants to conditions, it is possible for there to be more than one potential explanation of the findings. This is because it is impossible to manipulate only one variable. For example, an attitude manipulation might unintentionally manipulate mood, too, and so even if the experiment works out as hoped, there is no way to unambiguously distinguish whether the empirical success was due to attitudes or due to moods. Consequently, whatever the statistical analysis one uses, there may be no way to distinguish alternative models, such as an attitude model versus a mood model. When evaluating any research, it is a useful mental exercise to assess the extent to which the research design and statistics employed distinguish between alternative plausible models.

The Issue of Time

Let us return to the domino analogy. When the first domino falls over and thereby tips over the second domino, a certain amount of time must elapse. Likewise, when the second domino falls over and thereby tips over the third domino, some more time must elapse. No reasonable person expects all three dominos to fall over simultaneously; there is a time sequence that goes together with the sequence of events. Charlotte Ursula Tate (2015) wrote a nice special issue article that focused on the time issue. She quoted from the Baron and Kenny article that famously touted mediation analysis and I repeat that quotation here:

> This formulation in no way presupposes that mediators in social psychology are limited to individualistic or "in the head" mechanisms. Group-level mediator constructs such as role conflict, norms, groupthink, and cohesiveness have long played a role in social psychology.

> Moreover, with the increasing interest in applied areas, there is likely to be an increasing use of mediators formulated at a broader level of analysis.
>
> (Baron & Kenny, 1986, p. 1178)

After quoting, Tate (2015) went on to point out that the Baron and Kenny (1986) statement is problematic once time constraints are considered. For example, consider norms, which are long-lasting and exist prior to any sort of experimental manipulation or any life experiences that occur after the existence of the norm. Thus, there is no way that norms can be plausible mediators. A similar issue plagues the other group-level mediator constructs in the Baron and Kenny (1986) quotation. Moreover, consider other popular constructs, such as traits, that are defined as long-lasting and not changeable (though states are defined as changeable). There is no way, then, that traits can be plausible mediators.

In summary, when you run across a mediation analysis, you ought to consider whether the alleged mediator comes into existence before or after precursor variables in the alleged causal chain, and whether it is plausible that the precursor variables cause that mediator.

Causation by Definitional Fiat

A standard mediation ploy is to define causation as when there is a non-zero path coefficient. Because, as we saw earlier, it is tantamount to guaranteed that a path coefficient will not exactly equal zero, it follows that all the arrows in a mediation model are causal. Social science researchers often fall into a quagmire when it comes to definitions, with countless studies performed to show why one's favored definition is superior to alternative definitions. The reason such disputes fail to get settled is because definitions are not susceptible to empirical tests. Definitions are not true or false, but rather useful or not useful. Although I believe forcing causation by definitional fiat is not useful, and even harmful, let us stay with it a while longer to see what happens.

Once we insist that causation is always present, by definitional fiat, there is no longer an issue of the unsoundness of inferring causation from correlation. The causation must be there because we have defined it so! Well, then, if the causation must be there, then the next question is: What is the extent of that causation? And the answer, of course, is to perform a mediation analysis to find the path coefficients using Equations 8.3 to 8.5, or via a more complicated method. Once the sample path coefficients are determined, they can be used as the best estimate of population path coefficients.

If you have a feeling in the pit of your stomach that something has been pulled on you, it is because something has been pulled on you! In the first place, the whole line of reasoning starts with a definitional coup. Secondly, as you may recall from the previous discussion of the a priori procedure in Chapter 6, there is not necessarily a good reason to believe that the sample path coefficients are good estimates of the population path coefficients. In a recent article, my colleagues and I have proposed a method for determining the sample sizes necessary to obtain sample regression weights (including path coefficients) that are good estimates of corresponding population regression weights (Tong et al., 2022a). Consequently, this problem can be solved in the future merely by using the link to the program in that article that I included in Chapter 6. However, concerning previous research, where researchers have depended on power analysis to determine their sample sizes, there is no reason to believe that the sample path coefficients are good estimates of corresponding population path coefficients. As reviewed in Chapter 6, the purpose of power analysis is to aid in performing significance tests, not to have sample statistics that are good estimates of corresponding population parameters.

In fact, the opposite may be so when it comes to mediation models. In an extremely famous article in the prestigious *Journal of Business Research*, McQuitty (2004) argued that researchers should avoid too large sample sizes because then it would be tantamount to certain that a statistical significance test would reject tenable models. This article is so well regarded that the editor of another prestigious journal, *Journal of Global Scholars of Marketing Science*, invited McQuitty to revisit the 2004 article, and this latter article was published in 2018 (McQuitty 2018).

Then, in 2021, I and my colleagues published a paper, also in the *Journal of Business Research*, emphasizing two points relevant to the present discussion (Trafimow et al., 2021). One point is that limiting sample sizes forces sample statistics, including sample path coefficients, to poorly estimate corresponding population parameters. Thus, even ignoring all the other issues we have discussed thus far, there is little reason to believe that published path coefficients are good estimates of corresponding population parameters. Secondly, although the McQuitty (2004; 2018) argument makes sense, given that one is going to perform significance tests, there is no good reason to thusly shoot ourselves in the foot. From an estimation point of view, as opposed to a significance testing point of view, the McQuitty advice is plain bad. That such bad advice follows reasonably from a significance testing perspective constitutes yet another reason to abandon significance tests. And so, hearkening back to the Kline (2015) point, the combination of mediation analysis and significance testing is particularly harmful for the social sciences.

Nor is that all. Recall the demonstration, earlier in this chapter, of how a mediation analysis supports a causal model that is false for 67% of the participants. And yet, if we accept definitional fiat, we would be forced to say that the mediation analysis supports the causal model. The smart move is not to accept the definitional imposition.

Theory and Mediation analyses

There is a social science mantra that most mediation analysis aficionados chant whenever someone brings up that correlation need not indicate causation. And the mantra is that the criticism does not apply when there is a theory. When mediation analysis is combined with theory, causation follows. The idea is that the theory supports the proposed causal arrows in the mediation model, and the mediation analysis places values on those arrows, in the form of path coefficients. Thus, the theory and the mediation analyses are mutually supportive.

Because so many people believe the mantra, let us take our time to investigate it thoroughly. As a preliminary point, you might consider how much credence you place in social science theories. If you think most social science theories are questionable, then you might likewise question why you should believe in the associated mediation models. Furthermore, as we shall see, the justification falls apart when we consider various types of relations between theory and mediation analysis in the following subsections. For more details you might consult my recent article with Michael Hyman and Alena Kostyk (Trafimow, Hyman, & Kostyk, 2023).

There is a Comprehensive Theory

Let us consider one of the most comprehensive theories of the last half century that continues to be very popular in social psychology, management, and marketing. It is Fishbein's theory of reasoned action and was also used as an example in previous chapters (Fishbein & Ajzen, 1975; Fishbein, 1980). According to this theory, behavioral intentions (what people intend to do) are the immediate determinant of behaviors. In turn, attitudes (what people like to do) and subjective norms (people's opinions about what their important others think they should do) jointly determine behavioral intentions. Finally, beliefs about consequences and evaluations of those consequences determine attitudes, whereas beliefs about the opinions of specific others and the extent to which people are motivated to comply with them determine subjective norms. In addition to attitudinal and normative pathways to behaviors, Ajzen (1988) added perceived behavioral control. When perceived behavioral control is included in the theory, then Ajzen termed it the theory of planned behavior. And in its most recent incarnation (Fishbein & Ajzen, 2010), the theory was termed the reasoned action approach.

In a typical reasoned action or planned behavior type approach, of which there are hundreds in the literature, one might test the following nine bullet-listed mediation routes:

- Attitudes → behavioral intentions → behaviors,
- Subjective norms → behavioral intentions → behaviors,
- Perceived behavioral control → behavioral intentions → behaviors,
- Beliefs about consequences and evaluations of consequences → attitudes → behavioral intentions,
- Beliefs about what important others think and motivations to comply with them → attitudes → behavioral intentions,
- Control beliefs → perceived behavioral control → behavioral intentions,
- Beliefs about consequences and evaluations of consequences → attitudes → behavioral intentions → behaviors,
- Beliefs about what important others think and motivations to comply with them → attitudes → behavioral intentions → behaviors,
- Control beliefs → perceived behavioral control → behavioral intentions → behaviors.

Nor are these all, as researchers typically add new variables to the analysis, to generate many more potential mediation routes. The usual hope will be that there will be a statistically significant mediation route that involves a new variable, thereby justifying publication.

It is crucial to understand that the theory does not say that all the bullet-listed routes apply to every behavior. On the contrary, the theory emphasizes that some behaviors may be under attitudinal control but not normative control, vice versa, or varying degrees of each. And this flexibility extends to the other constructs in the expanded theory, such as perceived behavioral control. The flexibility is an important reason why the theory is one of the most highly cited theories across different social sciences.

However, when it comes to mediation analyses, such flexibility can be a disadvantage. To see this, suppose a researcher tests all the bullet-listed mediation routes and finds that only one of them works for the single behavior of concern. Because the theory allows all the routes, but insists on none of the routes, it follows inevitably that no matter which route or routes are supported by the mediation analysis, the result will be interpreted as consistent with the theory. The only way to obtain findings that would not be interpreted as supporting the theory would be if no mediation routes are statistically significant. And because there are so many possible mediation routes, it is unlikely in the extreme for this to happen.

Worse yet, it is possible to imagine two studies, with completely contradictory results, and interpret both as supporting the theory. To see this, let us suppose Martha performs a mediation analysis that supports the following mediation route: attitudes → behavioral intentions → behaviors. But Martha's analyses fail to convincingly support any other mediation route. In contrast, Joe supports the following: subjective norms → behavioral intentions → behaviors.

118 *General Methodological Issues*

But Joe's analyses fail to convincingly support any other mediation route. Thus, we have a contradiction across studies. Martha supports attitudes → behavioral intentions → behaviors and disconfirms subjective norms → behavioral intentions → behaviors whereas Joe's data show the reverse. Under mediation reasoning and given that the theory does not specify which mediation routes should hold for which behaviors, these contradictory findings would both be interpreted as confirming the theory!

Then, too, there remains the issue of auxiliary assumptions that provided much of our focus in Chapter 1 and Chapter 3. Whether a particular mediation route is supported or not supported, there is the ubiquitous problem of determining whether to attribute the finding to the theory or to auxiliary assumptions. Or going beyond, in line with the TASI taxonomy explained in Chapter 3, credit or blame can go not just to the theory or auxiliary assumptions, but to statistical or inferential assumptions too. The issue of different levels of assumptions is crucial for all kinds of research, not just mediation research. The upshot is that because it is so easy to interpret mediation analyses as supporting the theory, such support is not convincing.

The Mediation Model Is the Theory

In much mediation research, there is no overarching theory. Rather, by the time the reader of the journal article reaches the discussion section, it becomes clear that the mediation model *is* the theory, not that the mediation model is somehow derived from the theory. If shouting 'theory' is to be used to defend the mediation analysis, we end up in a vicious circle. The theory justifies the mediation analysis, and the mediation analysis justifies the theory. This is blatantly poor research practice, but unfortunately quite typical.

Moreover, as it is obvious that there is no preexisting theory in this case, that nonexistent theory cannot soundly justify that the alleged causal arrows in a mediation analysis really are causal.

The Mediation Model Is a Hodgepodge of Variables from Different Research Lines

This may be the most common form that mediation research takes. Suppose that a prior researcher has argued that A causes B causes C, so we have the following mediation model: $A \rightarrow B \rightarrow C$. And suppose a different prior researcher has argued that E causes F causes G, so we have the following mediation model: $E \rightarrow F \rightarrow G$. To be 'novel,' a third researcher might propose both. In the Hypotheses section of the Introduction, this third researcher might present these as separate hypotheses or even break them up into more hypotheses to generate an impressive list of hypotheses (e.g., $A \rightarrow B$, $B \rightarrow C$, $E \rightarrow F$, $F \rightarrow G$). However, the common practice is to also generate a complex mediation model that has everything in it. In terms of mediation practice, if the goal is to test separate hypotheses, they should not be included together in the same model. Rather, the hypotheses should be tested separately. More to the present point, however, the fact that one has put together a hodgepodge of relations from previous research scarcely qualifies as having a preexisting theory. Therefore, it is again unsound to use theory to justify the mediation analysis. What's more, the previous literatures used to generate the sets of arrows were likely themselves based on mediation analyses which, as we have seen scarcely provides a strong a priori case that the proposed mediating routes really are causal.

A rarer alternative might be for a researcher to find a literature that argues for the following set of arrows: $A \rightarrow B \rightarrow C$. But then find another literature that argues for the following set of arrows: $C \rightarrow D \rightarrow E$. Putting these together is taken as implying the following: $A \rightarrow B \rightarrow C \rightarrow D \rightarrow E$. In turn, this now becomes the 'theory.' But again, if the two literatures were both based on mediation analyses, there is scarcely a strong prior case for causation. And if the mediation model, $A \to B \to C \to D \to E$, is now the theory, we are back to the vicious circle of using the theory, which obviously was not preexisting, but merely a putting together of previous mediation findings, to justify the new mediation analysis and using the new mediation analysis to justify the theory. We again have a vicious circle. Moreover, remember that the more complex the mediation model becomes, the larger the set of underlying correlation coefficients, the smaller the probability that all are for the theoretically correct reason, and the smaller the probability that the mediation model is correct.

Application

Let us return to the use of definitional fiat to force that all arrows in a mediation model indicate causation. To generate an effective application out of such a mediation model, definitional fiat is obviously insufficient. It is necessary to switch to an interventionist causation conception, where manipulating the alleged cause forces an effect that propagates across the set of arrows that mark out the mediation route. This is often termed the transportability issue. But why should anyone believe that causation by definitional fiat should transport to an effective intervention? On the contrary, based on my nine years of editing *Basic and Applied Social Psychology*, it is rare, indeed, that an intervention based on prior mediation research is effective across the alleged causal chain. In fact, it is so rare that I have never seen it! Much more often, the best that can be said is that the effect propagates across one arrow, though typically with a very small effect size, and effects further down the causal chain are near zero.

Even mediation aficionados have admitted that much more is needed for transportability than is true of typical mediation research. Some additional assumptions are required such as that the researcher has employed a cross-lagged design (Gische et al., 2020; Pearl & Bareinboim, 2011; Schwartz et al., 2011). Another assumption is that the strength of the effect is known and applies equally to all people (Gische et al., 2020). Even if one believes that adding the extra assumptions renders mediation analyses transportable, I have yet to read an article where these extra assumptions are met. In fact, in a recent article in *Basic and Applied Social Psychology*, John Richters (2021) demonstrated that social science models do not even apply to everyone qualitatively because the underlying psychological structures and processes are not the same for everyone. That is, the constructs or processes in a social science theory or model are simply misconstrued for some people. This is not a matter of setting the value of a construct at zero for some people, but rather there is no sound way of setting any number whatsoever. Well, then, given Richters' demonstration that even qualitative homogeneity is unrealistic, the kind of quantitative homogeneity needed to render mediation analyses transportable is out of the question. Therefore, we see that causation via definitional fiat fails to transport to causation of the type that supports the effectiveness of an intervention. As a final point about transportability, consider that, to justify an intervention, it is insufficient that the intervention works statistically significantly; it must work well enough to justify the costs (Trafimow & Osman, 2022).

An Alternative Way to Demonstrate Mediation

Sometimes people ask me something along the following lines: "David, I get it that mediation analysis has very little to do with real mediation, but what else can we do to test for mediation?" I have an answer, though it requires much more work for the researcher than does a typical mediation study.

Let us return to the theorized causal chain: $A \rightarrow B \rightarrow C$. Instead of performing a correlational study, imagine a series of experiments. In Experiment 1, the researcher manipulates A and gets an effect on B and C. The good news, thus far, is that the researcher has a strong case that A causes B and C. The bad news is that the researcher does not have a strong case that the effect of A on C is mediated through B. A typical strategy would be to perform a mediation analysis, but we have already seen that this strategy is unconvincing. A better strategy would be to perform a second experiment using two independent variables in a 2 x 2 design. The researcher can again manipulate A; however, it is useful to add a second manipulation that either fixes B at a particular level or leaves it free to vary. If B truly mediates between A and C, then manipulating A should affect C, just as in Experiment 1, when B is free to vary. However, when B is fixed, then manipulating A should have no effect on C. As an analogy, consider again three dominos. Tipping over the first domino will cause the third domino to fall too, provided that the second domino is allowed to tip it over. However, if the second domino is held in place and not allowed to tip over, then tipping over the first domino will fail to tip over the third domino.

My suggested procedure for establishing mediation convincingly is not fanciful. I employed it myself quite some time ago to test an attribution theory I and my colleagues had proposed (Trafimow et al., 2005). The idea was that some kinds of moral violations cause strong negative affect whereas others cause weak negative affect. In turn, negative affect influences attribution strength (the negativity of the attribution that participants make about the person who committed the moral violation). Thus, negative affect is the mediating variable in the causal chain: type of violation $\rightarrow$ negative affect $\rightarrow$ attribution strength. After establishing that the type of violation influences both negative affect and attribution strength, I needed another experiment to demonstrate that the effect of type of violation on attribution strength is through negative affect. I used multiple strategies. One strategy was to perform an independent manipulation to drive negative affect to a ceiling, to fix it and reduce its ability to vary. When negative affect was thusly fixed, manipulating the type of moral violation had very little effect on attribution strength, whereas the typical strong effect of type of moral violation on attribution strength remained in the condition where negative affect was left free to vary. In another version of the same theme, I added a misattribution manipulation where participants were convinced to attribute their negative affect to an irrelevant source. In the misattribution condition, manipulating the type of moral violation had very little effect on attribution strength whereas the usual strong effect remained in the control condition. The larger point is that by being creative with respect to auxiliary assumptions, it is not necessary to depend on mediation analyses, though we had performed one of those too to make the reviewers happy. Creative experiments are much superior to mediation analyses to demonstrate mediation. Admittedly, there may be times when experiments are not feasible, but when they are, they should be favored over mediation paradigms.

Summary

In the mediation analyses of the planets (Trafimow, 2015a), we saw blatant and ridiculous errors, such as the error of concluding that planetary velocity importantly causes planetary mass. Obviously, there is something—or many things—wrong with mediation analyses. We then considered the complexity issue. Even when there are only three variables in a mediation model, so there are only three relevant correlation coefficients, the probability that all are for the correct reason, so that the mediation model is correct, is already well below a coin toss. And as more variables are added, so that the number of relevant correlation coefficients increases, the probability that the mediation model is correct decreases dramatically. And so, we already have a preliminary reason to distrust mediation analyses.

We then addressed a variety of other problems. There was the problem identified by James Grice and his colleagues (2015) that mediation analyses assume efficient causation along the arrows in the model. However, analyses of individual persons can contradict the seeming implications of mediation analyses. I provided an example where although a mediation analysis results in respectable numbers, 67% of the participants exhibited data patterns that contradicted the hypothesized mediational route. If one really takes mediation seriously, it would be better to analyze each person's pattern of responses than to conduct mediation analyses.

Another problem is the unhappy marriage of mediation analyses with null hypothesis significance testing, as Rex Kline (2015) showed. Although we saw in Chapter 4 that null hypothesis significance testing is generally unsound, the marriage forces extra problems that further call mediation paradigms into question.

Then, too, Rex Kline (2015) demonstrated a statistical indistinguishability problem. This is because when a statistical analysis is consistent with multiple models, there is no way to make a compelling case for any one of them. Mediation analyses are rife with this problem.

Charlotte Tate (2015) identified an additional problem, which is that it takes time for causation to propagate along a causal chain. If a mediation model proposes a mediating variable that is already fixed or that otherwise is inconsistent with respect to the passage of time necessary to render the causal model plausible, then the mediation model cannot be trusted. And as she demonstrated, mediation authorities have pushed such impossible mediation contexts.

Finally, but crucially, causation along a mediated route is so by definitional fiat rather than because the mediation model fits any reasonable philosophical conception of causation.

After discussing the foregoing general problems with believing that mediation analyses have much to do with real mediation, we discussed the most common defenses. One of them is that if there is a prior reason to believe in causal arrows, mediation analysis can put sound values to those arrows. The second defense is that theory justifies mediation analyses. We have seen that both defenses are insufficient.

Moving to application, we saw that causation by definitional fiat fails to imply that an intervention based on a mediation analysis likely would transport to an effective intervention. In fact, the applied literature shows just the opposite. There are many added assumptions needed to render transportability plausible, and there are no published studies of which I am aware where these are remotely plausible. If you expect that you can effectively apply the results of mediation analyses in the social sciences to perform interventions to better the human condition, you are likely to be disappointed.

Finally, we addressed another potential mediation defense, which is that there are no alternatives. However, there are alternatives based on restricting or not restricting the ability of the hypothesized mediator to move. When the hypothesized mediator is allowed to move freely, then manipulating the first variable in the causal chain should strongly influence the dependent variable, but when the hypothesized mediator is not allowed to move freely, then the effect should attenuate or disappear. Thus, mediation can be tested much more definitively by clever experiments than by mediation analyses.

In conclusion, you should be strongly suspicious of mediation analyses. In addition, please depend on these as little as possible in your own research.

Part II
Measurement Issues

9 The Classical Theory and Implications

Consider a bathroom scale. You stand on it and observe the reading, get off, and then get on again and take another reading. Suppose the two readings differ wildly. That would signal to you there is an important problem with the bathroom scale.

Or suppose the two readings are the same. That might increase your trust in the bathroom scale, though that trust might be qualified by the closeness of the two readings to your expectations of your weight. If your guess is that you weigh approximately 200 pounds, and the bathroom scale shows readings within some reasonable distance of that guess, there would be little reason to doubt that it works. In contrast, if the bathroom scale displays a reading of 250 pounds, you might begin to doubt it even if the readings are consistent across multiple attempts to weigh yourself.

Thus, there are two desirable characteristics that your bathroom scale can have. It is desirable that there is consistency across weighing attempts; this is often termed *reliability*. Secondly, it is desirable that the bathroom scale measures what it is supposed to measure. For example, it would be desirable for your bathroom scale to measure your weight, as opposed to measuring your weight plus some sort of systematic error, such as person weighing 200 pounds nevertheless consistently obtaining a reading of 250 pounds. That the bathroom scale measures what it is supposed to measure is often termed *validity*.

It may have occurred to you that there is a slight redundancy here. If the bathroom scale is unreliable, giving wildly different readings across weighing attempts, then it cannot be said to be valid either. Reliability is a necessary condition for validity. If there is no reliability, there is no validity. But reliability does not guarantee validity because the bathroom scale could be reliably wrong. Success with respect to reliability suggests there may be validity, but the suggestion begs further investigation.

Transitioning from Bathroom Scales to Psychology Measures

Psychology measures are less straightforward than bathroom scales. For one thing, as we saw in Chapter 1, weight is an observational term that can be contrasted with mass, which is a nonobservational term. To remind you, an object would have different weights if weighed on the Earth or on Mars, but the same mass. Of course, Newton's theory and auxiliary assumptions are sufficient for inferring mass from weight, but that should not deter us from carefully distinguishing between measuring something unobservable (e.g., mass) versus measuring something observable (e.g., weight). The inconvenient fact of the matter is that psychological traits, attitudes, intelligence, prejudice, and most of what social scientists care about cannot be observed. This contrasts sharply with measuring weight, which can be observed.

Secondly, most measurements in the social sciences are mediated by participants' mental processes. There is a large class of measures that involve participants making check marks on scales or a computerized analogous procedure. There is an increased level of ambiguity, compared to using bathroom scales, due to the difficulty in knowing all the relevant mental processes that figure into participants' responses to the test items.

Despite the lack of straightforwardness pertaining to measurement in the social sciences, relative to using bathroom scales, it is nevertheless possible to make progress. And such progress was made by a group of researchers spanning several decades in the first half or two-thirds of the twentieth century. There is insufficient space here to provide a proper historical perspective, so let us move directly to the main concepts. For comprehensive reviews, you may consult highly cited books by Lord and Novick (1968) and Gulliksen (1987) that retain their relevance today.

An Impossible, but Useful, Scenario for True Scores

It is obviously impossible to have someone complete a test, such as a personality test, wipe that person's mind so he or she is in the same mental state as before taking the test, have that person complete the test again, and so on for indefinite iterations. Nevertheless, the scenario is convenient because it clarifies a difference between systematic and random effects on test scores. Because the mind-wiping process renders all systematic factors the same across test-taking occasions, differences in a person's scores would be due to randomness. The expectation across the indefinite test-taking occasions—in more popular language this would be the average—equals the true score. In symbols, we have Equation 9.1 below:

$$T = \varepsilon X = \mu_X. \tag{9.1}$$

The person's true score T equals the expectation across indefinite test scores εX. The person's true score T is also the mean across indefinite test scores μ_X. Equation 9.1 provides the foundation for what is often called classical test theory, classical true score theory, or simply the classical theory.

Before continuing, let us ensure that we properly understand the philosophical implications of Equation 9.1. To reiterate, Equation 9.1 is based on an impossible scenario involving indefinite test-takings, with mind wiping prior to each successive test-taking. In addition, Equation 9.1 does not follow from any other equations: it is a definition. Its sole purpose is to define true scores into existence. Because it is a definition, there is no way to test empirically whether it is true or false, it is merely useful or not useful. We will see that it is useful. Finally, and this is perhaps the most controversial aspect of Equation 9.1, this equation does not require the existence of a construct being measured!

To see that I am not exaggerating, imagine the following bullet-listed test items:

- I like chocolate (scored –3 to +3),
- The number of letters in my last name (the score is the number of letters),
- My attitude towards exercising (scored –3 to +3).

It is obvious that the bullet listed items do not comprise a measure of any reasonable psychological construct. Nevertheless, if we imagine indefinite iterations, with mind wiping, of the test comprising the three bullet-listed items, it would be possible to calculate a true score. Thus, a true score need not map onto a psychological construct or trait.

Is this good or bad? Well, it depends on your perspective. Usually, the goal social scientists have is to measure a psychological construct, such as attitude, a personality trait, intelligence, and so on. To openly admit that such a construct need not exist, and yet the mathematical machinery can nevertheless run, is tough for some researchers. Not surprisingly, such researchers prefer more modern theories that do assume a score on a construct, such as item response theory that will not be covered here. Another potential disadvantage of the classical definition of a true score is that the mathematical machinery that comes out of it is less powerful than the mathematical machinery associated with more modern theories. Thus, more can be accomplished with more modern theories than with the classical theory.

And yet, despite the potential disadvantages, the classical theory continues to be popular. One reason is that because the classical theory has been around for longer, there is more of a tradition, and researchers are quite traditional. A second reason is that the potential disadvantage that true scores need not map onto any psychological constructs can be construed as a potential advantage too. Although a detailed discussion will await a future chapter, there are good reasons to suspect that scores on psychological tests do not correspond well with the traits they allegedly measure. For those researchers who suspect this, the lack of an assumption that true scores

128 *Measurement Issues*

map onto specific psychological constructs can be construed as an advantage rather than as a disadvantage.

And there is a related advantage. As Lord and Novick (1968) suggested in their famous book, the classical theory makes weaker assumptions than do more modern theories which, in turn, indicates that the assumptions are less likely to be problematic. Thus, as I have argued previously (e.g., Trafimow, 2021), in those cases where a weaker theory is nevertheless sufficient to achieve one's goals, it makes sense to use the weaker theory and enjoy a decreased probability of problematic assumptions. Put in the form of a rhetorical question: Why take a chance on extra assumptions if you do not need them? And as we will see, for the purpose of making the points I wish to make in this book, the classical theory is sufficient.

Reliability

Now that we have defined true scores into existence, we are ready to take on reliability. To set this up, let us define error. As everyone has a true score according to Equation 9.1, the error associated with each of the indefinite test scores is simply the difference between each of them and the true score. Equation 9.2 presents this in symbols:

$$E = X - T. \tag{9.2}$$

The error E is the difference between the observed score on a test X and the true score T. Equation 9.2 follows from how we defined a true score, with our impossible scenario and Equation 9.1. Therefore, it is not novel, but it is useful. For example, algebraically manipulating Equation 9.2 provides Equation 9.3:

$$X = T + E. \tag{9.3}$$

Equation 9.3 is useful because it provides a perhaps more intuitive way to understand what it means to have a score on a test. Specifically, one's score on a single test is influenced by both the true score and random error.

Moving to reliability, the less the random error, the better the reliability. Or to put this another way, the less the random error, the better observed scores will reflect true scores. Thus, far, we have only considered a single person, but let us now consider a population of people. Suppose that we have each person complete the test, and so we can know each person's score on that test. And suppose that we also know each person's true score. We do not, of course, but let us not be discommoded yet by lack of reality. Anyway, pretending that we know each person's observed score and each person's true score, we might ask how well true and observed scores go together? The lower the error variance, the better variance in true and observed scores will go together. More formally, we can define reliability according to Equation 9.4 below:

$$\text{reliability of the test} = \rho_{XX'} = \frac{\sigma_T^2}{\sigma_X^2}. \tag{9.4}$$

To understand Equation 9.4, let us first be clear about the notation. $\rho_{XX'}$ is an often-used symbol for the reliability of a test, or the extent to which a test correlates with itself under mind wiping to remove the effect of the first test-taking occasion on the second test-taking occasion. You might be more used to r as the symbol for correlation whereas I used ρ (rho) here. The reason is that r refers to a sample correlation coefficient but I want to think at the population level in explaining the classical theory. And ρ is the symbol for correlation coefficient at the population level. In turn, the reliability of the test is the ratio of true score variance σ_T^2 to observed score variance σ_X^2. Why is true score variance in the numerator and observed score variance in the denominator? The reason is that it is possible to derive Equation 9.4 from the previous equations and the definition of a correlation coefficient (e.g., Gulliksen, 1987). For a quick check, consider again Equation 9.3. It implies that observed score variance is larger than true score variance. In fact, Equation 9.3 implies that observed score variance σ_X^2 equals true score variance σ_T^2 plus error variance σ_E^2, as shown by Equation 9.5:

$$\sigma_X^2 = \sigma_T^2 + \sigma_E^2. \tag{9.5}$$

Therefore, to arrive at a number less than or equal to 1, it is necessary to have true score variance in the numerator and observed score variance in the denominator of Equation 9.4.

Although I usually omit derivations in this book for the sake of brevity and to avoid confusion, I'll make an exception with respect to Equation 9.5 because we will continue to use it in future chapters. Consider again, Equation 9.3: $X = T + E$. Well, then, according to the Covariance Law, the variance of a variable that is made up of two other variables equals the variances of the two variables plus twice the covariance between them. That is, $\sigma_X^2 = \sigma_T^2 + \sigma_E^2 + 2\sigma_{TE}$. However, because the errors are random, $2\sigma_{TE} = 0$, and can be cancelled. The leftover, after cancelling, is $\sigma_X^2 = \sigma_T^2 + \sigma_E^2$, or Equation 9.5.

Well, then, now that we know what reliability is, which is true score variance divided by observed score variance $\dfrac{\sigma_T^2}{\sigma_X^2}$, what does that imply? An important implication is that error variance σ_E^2 is bad because it decreases reliability. In the ideal case where there is no error variance, true score variance would equal observed score variance and so reliability would be perfect: $\dfrac{\sigma_T^2}{\sigma_X^2} = 1$. Alternatively, we might imagine the most horrible scenario where there is no variance in true scores and so reliability would equal zero: $\dfrac{\sigma_T^2}{\sigma_X^2} = \dfrac{0}{\sigma_X^2} = 0$. But there is another crucial implication too with respect to validity, which is where we go next.

Validity

Validity is a complicated issue, and future chapters will address much of that complexity. However, we need not be that complex yet, and so let us commence simply.

According to typical psychology textbook conceptions, a test is valid to the extent that it measures what it is supposed to measure. Which sounds straightforward until further reflection forces the following question: How would we know whether a test measures what it is supposed to measure? And here is where the complexities arise.

130 *Measurement Issues*

One way to know that a test is valid is that it correlates with something with which it ought to correlate. Consider some examples bullet-listed below:

- Scores on an extraversion test ought to correlate with social interactions,
- Scores on an attitude test ought to correlate with intentions to perform the behavior,
- Scores on an intelligence test ought to correlate with educational level,
- And so on.

On the one hand, there is an obvious problem with the bullet-listed examples. The problem is that it is easy to imagine obtaining the hoped-for correlation coefficients for wrong reasons. This is one reason why the ability of a test to predict something else need not be definitive as far as validity is concerned. On the other hand, however, if the bullet-listed correlation coefficients failed to appear, we would have reason to be quite concerned about the test. To keep things simple, the present section will focus only on the ability of a test to predict a criterion variable. In a word, we will focus on *predictive validity*. Also, for present purposes, it does not matter if scores on a test at one time predict scores on a test at another time, or whether tests are taken in the same experimental session and the correlation between them obtained. Either way, there is a single correlation coefficient, and we can speak of scores on a test predicting scores on a second test or on a criterion variable.

The Spearman Formula Relating Reliability to Validity

At this point, I happily bring up one of my psychology heroes, Charles Spearman, who published an article in 1904 whose importance would be very difficult to exaggerate (Spearman, 1904). Spearman derived a mathematical relationship between reliability and validity. The derivation is long and so I relegated it to an Appendix to this chapter rather than bog down the main text with it. The upshot, though, is that as tests become less reliable, the ability to observe impressive correlation coefficients decreases, and I will expand on that presently. Let us now consider the equation, denoted below as Equation 9.6:

$$\rho_{XY} = \rho_{T_X T_Y} \sqrt{\rho_{XX'} \rho_{YY'}}. \tag{9.6}$$

It is worthwhile to take our time and understand Equation 9.6 fully. The goal of the equation is to determine the extent to which the reliabilities of two tests, $\rho_{XX'}$ and $\rho_{YY'}$, influence the relationship between the correlation between true scores on the tests $\rho_{T_X T_Y}$ and observed scores on the tests ρ_{XY}. Suppose we set the reliability coefficients of the tests, $\rho_{XX'}$ and $\rho_{YY'}$, at 1.00 so that we have perfect reliability. In that case, the square root of the product of the reliability coefficients would likewise equal 1.00, and the observed correlation coefficient ρ_{XY} would equal the true correlation coefficient $\rho_{T_X T_Y}$. That would be the best-case reliability scenario.

The worst-case reliability scenario would occur if one or both reliability coefficients were to equal 0. In that case the whole right side of Equation 9.6 would equal 0, and the observed correlation coefficient would equal 0 too. That would obviously be disastrous for the researcher.

Of course, in most research, there are in-between scenarios where the reliability coefficients are between 0 and 1, but hopefully substantially closer to 1. Some authorities insist that reliabilities should exceed a floor of 0.70 whereas others prefer exceeding a floor of 0.80. These may sound like high bars but consider that a reliability coefficient equal to 0.70 only accounts for $0.70^2 = 0.49 = 49\%$ of the variance in its own scores, thereby leaving 51% of the variance unaccounted for. Insisting on a floor of 0.80 raises that value to 64%, but that still is not necessarily impressive.

To render the discussion of intermediate values easier, it is useful to collapse the two values, $\rho_{XX'}$ and $\rho_{YY'}$, into a single reliability product. Equation 9.7 accomplishes this:

$$\text{reliability product} = RP = \rho_{XX'}\rho_{YY'}. \tag{9.7}$$

Now instead of having two values $\rho_{XX'}$ and $\rho_{YY'}$ with which to contend, we only have a single value, RP, that ranges from 0 (worst reliability) to 1 (best reliability). This allows us to simplify Equation 9.6 to obtain Equation 9.8.

$$\rho_{XY} = \rho_{T_X T_Y} \sqrt{RP}. \tag{9.8}$$

And using our now defined reliability product RP, it is possible to create an easily comprehended figure that relates the true correlation coefficient $\rho_{T_X T_Y}$ to the observed correlation coefficient ρ_{XY}. Figure 9.1 illustrates the relationship.

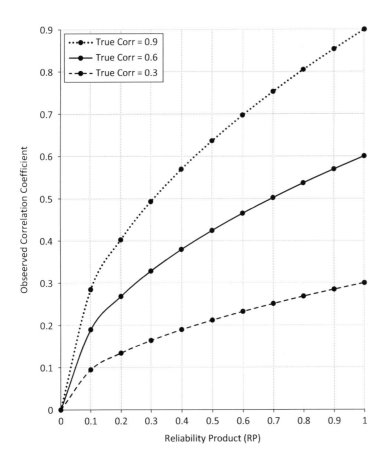

Figure 9.1 The observed correlation coefficient is expressed along the vertical axis as a function of the reliability product (RP) along the horizontal axis, with curves representing true correlation coefficients equal to 0.3 (bottom curve), 0.6 (middle curve), or 0.9 (top curve).

Let us first observe the top curve where the true correlation coefficient is set at 0.90 and read from right to left. When the reliability product equals 1, so there is perfect reliability, the observed correlation coefficient equals the true correlation coefficient equals 0.90. That is the good news. The bad news is that as the reliability product decreases, so does the observed correlation coefficient, which is why Equation 9.6 is often called the 'attenuation formula.' For example, suppose that the reliability product is 0.50, a realistic value if the reliability coefficient of each test approximately equals 0.70 (0.70 x 0.70 = 0.49), in which case the observed correlation coefficient would only equal 0.64. This is a substantial decrease from 0.90. Of course, the decreases in observed correlation coefficients as the reliability product decreases are less spectacular if we commence with small true correlation coefficients, such as 0.60 or 0.30. Nevertheless, even in these cases, the decreases should be sufficient to hopefully instill a desire to do whatever is reasonable to increase the reliability coefficients of the measures you use in your future research.

The Dis-Attenuation Formula

It may have occurred to you that if unreliability decreases observed correlation coefficients, perhaps there is a way to estimate what observed correlation coefficients would be in the presence of perfectly reliable measures. And you would be right! It is merely a matter of algebraically rearranging Equation 9.6, the attenuation formula, to arrive at Equation 9.9, the dis-attenuation formula.

$$\rho_{T_X T_Y} = \frac{\rho_{XY}}{\sqrt{\rho_{XX'} \rho_{YY'}}} \tag{9.9}$$

For example, suppose that the observed correlation coefficient is 0.3, a reasonably typical though unimpressive value in the social sciences. However, the researcher suspects that low reliability may have contributed to the problem. The researcher performs a study to assess the reliability coefficients of the measures, such as having participants complete the measures twice to obtain estimates of test–retest reliability (see next section for details). And let us suppose that the estimated reliability coefficients come out as follows: $\rho_{XX'} = 0.6$ and $\rho_{YY'} = 0.7$. The researcher then can use Equation 9.9 to estimate the value of the true correlation coefficient or what the correlation between the two variables would be under ideal conditions of perfect reliability: *estimated true correlation = est* $\rho_{T_X T_Y} = \dfrac{0.3}{\sqrt{(0.6)(0.7)}} = 0.46$. Thus, the dis-attenuation formula implies that the observed correlation coefficient is an underestimate of the true correlation coefficient. Furthermore, the more impressive true correlation coefficient can be argued to better describe the state of the real world than does the observed correlation coefficient because the true correlation coefficient is no longer contaminated by measurement error. For this reason, many classical theory afficionados argue that researchers should habitually dis-attenuate their observed correlation coefficients when reporting their data.

However, there are ways to push back on this argument. One potential problem is that estimating reliability coefficients is not necessarily as straightforward as I have pretended in the previous paragraph. There are many ways to estimate reliability and I cover a few of them in the following section. And if it is not completely clear how to estimate reliability coefficients, placing such potentially invalid estimates in the dis-attenuation formula can be argued problematic. A second potential problem is related to the first one. Suppose that the reliability estimates are too low. In that case, the researcher might over adjust, and report true correlation coefficients that are overestimates. It is even possible to end up with estimated true correlation coefficients that exceed 1. This would be an obvious problem as correlation coefficients have limits of –1 and +1. Lest this possibility seems too outlandish to be true, let us consider a case where the observed correlation coefficient = 0.80, the reliabilities of the measures are 0.80 and 0.90, but the estimated reliabilities are only 0.60 and 0.70, respectively. In that case, the proper dis-attenuation would be exemplified by the first bullet-listed calculation below whereas the actual dis-attenuation would be exemplified by the second one:

- $\text{est } \rho_{T_X T_Y} = \dfrac{0.8}{\sqrt{(0.8)(0.9)}} = 0.94,$

- $\text{est } \rho_{T_X T_Y} = \dfrac{0.8}{\sqrt{(0.6)(0.7)}} = 1.23.$

Clearly, the second bullet-pointed calculation results in an impossible value for the true correlation coefficient, thereby dramatizing the perils of over adjusting.

That said, there are potential comebacks. For one thing, although it is tantamount to certain that estimated reliability coefficients will not be exactly right, they may be reasonably close. In the case where the estimated reliability coefficients are too high, the researcher will under adjust, but even so, the estimated true correlation coefficient will still be closer to the true correlation coefficient than will the observed correlation coefficient. And this goes for when reliability coefficients are too low as well, in which case, even with over adjusting, the result will be more accurate than remaining with the observed correlation coefficient. Then, too, in the unfortunate cases where the calculated value exceeds 1, the researcher can simply cap at 1, thereby avoiding the problem of impossible correlation coefficients. Finally, recall the a priori procedure in Chapter 6, which includes a link to a program for determining the sample size necessary for obtaining sample correlation coefficients that are trustworthy estimates of population correlation coefficients. The problems of over adjusting or under adjusting can be greatly mitigated by using the a priori procedure to ensure that the estimated reliability coefficients can be trusted to be close to correct.

Of course, there remains the conceptual issue that a true score on a measure need not indicate a person's standing with respect to the characteristic of concern. To see this, recall that a true score is simply the expectation across indefinite test-taking occasions with mind wiping in-between. A consequence is that the substantive meaning of a true correlation coefficient with respect to the characteristic of concern is arguable and likely depends on particulars of the study.

So, should you dis-attenuate or not? At this point it would be premature to make a definitive statement. Rather, you should evaluate your assumptions, in the context of your expert knowledge about your substantive area, to decide. In addition, the extent to which you trust your estimated reliability coefficients ought to figure into your decision.

Practical Ways to Index Reliability (and Hopefully Thereby Increase Validity)

Although reliability is usually considered a less complex issue than validity, it nevertheless is quite complex. The reason for the complexity is that our definition of reliability, though theoretically satisfying, is difficult to put into practice. Recall that we defined reliability as true score variance divided by observed score variance σ_T^2/σ_X^2, but there is no way to observe true score variance. Ideally, we could give participants two versions of the test, which are parallel versions

134 Measurement Issues

of each other, and use the correlation between the two tests as the reliability coefficient. This would be an example of parallel tests reliability. However, it is extremely difficult to come up with parallel tests that have the following bullet-listed requirements:

- Each person has the same true score on both tests,
- The error variances of the two tests are the same.

Although some researchers attempt parallel tests, most researchers do not.

An alternative is to give participants the same test twice and use the correlation between them as the estimate of reliability. Such test–retest reliability has an advantage over parallel tests reliability because there is no need to worry about the bullet-listed requirements. However, a disadvantage is that scores the second time around might be influenced by having taken the test the first time. A disadvantage of parallel tests reliability and test–retest reliability is that both require time for participants to take two tests.

A way around this last disadvantage is to present participants with a single test, but correlate half of the test with the other half of the test. For example, one could correlate scores on the odd numbered items with scores on the even numbered items. A problem with splitting tests—that is, split-half reliability—is that the researcher obtains the reliability of only half the test. Consequently, it is necessary to make an appropriate adjustment to estimate the reliability of the whole test. Researchers typically use what is traditionally termed the Spearman-Brown prophesy formula, presented below as Equation 9.10.

$$\textit{estimated reliability of whole test} = \textit{est } \rho_{XX'} = \frac{2\rho_{AB}}{1+\rho_{AB}}. \tag{9.10}$$

If we designate the reliability coefficients of the two halves as A and B, then ρ_{AB} is the correlation coefficient between the two halves. In turn, to estimate the reliability coefficient of the whole test, we simply instantiate that value into Equation 9.10. For example, if the correlation coefficient between two halves equals 0.60, the estimated reliability coefficient of the whole test is $\frac{2(0.60)}{1+0.60} = 0.75$. In this example, the adjustment lifts the reliability coefficient from a 0.60 value that is under an often-used reliability threshold of 0.70, to 0.75 which is a value that is above the threshold.

A second method for computing reliability, based on a single test administration, is to use Cronbach's alpha (Cronbach, 1951). This is easily the most popular method and Equation 9.11 illustrates the computation:

$$\textit{Reliability as indexed by } \alpha_{standardized} = \frac{K\bar{r}}{1+(K-1)\bar{r}}. \tag{9.11}$$

Equation 9.11 includes the following:

- $\alpha_{standardized}$ is the reliability coefficient,
- $\bar{r}$ is the mean inter-unit (inter-item for present purposes) correlation coefficient, and
- K is the number of units (items for present purposes).

The Classical Theory and Implications 135

A close look at Equation 9.11 shows that Cronbach's alpha is influenced by two things. There is the average inter-unit correlation coefficient and the number of items. As either of these increases, so does Cronbach's alpha. Figure 9.2 illustrates.

To interpret Figure 9.2, consider the following. As the number of units increases, the curves are increasingly higher in the graph; that is, Cronbach's alpha is generally larger. Secondly, as the average inter-unit correlation increases, so does Cronbach's alpha. However, there are limits to both effects. One limit is when the average inter-unit correlation equals zero, in which case it does not matter how many units there are because Cronbach's alpha always decreases to zero. The other limit is when the average inter-unit correlation equals one, in which case it does not matter how many units there are because Cronbach's alpha always increases to one. The number of units matters the most when the inter-unit correlation is at an intermediate level. For example, imagine tests with 2, 4, 8, or 16 items, where each item is a unit, and the average inter-unit correlation equals 0.30. When there are 2, 4, 8, or 16 items, Cronbach's alpha equals 0.46, 0.63, 0.77, or 0.87, respectively. These are big differences!

To obtain an impressive Cronbach's alpha, there are two main ways to do it. One way is to include many items. For example, even when the average inter-unit correlation is an anemic 0.20, it is still possible to obtain respectable reliability by having 16 items, in which case Cronbach's alpha clocks in at a reasonably impressive value of 0.80. Secondly, even if there are only two items, if they correlate sufficiently, Cronbach's alpha can be impressive. For example, if the two items correlate at the 0.90 level, Cronbach's alpha is 0.95.

There has been much debate about how to think about Cronbach's alpha. Does Cronbach's alpha index reliability or does it index internal consistency? Authorities are divided about which it is. My own answer is that both sides are wrong!

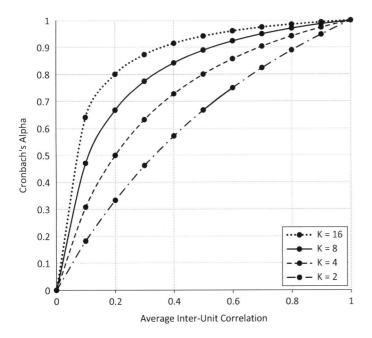

Figure 9.2 Cronbach's alpha is expressed along the vertical axis as a function of the average inter-unit correlation, when there are 2 items (bottom curve), 4 items (next to bottom curve), 8 items (next to top curve), or 16 items (top curve).

136   *Measurement Issues*

To see why, let us take both perspectives and see how matters play out. As Cronbach's alpha is in the reliability section of most measurement textbooks, it is convenient to start with reliability. To move in this direction, consider a rather nonsensical test with the following items.

- How many letters are there in your last name?
- Is your area code greater than 400?
- What is the number of the month in which you were born?

Although the test is nonsensical, let us consider reliability in the test–retest sense and in the Cronbach's alpha sense. Because the correct answers to the bullet-listed items are unlikely to change between test-taking occasions, provided there is not too long an interval, test–retest reliability ought to be very impressive. In contrast, because there is no reason to expect the items to correlate well with each other, Cronbach's alpha is likely to be very poor. Remembering the classical theory style of thinking that emphasizes repeated test-taking occasions, it is obvious that test–retest reliability is much more consistent with the classical spirit than is Cronbach's alpha. Thus, the divergence between test–retest reliability and Cronbach's alpha in the example suggests that Cronbach's alpha does not measure reliability, at least not in the classical theory sense of reliability.

A similar conclusion comes from using the classical definition of reliability as true score variance divided by observed score variance σ_T^2/σ_X^2. But these again depend on participants receiving at least two test administrations (e.g., two parallel tests), and so there is no reason to expect Cronbach's alpha, based on a single test administration, to map on well to σ_T^2/σ_X^2.

Now, let us consider internal consistency. Suppose that a researcher unintentionally includes eight items that measure anxiety and eight items that measure depression. We would, of course, expect impressive inter-item correlations among the eight anxiety items and among the eight depression items. But because anxiety and depression are correlated, the correlation between items measuring anxiety and items measuring depression will not be all that small. For example, perhaps the average inter-item correlation between items measuring the same construct is somewhere in the ballpark of 0.6 and the average inter-item correlation among items measuring different constructs is in the ballpark of 0.3. Well, then, the average might be somewhere in the ballpark of 0.4 to 0.5. With 16 items, that would result in a value for Cronbach's alpha somewhere in the ballpark of 0.90, a seemingly highly impressive value! But despite the impressive value, the plain fact of the matter is that the items are not internally consistent because half of them measure anxiety and half of them measure depression. Thus, Cronbach's alpha is not a valid index of internal consistency.

In summary, Cronbach's alpha indexes neither reliability, at least not in the classical theory sense of the word, nor does it index internal consistency. Frankly, it is not clear what it indexes. And yet, as I said earlier, it is easily the most popular reliability index in the social sciences. The ridiculous level of reliance that researchers place on Cronbach's alpha should change for the benefit of the field. And there is another problem with Cronbach's alpha, but that will have to await a later chapter.

The Effects of Unreliability on Regression Coefficients and Path Coefficients

We have seen that unreliability has a predictable effect on correlation coefficients; unreliability decreases them. But as we saw in Chapter 8, researchers often perform more complex correlational analyses that feature regression coefficients or path coefficients. As unreliability decreases

The Classical Theory and Implications 137

correlation coefficients, might it decrease regression coefficients and path coefficients too? In contrast to correlation coefficients, the effects of unreliability on regression coefficients and path coefficients are unpredictable in the sense that these can increase or decrease. I described the effects in detail in an article I published in 2021 (Trafimow, 2021), but here I will only present a few illustrative cases.

To see the unpredictability, suppose two variables are used to predict a criterion variable and we use the attenuation formula to account for the effects of unreliability, and then instantiate the attenuated correlation coefficients into both the regression weight equations and path coefficient equations discussed in Chapter 8. It is first useful to bullet-list the attenuated correlation coefficients using Equation 9.6 for each of the three possible underlying correlation coefficients:

- $r_{y1} = r_{T_y T_1} \sqrt{r_{yy'} r_{11'}}$,

- $r_{y2} = r_{T_y T_2} \sqrt{r_{yy'} r_{22'}}$,

- $r_{12} = r_{T_1 T_2} \sqrt{r_{11'} r_{22'}}$.

Instantiating the bullet-listed equations into equations 8.1 and 8.2 from Chapter 8 leads to the regression coefficients bullet-listed below:

- $\beta_1 = \dfrac{r_{T_y T_1}\sqrt{r_{yy'} r_{11'}} - \left(r_{T_y T_2}\sqrt{r_{yy'} r_{22'}}\right)\left(r_{T_1 T_2}\sqrt{r_{11'} r_{22'}}\right)}{1 - r_{T_1 T_2}^2 r_{11'} r_{22'}}$,

- $\beta_2 = \dfrac{r_{T_y T_2}\sqrt{r_{yy'} r_{22'}} - \left(r_{T_y T_1}\sqrt{r_{yy'} r_{11'}}\right)\left(r_{T_1 T_2}\sqrt{r_{11'} r_{22'}}\right)}{1 - r_{T_1 T_2}^2 r_{11'} r_{22'}}$.

These bullet-listed regression coefficient equations may look scary, but the simple way to understand them is merely to consider that they account for how lack of perfect reliability attenuates the underlying correlation coefficients that go into regression coefficient computations.

To see why unreliability can increase or decrease regression weights, suppose that all underlying true correlation coefficients equal 0.70, the reliability of the first predictor variable is 0.90, the reliability of the second predictor is 0.50, and the reliability of the criterion is 0.90. In that case, the estimated value for $\beta_1 = 0.38$ but the estimated value for $\beta_2 = 0.21$. As we had set all underlying correlation coefficients equal, the two regression coefficients ought to be equal too, but unreliability messes up that obvious outcome. In fact, if we set the reliability coefficients as all equal to 1, so there is perfect reliability, then the regression coefficients are both 0.33. Note that by adding unreliability to the system, we raised β_1 from 0.33 to 0.38 and we decreased β_2 from 0.33 to 0.21. Thus, we have a clear example of how unreliability renders regression coefficients unpredictable: unreliability can raise or lower the values.

A similar argument pertains to path coefficients. Instantiating the equations that account for unreliability into the path coefficient equations from Chapter 8 (Equations 8.3 to 8.5) yields the following.

- $p_{21} = r_{T_2 T_1}\sqrt{r_{22'} r_{11'}}$,

138 *Measurement Issues*

- $$p_{31} = \frac{r_{T_3T_1}\sqrt{r_{33'}r_{11'}} - r_{T_3T_2}\sqrt{r_{33'}r_{22'}}\, r_{T_2T_1}\sqrt{r_{22'}r_{11'}}}{1 - r_{T_2T_1}^2 r_{22'}r_{11'}},$$

- $$p_{32} = \frac{r_{T_3T_2}\sqrt{r_{33'}r_{22'}} - r_{T_3T_1}\sqrt{r_{33'}r_{11'}}\, r_{T_2T_1}\sqrt{r_{22'}r_{11'}}}{1 - r_{T_2T_1}^2 r_{22'}r_{11'}}.$$

The bullet-listed equations suggest some potentially scary consequences. Unreliability can cause path coefficients not only to decrease or increase, as we saw with the regression coefficient example, but even to appear or disappear. It is even possible for unreliability to cause path coefficients to change from negative to positive or from positive to negative. Let us consider an example of this last from Trafimow (2021). Suppose that the true correlation between Variable 1 and Variable 2 is 0.90, the true correlation between Variable 1 and Variable 3 is 0.13, and the true correlation between Variable 2 and Variable 3 is 0.10. Under perfect reliability, the path coefficients would be as follows: $\rho_{21} = 0.90$, $\rho_{32} = -0.089$, and $\rho_{31} = 0.211$. Note that the mediated pathway from Variable 1 to Variable 2 to Variable 3 ($1 \rightarrow 2 \rightarrow 3$) is negative because ρ_{32} is negative. However, if we reduce the reliability of Variable 1 to 0.60, all path coefficients change. Of special concern, now $\rho_{32} = 0.058$, a positive value. And so, what is really a negative mediation pathway now becomes a positive mediation pathway. If the mediation problems discussed in Chapter 8 were insufficient to cause you to worry, now you have yet another reason.

Other Worries

If you have reached this point in the chapter, it means you have survived the introduction of several equations, which is the good news. However, the bad news is that there is a hidden assumption behind the equations, which is that whatever it is that researchers measure is quantitative. If this is not so, then perhaps the equations mean less than that which is apparent, and perhaps our measures of social science constructs are meaningless. Although I will not go so far as to argue this, I will go so far as to mention work by Michell (1999) who has argued this.

Although Michell's arguments are complex and there is no way to do them justice here, an important component of his position concerns the lack of evidence that our measures are quantitative, combined with common sense reasons to suppose that they are not. Consider, for example, scores on a test ostensibly measuring extraversion, where participants respond to items marked "strongly agree" (2), "agree" (1), "neutral" (0), "disagree" (–1), "strongly disagree" (–2). Suppose that Jill responds to all items with "strongly agree" (2) and Jack responds to all items with "agree" (1), so that Jill's extraversion score equals 2 and Jack's extraversion score equals 1. Do you believe that Jill is twice as extraverted as Jack? If not, and it would be very difficult to defend such a belief, then there is a quantitative issue here. According to how math works, 2 is twice 1, but it is unlikely that matters work out in this way with respect to extraversion. Doubtless, some of the problem is that what is marked out as 0 on the scale, that is, a neutral response, could easily be argued not to be a true zero point. If there is no true zero point, there is no way to argue that 2 on the scale is twice the value of 1 on the scale.

Well, then, although this problem is inconvenient, perhaps it is not fatal. After all, 2 degrees Celsius in not twice as hot as 1 degree Celsius either and yet the Celsius scale is nevertheless often useful. A qualification of this apology is that scientists usually use the Kelvin scale, which does have a true zero point, as zero degrees Kelvin really does set a theoretical limit on how low it is possible for temperature to go. Thus, 2 degrees Kelvin really is twice as hot as 1 degree Kelvin. But the qualification aside, there can be little doubt that for normal everyday use by ordinary people, the Celsius scale remains useful. And even for scientific purposes, it is well-known how to convert between degrees Celsius and degrees Kelvin. Might extraversion be like Celsius, and likewise useful?

We have supposed that Jill scores 2 on extraversion and that Jack scores 1. Let us suppose, too, that Sarah scores 0 on extraversion. According to arithmetic, Jill is one extraversion unit higher than Jack, and Jack is one extraversion unit higher than Sarah. To use the Celsius analogy, 2 degrees Celsius is one degree higher than 1 degree Celsius, and 1 degree Celsius is higher than 0 degrees Celsius. But alas, in the case of Celsius, there is wide agreement that the difference between 2 and 1 equals the difference between 1 and 0. In the case of extraversion, this is less clear. Do you believe that the difference in extraversion between Jill and Jack is the same as the difference in extraversion between Jack and Sarah? If you do believe this, then that would justify the extraversion scale to an important extent. If you do not believe this, then that puts you in agreement with Michell (2011) and gives you good reason to worry about interpreting scores on social science measures. Perhaps a compromise position would be that social science measures are close enough to Celsius to be "good enough for government work."

Work by Morris and her colleagues not only casts doubt upon social science measures being quantitative, but even against the compromise position (Morris, Grice, & Cox, 2017). To understand their work, consider again the Jill, Jack, and Sarah scenario. As a minimal, but far from sufficient condition for believing that the extraversion scale is quantitative, we would at least expect that Jill's score of 2 indicates that she is more extraverted than Jack, with his score of 1. Also, we would expect that Jack is more extraverted than Sarah, with her score of 0. With this stricture in mind, consider the studies Morris and her colleagues performed with respect to neuroticism. They presented participants with pairs of persons and asked, straight out, for judgments of which member of each pair is more neurotic. Suppose a participant indicates that Person A is more Neurotic than Person B, and that Person B is more neurotic than Person C. In that case, when given an opportunity to judge Person A and Person C, the judgment should be that Person A is more neurotic than Person C. The mathematical word for this is *transitivity*; if A is greater than B, and B is greater than C, then A is greater than C. Nevertheless, in two experiments, Morris and her colleagues found a substantial percentage of transitivity violations, thereby calling into question a minimal requirement for faith in the quantitative nature of social science measures. For icing on the cake, Morris et al. also performed a third experiment, but using height rather than neuroticism. In this case, they obtained dramatically fewer transitivity violations, thereby suggesting that it was the extraversion measure itself that was the problem, rather than the general methodology being the problem. That said, however, an alternative explanation might be cobbled together out of an assumption that there may be more randomness with respect to neuroticism than height judgments, and so apparent transitivity violations are due to that rather than because neuroticism is not quantitative.

Then, too, there is a recent article by friend John Richters (Richters, 2021). The argument is complex, and so I will render a simplistic version of it here, with a recommendation that you read the article to get the full story. According to Richters, researchers using measures of social science constructs, such as extraversion, neuroticism, and so on, tacitly assume that the same underlying psychological structures and processes work the same way for everyone. This is not to say that everyone will have the same score, but rather the underlying causes of scores are the same for everyone. As an example, pea plants might differ in height, but the combination of genetic and environmental factors that influence growth arguably apply to all pea plants.

140 *Measurement Issues*

Thus, staying with pea plants, although there are quantitative differences between them, there is no difference qualitatively with respect to the factors underlying height. There is qualitative homogeneity but not quantitative homogeneity. Likewise, Richters argued that social science researchers tacitly assume qualitative but not quantitative homogeneity. However, Richters also argued that the qualitative homogeneity assumption is not tenable in the social sciences. If you agree with Richters, that could provide another reason to worry about measures of social science constructs.

Chapter Summary

We commenced with the classical theory, featuring a discussion of true scores and implications. One of these is that a true score need not refer to any single social science construct, which can be advantageous or disadvantageous. We then moved on to reliability, and the classical definition, which is true score variance divided by observed score variance σ_T^2/σ_X^2.

We subsequently discussed predictive validity and how unreliability impinges on it. This discussion featured Spearman's (1904) famous attenuation formula. We saw that unreliability can impressively attenuate observed correlation coefficients relative to corresponding true correlation coefficients that would be obtained with perfect reliability. In addition, it is possible to algebraically rearrange the attenuation formula to dis-attenuate—that is, to estimate true correlation coefficients based on observed correlation coefficients and estimates of the reliability coefficients of the measures. However, there is some controversy with respect to whether it is wise to dis-attenuate.

There is no way to use Spearman's work unless there is a way to assess reliability. We discussed several ways, including their pros and cons. This discussion included an argument that single administration reliability assessments, such as split-half reliability and Cronbach's alpha, may differ crucially from of the classical theory conception of reliability. In addition, we saw that although Cronbach's alpha is widely considered to index internal consistency, it does not.

Chapter 8 included an extensive discussion of mediation analyses and why it is not trustworthy as typically used in the social sciences. However, the discussion in Chapter 8 did not include anything about how measurement unreliability can further destroy sensible interpretation of path coefficients. The present chapter provided that discussion. That social science measures are not perfectly reliable can make ostensibly causal arrows appear when they are not there, disappear when they are there, or even change from positive to negative causation, or the reverse. I provided an example of how measurement unreliability can cause the latter and referred you to one of my recent articles for the rest.

Finally, there are philosophical worries. These include whether social science measures are quantitative, whether they violate transitivity, and whether it is justified to assume qualitative homogeneity. There is much for you to think about!

As a postscript, although I did not want to bog down the main text with a proof of Spearman's formula, I included it in the Appendix to this chapter.

Appendix

Let's start with the assumptions. These are given below

- $X = T + E$
- $\varepsilon(X) = T$

The Classical Theory and Implications 141

- $\rho_{ET} = 0$
- $\rho_{E_1 E_2} = 0$
- $\rho_{E_1 T_2} = 0$

We have already discussed the first two assumptions in the main text. The latter three assumptions are consequences as they follow from the first two assumptions, which assume that errors are random. It is forced that error scores and true scores are uncorrelated, that error scores for two tests are uncorrelated, and that error scores on any test are uncorrelated with true scores on another test.

Also, if two tests have observed scores X and X' that satisfy the foregoing assumptions, and if, for every population of examinees, $T = T'$ and $\sigma_E^2 = \sigma_{E'}^2$, then the tests are called parallel tests.

Finally, if two tests have observed scores X_1 and X_2 that satisfy the foregoing assumptions, and if, for every population of examinees, $T_1 = T_2 + c_{12}$, where c_{12} is a constant, then the tests are called *essentially τ-equivalent tests*.

Given the above assumptions, can we derive the correction formula? The answer is "yes!"

Consider first the definition of a correlation coefficient as the covariance divided by the standard deviations of the two variables.

$$\rho_{XZ} = \frac{\sigma_{XZ}}{\sigma_X \sigma_Z}$$

There is also a theorem about covariances that goes as follows.

$$\sigma_{(W+X,Y+Z)} = \sigma_{WY} + \sigma_{WZ} + \sigma_{XY} + \sigma_{XZ}$$

Based on the above and the fact that observed score equals true score plus error, we can get the following. To do this, we make "W" the true score for the first test and "X" the error for it. Then we make "Y" the true score for the second test and "Z" the error for it. Another way to say this is to put it in terms of the equation below.

$$\sigma_{(W+X,Y+Z)} = \sigma_{(T_X+E_X, T_Z+E_Z)}$$

Given all of this, we have the equation below.

$$\rho_{XZ} = \frac{\sigma_{T_X T_Z} + \sigma_{T_X E_Z} + \sigma_{E_X T_Z} + \sigma_{E_X E_Z}}{\sigma_X \sigma_Z}$$

By the assumptions, or more generally the fact that all errors are random, the covariances in the numerator containing the errors necessarily equal 0 and can be cancelled. This results in the equation below.

$$\rho_{XZ} = \frac{\sigma_{T_X T_Z}}{\sigma_X \sigma_Z}$$

142 Measurement Issues

Let's rearrange the terms to get the covariance between true scores by itself. This gives us the following.

$$\sigma_{T_X T_Z} = \rho_{XZ} \sigma_X \sigma_Z$$

Now we need to deal with the correlation between true scores. Going back to the definition of correlation, we start with the following.

$$\rho_{T_X T_Z} = \frac{\sigma_{T_X T_Z}}{\sigma_{T_X} \sigma_{T_Z}}$$

Now, we substitute for the covariance between true scores in the immediately foregoing equation using the equation two steps back.

$$\rho_{T_X T_Z} = \frac{\rho_{XZ} \sigma_X \sigma_Z}{\sigma_{T_X} \sigma_{T_Z}}$$

Let's do some more algebra.

$$\rho_{T_X T_Z} = \frac{\rho_{XZ} \sigma_X \sigma_Z}{\sigma_{T_X} \sigma_{T_Z}} = \frac{\rho_{XZ}}{\frac{\sigma_{T_X}}{\sigma_X} \frac{\sigma_{T_Z}}{\sigma_Z}}$$

Obviously, the denominator in the above equation is a pain. Also, we want it in terms of the reliability coefficients of the tests. So, let's go back and figure this out. As usual, starting with the definition of a correlation, but applying it to the correlation between a test with its parallel test, we have the following.

$$\rho_{XX'} = \frac{\sigma_{XX'}}{\sigma_X \sigma_{X'}}$$

It is worth remembering that the observed score is the true score plus error. It is also worth remembering that the standard deviations of the two tests are equal by the assumption of parallel tests. All these considerations give the following equation.

$$\rho_{XX'} = \frac{\sigma_{(T+E)(T'+E')}}{\sigma_X^2}$$

By the covariation theorem we used earlier, we have the following.

$$\rho_{XX'} = \frac{\sigma_{TT'} + \sigma_{TE'} + \sigma_{ET'} + \sigma_{EE'}}{\sigma_X^2}$$

Three of the covariance terms in the numerator contain random error, and so they all equal zero and can be cancelled. This renders the equation below.

$$\rho_{XX'} = \frac{\sigma_{TT'}}{\sigma_X^2}$$

In addition, because the two tests are parallel, the covariance of a test and a parallel test is simply the variance of the test. I present this below.

$$\rho_{XX'} = \frac{\sigma_{TT'}}{\sigma_X^2} = \frac{\sigma_T^2}{\sigma_X^2}$$

Put another way that will be useful in a minute, we can take the square root of both sides and get the following.

$$\sqrt{\rho_{XX'}} = \sqrt{\frac{\sigma_T^2}{\sigma_X^2}} = \frac{\sigma_T}{\sigma_X}$$

Now, I copy an equation from before.

$$\rho_{T_X T_Z} = \frac{\rho_{XZ} \sigma_X \sigma_Z}{\sigma_{T_X} \sigma_{T_Z}} = \frac{\rho_{XZ}}{\dfrac{\sigma_{T_X}}{\sigma_X} \dfrac{\sigma_{T_Z}}{\sigma_Z}}$$

Consider the equation two steps back. Note that the T in the numerator standard deviation can refer to the true score of any test (e.g., test X or test Z). And note that the X in the denominator standard deviation can refer to the observed score of any test (test X or test Z). Consequently, we can substitute from that equation, into the foregoing equation, the square root of the consistency coefficients. This gives us the dis-attenuation formula!

$$\rho_{T_X T_Z} = \frac{\rho_{XZ} \sigma_X \sigma_Z}{\sigma_{T_X} \sigma_{T_Z}} = \frac{\rho_{XZ}}{\dfrac{\sigma_{T_X}}{\sigma_X} \dfrac{\sigma_{T_Z}}{\sigma_Z}} = \frac{\rho_{XZ}}{\sqrt{\rho_{XX'} \rho_{ZZ'}}}$$

In turn, the attenuation formula is simply an algebraic rearrangement of the dis-attenuation formula.

$$\rho_{XZ} = \rho_{T_X T_Z} \sqrt{\rho_{XX'} \rho_{ZZ'}}$$

10   Potential Performance Theory

I will start the present chapter by telling you a story of my complete lack of knowledge about something important, and what came of that lack of knowledge. I grew up in suburb of Chicago, so naturally I became a fan of all Chicago sports teams. Being a sports fan may be the ultimate

DOI: 10.4324/9781003365167-12

in irrational behavior, and so I plead guilty of irrationality. On one rare occasion, I took the time to watch a full Chicago Bears game instead of doing what I usually do, which is settle for a few minutes of highlights, and I was punished for my irrationality. The Bears lost and lost big!

I took a walk after the game and pondered the horrible catastrophe. I thought about task performance, as the Bears had performed badly. The problem is that although there is, and long has been, an impressively large literature on task performance, I knew absolutely nothing about that literature. The obvious thing to do, of course, was start reading the task performance literature. But I rarely do what I am supposed to do and so I started theorizing, instead, using my own ignorance as a base. Having a nice day, a clear blue sky, and being a bit high on adrenaline from walking doubtless helped too. Knowing nothing about task performance or about the factors that increase it or decrease it, I naturally sought a way of making progress that did not depend on substantive knowledge. One way out was to assume that there are random and systematic factors at play for the performance of any sort of task. It occurred to me that if randomness could be handled mathematically, then systematicity would be left over.

Then, too, in the back of my mind there was an issue that has long troubled me, which is that the social sciences are mostly about statistical conglomerations, such as means and correlation coefficients, that may have little to do with individual people. Could thinking about randomness and systematicity pay dividends at the level of individual people? Perhaps so.

There is one more preliminary, which is that many tasks are dichotomous: an answer to a true–false question is either correct or incorrect, a person finds her keys or does not, the Chicago Bears win or lose a game, and so on. The present chapter concerns dichotomous tasks.

The Deleterious Effects of Randomness on Task Performance

Most people, including social science researchers, underestimate the deleterious effects of randomness on task performance. For example, as computers continued to come into vogue in clinical psychology in the 1970s and 1980s, clinical psychology researchers became increasingly interested in using computers to make diagnoses. It became apparent that computers usually outperformed trained clinicians. This is not because the trained clinicians were somehow stupid or incompetent, it is because the trained clinicians were human beings, with human vulnerability to random inconsistency. In contrast, computers are perfectly reliable. Recalling the lessons learned in Chapter 9 about how unreliability (random error) decreases correlation coefficients, you can now see that computers have an important advantage over human beings. To nail this point home, consider that in one iteration of this sort of research, researchers questioned the few clinicians who outperformed the computer. When researchers included input from the star clinicians into the program, the computer outperformed even the stars. The reliability advantage is difficult to beat! We will encounter more on this later in the chapter. For now, it is sufficient that you keep in the back of your mind that the degree of randomness in people's performances strongly influences the degrees of success they can attain.

There is a reason for harping on the deleterious effects of randomness on task performance. Specifically, I will explain a theory, termed potential performance theory, that parses a person's performance across multiple trials, such as multiple true–false questions, into random and systematic components. In turn, the parsing implies the exciting possibility of estimating what the person's performance would have been in the absence of randomness. Or put another way, the parsing implies how to estimate the person's potential performance, if randomness in responding could be eliminated. For this reason, the theory is termed *potential performance theory* (e.g., Trafimow & Rice, 2008). As I will explain later, potential performance theory can imply surprising solutions to seemingly intractable problems.

Defining the Phi Coefficient, with Morality an Example

Because we are concerned with people's dichotomous responses across trials, the standard correlation coefficient is insufficient. It is necessary to introduce a type of correlation coefficient that works across dichotomous examples. The easiest way to make the introduction is through an example about moral choices. Why use moral choices? There is much controversy about morality, which makes it a 'squishy' topic. If I can show that potential performance theory works even for morality, then it ought to work for less squishy types of tasks, such as search tasks, academic tasks, and so on.

Suppose that Diedre and Joseph each complete 50 moral dilemmas. For each moral dilemma, each person can make Choice A or Choice B. Table 10.1 is the summary table.

In Table 10.1, the major diagonal (cells a and d) is where Diedre and Joseph agree. The minor diagonal (cells b and c) is where Diedre and Joseph disagree. If we assume that agreement is positive, we might designate the cells along the major diagonal as indicating 'success' and the cells along the minor diagonal as indicating 'failure.' Thus, we hope for large frequencies along the major diagonal and small frequencies along the minor diagonal. It is possible to convert Table 10.1 into a special kind of correlation coefficient for dichotomous options, called a phi correlation coefficient or simply phi coefficient r_ϕ. Equation 10.1 provides the formula:

$$r_\phi = \frac{|ad-bc|}{\sqrt{R_1 R_2 C_1 C_2}} = \frac{|ad-bc|}{\sqrt{(a+b)(c+d)(a+c)(b+d)}}. \tag{10.1}$$

Let us rewrite Table 10.1 as Table 10.2, where we fill in the cells with specific values. We can then instantiate those values into Equation 10.1 to obtain a result.

Based on the values in Table 10.2, the phi coefficient is as follows: $r_\phi = \dfrac{|(20 \cdot 20)-(5 \cdot 5)|}{\sqrt{25 \cdot 25 \cdot 25 \cdot 25}} = 0.60$.

In other words, the correlation between Diedre's answers and Joseph's answers is 0.60. We will make repeated use of Equation 10.1. It is not necessary that the row or margin frequencies equal each other, as in Table 10.2, though it is elegant when it happens. In most cases, there will be some inequality.

Absolute and Relative Morality

There are some who believe in absolute morality in the sense that whenever there is a moral choice to be made, there is an objectively correct answer. In contrast, there are others who believe that there are no objectively correct answers, and the best we can do is assess agreement between people. Table 10.2 takes the latter perspective, but that does not have to be so. Suppose

Table 10.1 Summary table of the choices that Diedre and Joseph could make on the 50 moral dilemmas.

Diedre		Joseph		
		Choice A	Choice B	Row Margins
	Choice A	Cell a	Cell b	R_1
	Choice B	Cell c	Cell d	R_2
	Column Margins	C_1	C_2	

Table 10.2 Summary table of the choices that Diedre and Joseph make on the 50 moral dilemmas, an example

		Joseph		
Diedre		Choice A	Choice B	Row Margins
	Choice A	a = 20	b = 5	25
	Choice B	c = 5	d = 20	25
	Column Margins	25	25	

that we were to replace Joseph's choices with choices derived from some sort of objective moral algorithm. In that case, the table would have reflected the correlation between Diedre's choices and objective choices. If we were to define the objective choices as 'morally correct,' Table 10.2 would indicate Diedre's moral performance relative to objective correctness.

Hopefully, you recall the dis-attenuation equation from Chapter 9, Equation 9.9. I rewrote it below as Equation 10.2, with a change in symbolism to make it easier to see the connection with the present issue:

$$R = \frac{r_\phi}{\sqrt{r_{XX'} r_{YY'}}} \quad \text{or} \quad R = \frac{r}{\sqrt{r_{XX'} r_{YY'}}}. \tag{10.2}$$

In Equation 10.2, R is the best estimate of the true correlation, and r_ϕ is the obtained correlation coefficient or phi coefficient. To make the equation more palatable, we can simply drop the phi subscript and use r as the symbol for the observed correlation coefficient. Finally, $r_{XX'}$ and $r_{YY'}$ are the observed reliability coefficients for each entity (such as Diedre and Joseph).

To relate Equation 10.2 to morality, consider again that some consider morality to be absolute whereas others consider it to be relative. If you believe in absolute morality, then there is no issue about agreement between two people who are not perfectly reliable. Rather, there is only the issue of agreement of the person of concern with an objective—and, therefore perfectly reliable—algorithm. In this case, $r_{YY'}$ can be set at 1 (perfect reliability), and the only potential reliability problem is the extent to which the person is not perfectly reliable. In this case, Equation 10.2 reduces to Equation 10.3:

$$R = \frac{r}{\sqrt{r_{XX'}}}. \tag{10.3}$$

Of course, if two people are being compared, Equation 10.3 is inappropriate and Equation 10.2 should be used.

Thus, the general strategy is as follows. First, the researcher collects data from a person and an objective source, or from two persons. The table of data, in the form of Table 10.1, and exemplified by Table 10.2, can be converted into a correlation coefficient using Equation 10.1. In turn, once that correlation coefficient has been obtained, it is possible to use Equation 10.3 if there is an objectively correct answer, or Equation 10.2 if not, to dis-attenuate the correlation coefficient obtained via Equation 10.1.

148 *Measurement Issues*

With this general strategy in mind, let us again consider the example of Diedre and Joseph. We saw earlier that Table 10.2 implies a correlation coefficient equal to 0.60. This observed level of performance is due to both random and systematic factors, but how much of each? To figure this out, we need to know the reliability with which Diedre responded and the reliability with which Joseph responded.

Suppose that Diedre and Joseph had completed the moral dilemmas not once, but twice. Thus, we could evaluate the extent to which Diedre's scores on the first test-taking occasion correlate with her scores on the second test-taking occasion. And we could evaluate the extent to which Joseph's scores on the first test-taking occasion correlate with his scores on the second test-taking occasion. These values could then be instantiated into Equation 10.2. For instance, suppose that Diedre's reliability coefficient is 0.80 and Joseph's is 0.75. Remembering that the correlation between Diedre's and Joseph's responses is 0.60, using Equation 10.2 implies the following: $R = \frac{0.60}{\sqrt{0.8 \cdot 0.75}} = 0.77$. Put another way, if Diedre and Joseph had responded with perfect reliability, the correlation between their scores would have been 0.77 rather than 0.60, a sizable difference.

Although the dis-attenuated correlation coefficient is nice to have, it would be even more useful to obtain a dis-attenuated table, such as Table 10.2, but corrected for unreliability. There are two ways to accomplish this. One way is to think in terms of standard tables, where we assume all margin frequencies are equal. That is, we assume R_1, R_2, C_1, and C_2 equal each other. A disadvantage is that this is rarely so. An advantage, however, is that standard tables are useful for general demonstrations, as will become clear in the following subsection.

Standard Tables

Rosenthal and his colleagues (e.g., Rosenthal & Rosnow, 1991; Rosenthal & Rubin, 1979, 1982) have demonstrated that, for dichotomous responses, it is possible to convert a correlation coefficient into a percentage of successes or percentage of failures. However, it is necessary to assume that the margin frequencies all equal each other. If this assumption is not true, you should use the equations in the following subsection rather than the ones in the present section. But assuming, for now, that the assumption is okay, we can calculate the proportion of potential successes S and failures F, using Equation 10.4:

$$S = \frac{R+1}{2} \text{ and } F = 1 - S. \tag{10.4}$$

In turn, with Equations 10.2 and 10.4 as assumptions, Trafimow and Rice (2008, Appendix A) proved Equation 10.5:

$$S = \frac{2s - 1 + \sqrt{r_{XX'} r_{YY'}}}{2\sqrt{r_{XX'} r_{YY'}}}. \tag{10.5}$$

Equation 10.5 introduces a new symbol, s, which is the observed proportion of successes. The idea of Equation 10.5 is to dis-attenuate the observed successes from the deleterious effects of unreliability.

For example, returning to Table 10.2, Diedre and Joseph agreed on 40 items out of 50 possible. So, the observed success rate equals 80%. However, let us use Equation 10.5 to

Potential Performance Theory 149

find the potential percentage of successes, if Diedre and Joseph were perfectly reliable, again using 0.80 and 0.75 for the obtained reliability coefficients for each person, respectively:

$$S = \frac{2s - 1 + \sqrt{r_{XX'}r_{YY'}}}{2\sqrt{r_{XX'}r_{YY'}}} = \frac{2 \cdot 0.80 - 1 + \sqrt{0.80 \cdot 0.75}}{2\sqrt{0.80 \cdot 0.75}} = 0.89 = 89\%.$$ Thus, we see that Diedre and Joseph could potentially have had a success rate of 89% whereas their observed success rate was only 80%. Randomness decreased their performance by 89% − 80% = 9%.

Let us reconsider the same example, but this time replacing Joseph with an objective responder with perfect reliability. In that case, $r_{YY'} = 1$ and so Equation 10.5 reduces to Equation 10.6:

$$S = \frac{2s - 1 + \sqrt{r_{XX'}}}{2\sqrt{r_{XX'}}}. \tag{10.6}$$

In turn, using Equation 10.6 results in the following computation:

$$S = \frac{2s - 1 + \sqrt{r_{XX'}}}{2\sqrt{r_{XX'}}} = \frac{2 \cdot 0.80 - 1 + \sqrt{0.80}}{2\sqrt{0.80}} = 0.84 = 84\%.$$ Thus, if Diedre were to be perfectly reliable, her moral performance would increase by 84% − 80% = 4%.

There is one more issue to consider before moving to nonstandard tables. Equation 10.6 is very useful if you are interested in determining potential performance or the difference between observed and potential performance. But what if you are interested in estimating what observed performance would be at various levels of reliability? We need some more mathematics for this, but it is not difficult.

Once you have established S using Equation 10.5 or Equation 10.6, you can use that value to estimate the observed score under any level of reliability you might desire to investigate. Thus, we need three variables. The first variable is that which you wish to compute, which is the desired success level under given levels of reliability s_{des}. The second variable is the desired reliability of the first person $r_{des-XX'}$. The third variable is the desired reliability of the second person $r_{des-YY'}$. As usual, if there is an absolute standard for success, then $r_{des-YY'} = 1$. Thus, Equation 10.7 provides the desired success rate in the context of agreement with another person and Equation 10.8 provides the desired success rate in the context of an absolute standard.

$$s_{des} = S\sqrt{r_{des-XX'}r_{des-YY'}} + 0.5 - 0.5\sqrt{r_{des-XX'}r_{des-YY'}} \tag{10.7}$$

$$s_{des} = S\sqrt{r_{des-XX'}} + 0.5 - 0.5\sqrt{r_{des-XX'}} \tag{10.8}$$

To see the value of these equations, let us perform a quick demonstration of the implications of Equation 10.8, which is the simpler one. The idea would be to imagine an objectively correct answer to each of the moral scenarios, so that we do not have to worry about $r_{des-YY'}$, and so the only variables that count in determining s_{des} are S and $r_{des-XX'}$. We can set S at various levels (1.0, 0.80, 0.60, 0.40) and let $r_{des-XX'}$ vary from 0 to 1 to see what happens to s_{des}. The results are graphed in Figure 10.1.

150 *Measurement Issues*

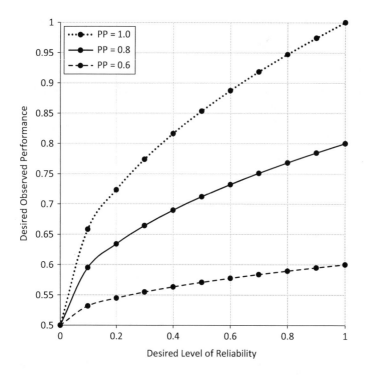

Figure 10.1 The desired observed performance ranges along the vertical axis as a function of the desired level of reliability, with separate curves for when potential performance is 1.0 (top curve), 0.8 (middle curve) or 0.60 (bottom curve).

To interpret Figure 10.1, first consider that the vertical axis ranges from 0.5 to 1.0. This is because 0.50 represents random guessing. Although potential performance theory equations can be adjusted for cases where people are at such a systematic disadvantage that they perform below randomness, this is highly unusual, and the present chapter only concerns those cases where people are expected to score above the level of randomness. In addition, if there are more than two choices, such as multiple choice items, random responding could be at a level below 0.5, though we will not be concerned with that here.

Next, consider that the desired level of reliability varies along the horizontal axis and there are different curves assuming different levels of potential performance. For an extreme low example, suppose that you wish to estimate the observed performance of a person when that person's reliability is 0. In that case, the person cannot be expected to perform better than 0.50—the chance level—no matter how good the potential performance. At the high extreme, if the person's reliability is perfect, then the observed performance will equal the potential performance. The figure illustrates various gradations between these two extremes and demonstrates that both potential performance and reliability are crucial.

Nonstandard Tables

Although Figure 10.1 demonstrates the usefulness of standard tables and associated equations, an important limit is that standard tables do not deal well with unequal margin frequencies. As

Potential Performance Theory 151

a reminder, these are R_1, R_2, C_1, and C_2. The general strategy for nonstandard tables starts from the fact that important information can be gleaned directly from the data. That is, R_1, R_2, C_1, and C_2 are directly determinable from the data, as we have seen. In addition, Equation 10.2 (or Equation 10.3 when there is an absolute standard of success) provides the potential correlation between two people (or a person and an absolute standard) R. Thus, we know R, R_1, R_2, C_1, and C_2 for any person or pairs of persons for whom we have collected data. The trick is to recreate Table 10.2, but with adjusted or potential values in the cells, while preserving the original margin frequencies. That is, instead of settling for observed cell frequencies a, b, c, and d, we also wish to estimate potential cell frequencies A, B, C, and D. Of course, if you are not interested in preserving the original margin frequencies, then you can use the equations associated with standard tables in the previous section.

To obtain the potential cells, A, B, C, and D, you can use Equations 10.9 through 10.12. We provided the derivation in Appendix B of Trafimow and Rice (2008).

$$A = \frac{R\sqrt{R_1 R_2 C_1 C_2} + C_1 R_1}{R_1 + R_2} \tag{10.9}$$

$$B = \frac{R_1(R_1 + R_2) - \left(R\sqrt{R_1 R_2 C_1 C_2} + C_1 R_1\right)}{R_1 + R_2} \tag{10.10}$$

$$C = \frac{C_1 R_2 - R\sqrt{R_1 R_2 C_1 C_2}}{R_1 + R_2} \tag{10.11}$$

$$D = \frac{C_2(R_1 + R_2) - \left[R_1(R_1 + R_2) - \left(R\sqrt{R_1 R_2 C_1 C_2} + C_1 R_1\right)\right]}{R_1 + R_2} \tag{10.12}$$

Alternatively, there is an easier way. Once you have obtained A using Equation 10.9, you can get the other potential cells as follows.

$$B = R_1 - A \tag{10.13}$$

$$C = C_1 - A \tag{10.14}$$

$$D = C_2 - B = R_2 - C \tag{10.15}$$

To see how this works, let us consider again the example where Diedre and Joseph respond to 50 moral decision items according to Table 10.2, and with reliabilities of 0.80 and 0.75, respectively. We have already seen that the phi coefficient is 0.6 and the potential correlation coefficient is 0.77. Finally, all the margin frequencies equal 25. Instantiating all these values into the foregoing equations renders the following cell values:

152   *Measurement Issues*

- $A = 22.18$,
- $B = 2.82$,
- $C = 2.82$,
- $D = 22.18$.

In addition, the observed percentage of successes is 80% and the potential percentage of successes is 89%, for a difference of 9%. If you recall our use of standard tables, these values are the same as the values we had obtained previously.

In that case, you might wonder, why accept the increased workload associated with non-standard tables? The answer is that in the example, all margin frequencies were kept equal and so both types of tables give the same answers. However, the margin frequencies need not be the same. Let us change the example so that we have the following cell and margin frequencies, illustrated in Table 10.3. And, for the sake of simplicity, let us remain with the reliability coefficients of 0.80 and 0.75 for Diedre and Joseph, respectively.

In Table 10.3, the row frequencies are unequal; the first is 22 and the second is 28. Therefore, we cannot use the equations associated with standard tables. We are forced to use the equations associated with nonstandard tables. The new potential cell frequencies are as follows:

- $A = 18.75$,
- $B = 3.25$,
- $C = 6.25$,
- $D = 21.75$.

In addition, the observed percentage of successes is 74% and the potential percentage of successes is 81%, for a difference of 7%.

Assessing Reliability

The key to making the foregoing equations work is to have a way to index each person's reliability coefficient. The obvious solution is to have participants complete two blocks of trials. With two blocks of trials, a person's responses on trials in the first block can be correlated with trials on the second block. This is the solution we adopted in the studies to be described subsequently to the present section.

In the scenario involving Diedre and Joseph on responses to moral dilemmas, it is easy to consider 2 x 2 tables. Only instead of having a table indicating frequencies of both people

Table 10.3 Summary table of the choices that Diedre and Joseph make on the 50 moral dilemmas, but with the example changed so that the row margin frequencies differ

Diedre		Joseph		
		Choice A	Choice B	Row Margins
	Choice A	$a = 17$	$b = 5$	22
	Choice B	$c = 8$	$d = 20$	28
	Column Margins	25	25	

Table 10.4 Summary table of the choices that Diedre makes on the 50 moral dilemmas, across two blocks of trials.

		Block 2		
Block 1		*Choice A*	*Choice B*	*Row Margins*
	Choice A	$a = 23$	$b = 2$	25
	Choice B	$c = 2$	$d = 23$	25
	Column Margins	25	25	

making similar or different choices, with Table 10.2 an example of that, for reliability purposes we are interested in only a single person and her choice frequencies across two blocks of trials. That is, we are interested in the frequency of making Choice A on both blocks of trials, making Choice A on the first block and Choice B on the second block, making Choice B on the first block and Choice A on the second block, or making Choice B on both blocks. Table 10.4 provides an example for Diedre.

Given a table of frequencies, such as Table 10.4, it is easy to calculate consistency using Equation 10.1. In the case of Table 10.4, we have the following:

$$r_\phi = \frac{|ad - bc|}{\sqrt{R_1 R_2 C_1 C_2}} = \frac{|23 \cdot 23 - 2 \cdot 2|}{\sqrt{25 \cdot 25 \cdot 25 \cdot 25}} = 0.84.$$ Of course, to continue with the Diedre and Joseph

scenario, it should be equally possible to calculate a reliability coefficient for Joseph. And thus, you have all the pieces needed to use potential performance theory in your own research.

Real Research Examples

The foregoing discussion was, of course, highly theoretical. In contrast, the present section describes real research examples where potential performance theory aided in addressing questions that otherwise could not be addressed.

The Suboptimality Problem in Automation Aided Performance

Suppose that humans search aerial photographs for tanks. In addition, there is an automated aid (e.g., the computer) that gives its opinion of whether there is a tank in the photograph or not. Suppose that the computer is 90% accurate and the humans are told that the computer is 90% accurate. As humans perform much less well than that, they should trust the computer unless they are sure they see a tank. However, even when this is carefully explained to humans, the combination of a human and an automated aid nevertheless results in lower performance than that achieved by the automated aid alone. In a word, the human-automated aid interaction is *suboptimal*. This impressive and ubiquitous suboptimality has confounded researchers in the area for decades. However, as we shall see, potential performance theory provides an elegant answer.

My colleagues and I performed a study to solve the puzzle (Rice, Trafimow, & Hunt, 2010). Our thinking was that perhaps the problem is not something systematic about humans, such as using a poor strategy, but rather the problem is that humans are unreliable. We have seen that, according to the mathematics of potential performance theory, unreliability can strongly influence performance. Our hope was that we could perform a typical experiment in the area and analyze the data using potential performance theory not only to assess the usual observed performances, but also to calculate potential performances that take human unreliability into account.

Thus, we had participants perform a large set of trials that involved looking at different photographs, with an automated aid, and indicating whether there was or was not a tank in each of them. In addition, our participants went through all the photographs twice so we could assess each one's reliability.

Consistent with our potential performance theory-based thinking, we found that potential scores were larger than observed scores. More to the point of solving the puzzle, although the combination of humans and an automated aid was suboptimal, as usual, potential performances tended to be near-optimal, or even better. Remember that potential performance dis-attenuates for the deleterious effects of randomness and so we at last have the answer to the puzzle that has confounded researchers for decades. In short, the problem is human unreliability and has little to do with systematic factors such as humans using poor strategies.

Signal Detection Theory: Is There an Unrealized Source of Systematicity?

Suppose that participants are exposed to tones masked by noise to make them difficult to detect, and the task is to say whether the tone occurred during one interval or another interval. Psychology researchers interested in perception often use such two-interval forced choice tasks. The most popular theory for understanding human performance on such tasks has been signal detection theory, which has been favored for many decades since it was made popular in 1961 (Swets, Tanner, & Birdsall, 1961).

According to signal detection theory, there is neural noise that is associated with each of the two options. If the signal is strong (e.g., a very loud tone), it cuts through the neural noise and the person is likely to answer correctly. But if the signal is weak (e.g., a very soft tone), detection is difficult, and errors are likely.

Because of the neural noise associated with each option, there are underlying neural distributions and people must establish a criterion for deciding between options. If the signal is weak, which are the cases of interest to researchers, these underlying distributions overlap, thereby guaranteeing that there will be some errors. In our sound detection study, participants will sometimes choose the wrong interval. According to signal detection theory, there is only a single systematic factor, which is where people place the decision criterion, and all else is random. In fact, there might be further randomness in that people may be inconsistent across trials in where they place the criterion for deciding. As there is much room for including additional sources of randomness in the theory, it is perhaps not surprising that much research since the original work by Swets et al. (1961) has involved the proposal of additional sources of randomness to account for imperfections in human performance.

The continual adding of sources of randomness suggests a question. Will signal detection researchers ever have a complete description of human performance by continually adding sources of randomness? Or to put it another way, once all sources of randomness have been included in the theory, along with the systematic factor of where people place the decision criterion, will there be anything left? The question is important because a negative answer would imply that researchers are justified in searching for all sources of randomness with a strong likelihood of eventually having a complete theory. In contrast, a positive answer would suggest that there is a source of systematicity that signal detection theories are failing to consider, and their efforts might be better devoted in that direction.

Although the question may seem an impossible one to answer, potential performance theory provides a potential solution. Suppose it were possible to use a magic wand to take all randomness out of people's performances. In this magical case, performance ought to be perfect. In our hypothetical magic wand experiment, barring people purposely giving wrong answers or setting a ridiculous criterion, performance ought to be perfect according to signal detection theory. If performance is not perfect when all randomness is removed, this would indicate that there is a systematic factor not in signal detection theory that is necessary for it to be complete.

As you may have anticipated, although we have no magic wand, we do have potential performance theory. It is merely necessary to have participants run through two blocks of sound detection trials to assess each of their reliability coefficients, and then use potential performance theory to calculate their potential scores, that is, how they would have performed in the absence of randomness. In short, potential performance theory can approximate our desired magic wand, as I showed with the aid of two colleagues, Justin MacDonald, and Stephen Rice (Trafimow, MacDonald, & Rice, 2012).

What happened? We performed three experiments, two auditory and one visual. In the visual experiment, participants were exposed to a difficult-to-detect pink dot and had to indicate the interval where it occurred. The results were remarkably consistent across the three experiments. Extremely high scorers did average out to 100% success in potential performance, after accounting for randomness. This supports the signal detection theory assumption that all is random other than the setting of the decision criterion. However, lower scorers' potential performances averaged out considerably under 100% in all three experiments. Thus, there must be a systematic factor missing from signal detection theory. Therefore, it is false that searching for more sources of randomness will eventually result in a complete theory. There is a systematic factor missing from the theory, and it is that for which signal detection researchers need to search.

Practice May Improve Performance, but Why?

Taking again a search task, where participants look at aerial photographs and attempt to find a target, it would be reasonable to expect that participants would improve with practice. Supposing this is so, there remains the question of why. One possibility is that people improve with respect to systematic factors whereas the other possibility is that people become less random. Of course, both or neither may be true. What's more, it is even possible that the same people improve for different reasons at different times. Finally, there may be some people who do not improve. The typical characterization of a null effect would be that nothing happened. However, it is possible that there was improvement or decrement with respect to either reliability or potential performance that offset, thereby seemingly implying that nothing happened, whereas the truth could be that two changes occurred.

Obviously, given the usual emphasis on group statistics, such as means, correlation coefficients, and so on, there is no way to explore this difficult issue. However, with potential performance theory, and its facility for studying individuals, the issue suddenly becomes tractable. As a demonstration, I and my colleague, Stephen Rice, performed a study in 2009 to investigate (Trafimow & Rice, 2009).

We had 24 participants complete five sessions of trials. Each session was divided into two blocks of 50 trials each. Thus, there were 100 trials in each session and 500 trials in total for each participant. An advantage of having two blocks per session is that we were able to assess each participant's reliability within each session. Thus, we were able to obtain both reliability and observed performance for each participant for each session. In turn, using the foregoing equations, we also were able to assess potential performance for each participant at each session. The ability to make these session-by-session assessments enabled us to calculate changes in reliability across sessions, changes in observed performance across sessions, and changes in potential performance across sessions. And from these, we could calculate the extent to which changes in observed performance could be attributed to changes in reliability, systematic factors, or both.

So, what were the results? At the level of group statistics, mean performance levels improved across sessions, as did mean reliability coefficients, and mean potential performances. If we were to settle for group level statistics, we would conclude that practice improves everything. Case closed.

However, we need not settle for group level statistics. When we look at individuals, the picture becomes much more nuanced. Consider the bullet-listed results that pertain to individuals.

- One participant improved with respect to systematic factors across sessions (potential score increased) with little improvement in reliability. Thus, the participant's observed improvement was due to improved systematicity but not to improved reliability.
- Five participants improved in reliability with very little improvement in potential performances. Thus, these participants improvements were due primarily to decreased randomness.
- Fourteen participants improved substantially with respect to both reliability and systematicity. For these participants, practice really did provide an across-the-board benefit.
- Four participants failed to show much improvement across sessions. Although three of the four failed to change much with respect to either reliability or systematicity, one participant improved impressively in reliability but with an offsetting deficit in potential performance (systematicity). The benefit and deficit roughly cancelled each other out, resulting in little change in observed performance. For this participant, the lack of an effect on observed performance masks two offsetting effects rather than indicating that 'nothing happened.'
- It is possible for people to improve for different reasons at different stages of practice. As an example, one participant improved markedly during the first session on reliability, but not on systematicity. There was then a lack of improvement with respect to reliability, potential performance, or observed performance in moving to the third and fourth sessions. Finally, however, this participant improved markedly from the fourth session to the fifth session with respect to potential performance but not with respect to reliability. Thus, for this participant, an improvement in reliability was the original cause of improvement in observed performance but, near the end, an improvement in systematicity caused the improvement in observed performance. The same person can improve for different reasons at different stages of practice, and potential performance theory can uncover this.

Finally, there were tests of the assumptions of the theory. For one thing, it is possible to use the foregoing equations to use reliability coefficients and potential performances to predict observed performances. If the theory is correct, there should be an impressive correlation between predicted performances and observed performances. That correlation was 0.98. A possible argument against this impressive correlation coefficient might be that there could have been absolute differences between predicted and observed performances but that correlations are not sensitive to them. To test this, we computed the difference between each person's predicted and observed scores, took the absolute value, and averaged across them. The average absolute deviation was only 0.007, thereby further supporting potential performance theory.

Philosophical Issues

Although there are many more potential performance theory applications than covered in the previous section, sufficient examples were provided for you to gain an idea of the power of the

Who Is More Moral?

Let us return to Diedre and Joseph, under the supposition that their morality is measured relative to an absolute standard, such as a deontologist standard. Relative to the standard, Diedre's scores for actual performance and reliability are 75% and 0.90, respectively. For Joseph, the scores are 70% and 0.20, respectively. Who is more moral, Diedre or Joseph?

If we ignore everything we have learned in this chapter, the answer seems obvious. As Diedre is at 75% and Joseph is at 70%, Diedre is more moral than Joseph.

However, under the umbrella of potential performance theory, the issue is less clear-cut. If we run out the potential performance theory calculations, Diedre's potential performance level is 76% whereas Joseph's is 95%. The reason Joseph's observed performance is worse than Diedre's is because Joseph's moral responses are more subject to randomness. These values suggest the possibility that Joseph may have it over Diedre when it comes to a systematic moral strategy, but that such moral superiority is hidden by a greater susceptibility to randomness. That said, however, it is possible to argue the other way too. It is possible to contend that susceptibility to randomness in morally relevant situations constitutes a moral deficiency, and Joseph is rightly penalized for that at the level of observed performance. The point of the example is less about coming to a decision that Diedre is morally superior to Joseph, or the reverse, and more about rendering salient that potential performance theory suggests an important philosophical issue of which we otherwise would remain ignorant.

Autonomy 1

One of the most interesting topics in the morality area concerns people's autonomy, their ability to make their own choices. A standard philosophical contention is that if people perform behaviors, whether good or bad, they are neither creditworthy nor blameworthy if they have no control over those behaviors. It is only when people do have control over their behaviors that they justly can be credited or blamed.

The area of medical ethics is one of the main areas where autonomy arguments come up repeatedly. To see the relevance, suppose that it were possible to improve some sort of behavior with brain implants that continually release a therapeutic chemical. On the one hand, it is possible to argue that the patient benefits, and so the treatment is ethical provided a lack of side effects, the cost is not prohibitive, and it has all the usual qualifications that pertain to medical treatments. On the other hand, it is possible to argue that the continual release of the chemical robs the person of her autonomy. If the chemical is responsible for the person's behaviors, the way is opened to argue that perhaps the person is no longer in control; the brain implant has decreased her autonomy.

However, with the aid of potential performance theory, we can make progress with respect to the autonomy question. To move in that direction, suppose a person's behavior is completely random. Would you believe that the person nevertheless has autonomy, or would you argue on the contrary, that a person whose behaviors are completely subject to random winds scarcely has autonomy? If you take the latter perspective, then it follows that anything that increases the reliability of a person's behaviors has at least the possibility of improving autonomy. If a person's brain disorder causes random self-harming behaviors, for example, a brain implant releasing a chemical that decreases them could be argued to increase autonomy by decreasing randomness. On the other hand, one could argue, too, that the brain implant merely changes one form of lack of autonomy—randomness, to another form of lack of autonomy—control by brain implant. Or perhaps both happen to some extent. That is, it is possible that some of the effect of the brain implant is to increase the reliability of behavior, but another effect is to increase the extent to which the brain implant controls the person's behavior.

The issue may come down to numbers, or at least subjective numbers. To see this, suppose that the brain implant increases the person's reliability from 0.2 to 0.9. In addition, however, suppose the person's potential performance, in this case the extent to which the person's behaviors are due to her own will as opposed to being due to the brain implant, decreases from 80% to 75%. What is the net effect on observed performance—the extent to which the person behaves consistently with her own will? Using Equation 10.8, we arrive at an answer. To see it, let us calculate observed performance before and after the brain implant.

- Before: $observed\ performance = 0.80\sqrt{0.2} + 0.5 - 0.5\sqrt{0.2} = 63\%$.
- After: $observed\ performance = 0.75\sqrt{0.9} + 0.5 - 0.5\sqrt{0.9} = 74\%$.

Thus, we see that the two opposing forces work out in favor of using the brain implant.

However, this need not be so. Remember that the values were hypothetical. We could try alternative hypothetical values that lead to the opposite conclusion. For example, suppose we change one value, potential performance after the brain implant, from 75% down to 60%. In this case, observed performance after the brain implant would drop to 59%, which is worse than the 63% value with which we commenced. In this case, the negative effect of the brain implant on potential performance is more important than its positive effect on reliability. The larger point is that the autonomy issue depends importantly on the subjective values one instantiates into potential performance theory equations. Unfortunately, medical ethicists are mostly unaware of this application of potential performance theory, though I have published the argument in the highly regarded *American Journal of Bioethics* (Trafimow, 2015b).

Autonomy 2

More generally than in the previous subsection, potential performance theory suggests a different way to think about free will that does not depend on the usual arguments about the relative impact of long-term issues such as genetic predispositions, and the more immediate impact of situational factors. Suppose people will the performance of a behavior or not. And suppose people perform the behavior or not. There are four possibilities. A person may will the behavior and perform it, will it and not perform it, not will it and perform it, or not will it and not perform it. If we imagine a large set of possible behaviors that a person may will or not will, and perform or not perform, we could set up a frequency table such as the ones you have already seen in this chapter.

Given such a table, we can set up definitions.

- The percentage of occasions where the person's behavior matches her will can be defined as her observed free will.
- The person's reliability of wills and behaviors can be defined with respect to consistency across similar situations where the will is relevant and where the behavior is relevant.
- The person's potential performance can be defined as the percentage of occasions where the person's behavior would match her will in the absence of randomness.

Does a particular operation, intervention, or policy change increase or decrease observed free will? That depends on its effect on reliability and potential free will. Although both effects may be in the same direction, they may be in opposing directions, as we saw in the previous subsection with respect to brain implants. Some colleagues and I recently published this application of potential performance theory in the *Journal of Business Ethics* (Hyman, Kostyk, & Trafimow, 2023).

Taking a potential performance theory perspective implies that, to discuss issues such as free will and autonomy honestly, one needs to attempt to place values on potential free will and reliability. If the requisite data are unavailable, and they usually will be unavailable, then it is necessary to use subjective values, and suffer the discomfort associated with subjectivity. And moving in this direction might cause protagonists to explain why they think the effects of an operation, intervention, or policy change would be deleterious or helpful to potential free will or reliability, and by how much. If the anticipated effects are in opposite directions, the how much issue may be critical, as we saw in the previous subsection.

Chapter Summary

We commenced with the phi coefficient, which is useful for dichotomous data. In addition, we saw that it is possible to dis-attenuate the phi coefficient provided that the researcher has obtained reliability data for each entity of concern. The entities could be people, such as Diedre and Joseph. However, the entities need not be people, such as an objective ethical standard, an automated aid, and so on. Whatever the nature of the entities involved, dis-attenuating the phi coefficient results in a potential correlation coefficient—the correlation between the entities that would be observed with perfect reliability, that is, all randomness removed.

In turn, the potential correlation coefficient can be used in the context of standard or nonstandard tables. For standard tables, we assume that the margin frequencies are all equal, whereas for nonstandard tables we retain all information about margin frequencies. Standard tables enjoy the advantage of being mathematically simple and useful for general demonstrations. Nonstandard tables are necessary for most real data where equal margin frequencies are unlikely. Either way, I provided equations that enable researchers to estimate potential performance. That is, performance in the absence of randomness. In turn, it is easy to estimate the extent of possible improvement that can be attained simply by increasing the reliability of responding. It is also easy to estimate the extent of possible improvement that can be attained by increasing the favorability of systematic factors. An obvious area of potential application might be education.

There have been many potential performance theory applications. Three of them were discussed here. We saw how potential performance theory provides a solution to the hitherto intractable puzzle about why person-automated aid combinations perform less than optimally. In brief, the reason is because people are unreliable, even in combination with an automated aid. When we used potential performance theory to dis-attenuate for the deleterious effects of random responding, potential performances met or exceeded the standard of optimality.

Secondly, we saw how it is possible to use potential performance theory to disconfirm a central assumption of a dominant perception theory, signal detection theory. Participants completed two-interval forced choice trials, and we used potential performance theory to dis-attenuate for the effects of randomness. If signal detection theory is true, then potential performances should have been perfect. Although this happened for the high scorers, for everyone else, potential performances fell substantially short of perfection. Therefore, there must have been a systematic factor at work not accounted for by signal detection theory. In a word, signal detection theory is false.

Thirdly, we saw how potential performance theory aids in understanding the process of practice on task performance. Although, at the level of group data, practice has beneficial across-the-board effects, this need not be so at the level of individuals. There are many subtle differences between individuals that often contradict the group level implications. The process of practice works differently for different people.

In addition, we explored a few philosophical potential performance theory implications. One of these pertained to the assessment of morality and whether such assessments should depend on observed moral performance, potential moral performance, or both. A second pertained to bioethics, and a way to think about autonomy in that context. A third pertained to the more general autonomy question of how to think about free will; with autonomy being defined as the percentage of times behaviors match corresponding wills.

I would like to end with a final point. Recall that I started the chapter with an explanation of my profound ignorance with respect to the extensive task performance literature. And yet, despite this profound ignorance, I was able to discover potential performance theory. There is a lesson in here for you. Consider the academic mantra about the importance of knowing the relevant literature for the research you are performing. And I have no desire to dispute that mantra, as knowledge is generally good to have. But there is a crucial discrepancy. And the discrepancy is that it is all too easy to interpret the mantra as indicating that you are not allowed to have any original ideas until you gain knowledge of the relevant literature. My hope is that you will take the present chapter as a strong counterexample. It is sometimes possible to have an original idea, even when in a state of profound ignorance about an area. You should always think for yourself and not let ignorance dissuade you from creative thinking. On the one hand, your thoughts may come to nothing, or you may reinvent the wheel. On the other hand, there is the possibility that you might be on to something great. To reiterate a theme in this book, you always have the right to think for yourself.

11 Auxiliary Validity

The present chapter and the next one both concern validity. You might wonder why validity deserves two chapters, as well as part of Chapter 9. Or ask as a pointed question: Why should you care about validity of measurement?

162 *Measurement Issues*

To see why, imagine a social science universe where all tests have nothing to do with the constructs they were created to measure. In that case, it would be impossible to test any theories, because empirical defeats could plausibly be blamed on invalid tests and empirical victories could be credited to invalid tests. Nor would application work with invalid tests. The bottom line is that the social sciences need valid tests to achieve desired objectives.

But what do we mean, or what should we mean, when we say that a test of a construct is valid or invalid? In Chapter 9 we talked about the ability of a test to correlate with a criterion test and termed it *predictive validity*. There is one sense in which predictive validity is a perfectly good way to think about validity and another sense in which it is not. If you imagine a hypothetical test that predicts nothing, there would be obvious reason to question its validity or whether it is useful for anything. Thus, predictive validity might be considered a minimum condition that a test must meet to have a chance of being considered valid. However, predictive validity is not enough. Suppose an alleged attitudes test and the goal of predicting scores on a behavioral intentions test; but suppose, too, that the alleged attitudes test really tests moods instead of measuring attitudes. Because moods are relevant to behavioral intentions, the alleged attitude test successfully predicts behavioral intentions, thereby demonstrating predictive validity.

Most likely you are not satisfied with this scenario. It feels unsatisfying to have successful prediction but for the wrong reason. Although we have not yet put our finger on validity writ large, even with this lack it is obvious that predictive validity may be a necessary condition for satisfaction, but it is certainly not a sufficient condition. We must look further.

Construct Validity

Although there are many kinds of validity, we will skip them here and move ahead to that which is by far the most emphasized type of validity, *construct validity*. The concept was introduced in a classic paper by Cronbach and Meehl (1955) and has been the most desired type of validity. For most substantive researchers, construct validity is the holy grail. If a research team can state that they have demonstrated that their test has construct validity, few question further. In short, if you have construct validity, you have validity!

So, what is this magical elixir termed construct validity? The easiest way to understand the concept is to imagine a theory with at least two constructs, that we can label X and Y. Suppose that our simple theory is that X causes Y (e.g., attitudes cause behavioral intentions, threat causes prejudice, and so on). Of course, as we learned in Chapter 1, X and Y are nonobservational terms; they refer to entities we cannot observe, such as prejudice, love, depression, and so on. Therefore, to test the theory, it is necessary to bring the nonobservational terms in our theory down to the level of observational terms in empirical hypotheses. For instance, we might create a measure of X that we label x, and a measure of Y that we label y. Because there is no way to observe X and Y, there is likewise no way to test, directly, the theory that X causes Y. Or, stated in a weaker form, there is no way to test whether X and Y are correlated constructs. In contrast, x and y are observable and so it is possible to test whether x and y are correlated to gain initial support that x causes y. If the theory indicates X and Y should be correlated and we perform a study finding that x and y correlate, then we likely would interpret that empirical correlation coefficient as supporting the theory.

It is possible to be more specific. Let us again consider the theory X causes Y ($X \rightarrow Y$) and the empirical hypothesis x causes y ($x \rightarrow y$). There is a clear relationship here. The reason for posing $x \rightarrow y$ is precisely because we believe or at least hope to test $X \rightarrow Y$. We interpret any evidence for $x \rightarrow y$ as supporting $X \rightarrow Y$. Thus—and this is the essence of construct validity—we have a matching of empirical and theoretical relations. The empirical relation $x \to y$ matches the theoretical relation $X \to Y$. We draw two conclusions. One conclusion is that we have increased support for the theory $X \to Y$. Secondly, we have better reason to believe that x is a valid measure of X, and that y is a valid measure of Y. We support the theory and the validity of the tests simultaneously.

Of course, a single correlation coefficient is rather weak evidence for the empirical relation $x \to y$, and hence for the theoretical relation $X \to Y$ too. Perhaps stronger evidence, if feasible, could be obtained by manipulating x in a true experiment and getting the predicted effect on y. Or if a true experiment is not feasible, perhaps we could have multiple tests of X, that we might label x_1, x_2 and so on, and multiple tests of Y, that we might label y_1, y_2, and so on. We would hope for impressive correlations among x_1, x_2 and so on, because they are ostensibly measuring the same construct. For a similar reason, we would hope for impressive correlations among y_1, y_2, and so on. Finally, if the theory is true, the various tests of X ought to predict the various tests of Y. Obtaining all these findings would further support (a) the theory and (b) the validity of the tests. The summary word for the network of theoretical and empirical relations is a *nomological network*. The more extensive the nomological network, the better the support for the theory and the better the support for the validities of the tests.

Hopefully, our theoretical entity X is not connected only to Y but to other constructs too. So, we might have the following relations as part of our theory involving X, such as $X \to A$, $X \to B$, and so on. In turn, we might have multiple tests of A, B, and other theorized constructs that we believe are caused by X or that cause X. If the tests of each construct correlate highly with each other, and correlate somewhat with the tests of X too, there would be yet more reason to have confidence in both the theory and the validity of the tests. Again, as the extent of the nomological network increases, support for the theory and the validity of the tests increases too. Construct validity increases.

Then, too, a clever twist can be achieved by showing something called *discriminant validity*. Imagine a plausible criticism that the alleged tests of X measure something else, which we might label X'. A strong refutation could be accomplished by showing that tests of X do not correlate well with tests of X', or at least much less well than with each other. Such discriminant validity contributes to be the case for construct validity.

Finally, because most substantive researchers do not understand construct validity, let us describe the misunderstanding and show it for what it is. Most substantive researchers interpret construct validity as showing that the test measures what it is supposed to measure. And of course, it would be great to show that. But that is a very difficult goal to achieve, and the difficulty is recognized by researchers who have a sophisticated understanding of construct validity. Hence, although increasing construct validity helps in making the case that the tests measure what they are supposed to measure, construct validity is not the same thing as validity writ large. Rather, to put it in a phrase, construct validity is about showing that empirical relations match theoretical relations. It is such matching that is the essence of construct validity. What's more, although most substantive researchers claim to have demonstrated the construct validity of their tests, my own opinion is that such claims are usually false.

The Usual Case for Construct Validity

Most construct validity claims depend on a mathematical technique called factor analysis. It is too complicated to do justice to here, but it is possible to provide enough of a flavor for you to get the general idea. Suppose a researcher has many test items. She might submit them to a factor analysis. The factor analysis program will find the correlations or covariances among all the items and, based on them, create mathematical factors. The program will also determine how much each item correlates with each factor. The usual interpretation of factors, though I would encourage skepticism about this, is that the factors represent underlying dimensions that capture the essences of the items. Suppose the result is that there are two factors, and items 1, 2, 3, and 4 correlate highly with the first factor, but items 5, 6, 7, and 8 correlate highly with the second factor. To make the case stronger, let us also suppose that the first set of items does not correlate well with the second factor, and the second set of items does not correlate well with the first factor, so that we have what might be considered a very clean factor structure.

Many would consider this as providing a strong case for construct validity. Items 1, 2, 3, and 4 correlate well with each other and with Factor 1, and items 5, 6, 7, and 8 correlate well with each other and with Factor 2, thereby demonstrating what researchers like to call *convergent validity*. Items that ought to go well together actually do go well together. In addition, the fact that items do not correlate well with the other factor is usually taken to demonstrate *divergent validity*. With convergent and divergent validity having been demonstrated, we appear to have a reasonably complete case for having achieved the holy grail of construct validity. But appearances are deceiving.

One problem is that I have omitted something extremely important, which is there was no mention of the theory! You cannot have construct validity if there is no theory. After all, if there is no theory, then there is no way for empirical relations to match nonexistent theoretical relations. Whenever a researcher claims to have demonstrated construct validity, ask yourself whether there is a theory. If not, the construct validity claim is immediately false.

Even if there is a theory, that does not mean that construct validity has been established. Let us return to $X \rightarrow Y$. We saw earlier the advantage of supporting $x \rightarrow y$ as a way of supporting $X \rightarrow Y$ and the validities of the tests. But in our factor analysis we were only concerned with X, or perhaps two subconstructs of X, as there were two factors, but where is Y? Or to repeat the question using an empirical term instead of the theoretical term, where is y? The hippopotamus in the room is that there is no Y or y in the factor analysis. So, even if there is a theory, the factor analysis still fails to establish an empirical relation that matches the theoretical relation. Construct validity still has not been established. To prevent yourself from being fooled about construct validity claims, there is a question you should ask yourself every time you encounter such a claim. Exactly what empirical relations match exactly what theoretical relations? Or in symbols, which empirical $x \rightarrow y$ relation or relations maps onto the theoretical $X \rightarrow Y$ relation? If you cannot glean an answer from the article you are reading, and in most cases you cannot, then you should not believe the construct validity claim.

The foregoing is not to say that factor analysis is irrelevant. Establishing a clean factor structure can be a preliminary step to coming up with construct valid tests. However, the factor analysis is the easier preliminary part. The real task is to demonstrate that empirical relations match theoretical relations. So, do not get fooled!

A Preliminary Problem with Construct Validity

Although construct validity, with its explicit concern for theory and for the matching of empirical and theoretical relations, is a step up from mere predictive validity, there nevertheless is a problem. Recall from Chapter 1 that empirical predictions come not just from theory, but from auxiliary assumptions too. Although there is no reason why researchers concerned with construct validity cannot consider auxiliary assumptions, the fact of the matter is that auxiliary assumptions receive short shrift, as is all too often the case. It is too early to explain exactly how this becomes a problem for construct validity, but I promise to satisfy you about that before completing the next section.

Auxiliary Validity

In 2012, I introduced the notion of auxiliary validity to the social sciences (Trafimow, 2012a). Auxiliary validity depends on the quality of the auxiliary assumptions one makes that link theoretical constructs to their observable tests. It is quite possible to have auxiliary validity and not have construct validity or to have construct validity and not have auxiliary validity.

Attending, again, to the fact that there is no way to derive predications from a theory without auxiliary assumptions, let us consider the role auxiliary assumptions play in coming up with tests of constructs. The sad fact of the matter is the auxiliary assumptions that go into tests of prejudice, depression, love, and so on are mostly tacit. That admitted, let us consider rare cases where some important auxiliary assumptions are spelled out. One such example is in theory of reasoned action research (e.g., Ajzen & Fishbein, 1980; Fishbein, 1980; Fishbein & Ajzen, 1975; 2010). We have already commented on the theoretical part in Chapter 3, but to remind you, behavioral intentions are the immediate determinant of behavior. In turn, attitudes and subjective norms jointly determine behavioral intentions. Finally, various sorts of beliefs and how they are evaluated determine either attitudes or subjective norms. But how do you measure these constructs? What are some reasonably good auxiliary assumptions to propose?

Fishbein thought carefully about behaviors in a way that few others have, and realized that every behavior involves an action with respect to a target, at a time, and in a context. For example, if a researcher is considering blood donation, it is not sufficient to measure attitudes, behavioral intentions, and so on toward donating blood. This is because nobody donates blood in general, but rather at a specific time and in a specific context. A person might have a positive attitude towards blood donation, in general, but a negative attitude towards their donating (action) blood (target) at a single time (time) at a single blood donation facility (context). To successfully predict people's blood donation behaviors, it is necessary to ask about attitudes, intentions, and so on with respect to their donating blood at a particular time and at a particular blood donation facility. It is only if all tests of all variables correspond with respect to action, target, time, and context that satisfactory prediction is likely.

And research has backed this up. Davidson and Jaccard (1979) systematically varied the extent to which tests of theory of reasoned action variables corresponded with respect to the four elements of behavior: action, target, time, and context. They found that when correspondence was complete, correlation coefficients were in the 0.70 neighborhood, which is very impressive by psychology standards. But a mismatch with respect to even one element dropped correlation coefficients to triviality. Thus, work in this area stands out because of the careful attention paid to auxiliary assumptions.

That said, even here there have been problems at the auxiliary assumption level. Specifically, although there is wide agreement that the theory, accompanied by the principle of correspondence of measurement, works well for prediction, several researchers have criticized the theory for not being useful at the level of intervention. There was even a special issue in *Health Psychology Review* about it in 2015. The general controversy is unimportant for present purposes, but what is important is that the intervention studies that have failed have not been as careful as Fishbein has traditionally been about auxiliary assumptions. If a theory of reasoned action-based intervention does not work, it could be because the intervention fails to affect the key variable as opposed to the theory being false. For example, suppose that I perform correlational research to show that attitudes towards eating broccoli, measured with respect to all four elements of behavior, predict corresponding broccoli eating behavior. In Study 2, I perform an intervention to better people's attitudes towards their eating broccoli, but the intervention does not work. Is this the fault of the theory or is it because the intervention failed to influence participants' attitudes towards their eating broccoli at the time, and in the context, in which broccoli eating is measured? And let us be clear that even if the intervention improves general attitudes towards broccoli, or even broccoli eating, that is quite a far distance from that which is necessary, which is participants' attitudes towards their eating broccoli at the time and in the context in which the behavior is measured. I have made this point multiple times, both by myself (Trafimow, 2015c) and in collaboration with Tom St Quinton and Ben Morris (St Quinton, Morris, & Trafimow, 2021).

With an example out of the way, we are now ready to recognize that the only way for a measure to be valid is if the auxiliary assumptions are true. If the auxiliary assumptions are not true, the measure is not valid. Or in a positive vein, if the auxiliary assumptions are true, then the measure is valid. To gain a birds-eye view of auxiliary validity, consider Figure 11.1.

Figure 11.1 shows the theoretical relation between two constructs (top arrow) and the empirical relation between tests of the two constructs (bottom arrow). As we have seen, for construct validity, what matters is the extent to which the empirical relation matches the theoretical relation. Or in terms of the figure, construct validity depends on the extent to which empirical findings support the bottom arrow. Given such empirical support, the bottom arrow can be argued to match the top arrow, and there is an increase in construct validity. But moving to auxiliary validity, it does not matter whether the empirical findings support the bottom arrow. Rather, what matters is the extent to which it is possible to support the vertical arrows. If the vertical arrows are strongly supported, and I will say more about how to do this in the next section, then auxiliary validity is boosted. Or, if empirical findings fail to support the vertical arrows, then auxiliary validity is compromised.

To clarify the contrast between construct validity and auxiliary validity, let us continue with the theory of reasoned action example. Suppose that the auxiliary assumptions behind an attitude measure are incorrect, so that the attitude measure indexes mood rather than attitude. Nevertheless, suppose that mood is relevant to behavior, and so there is a reasonable correlation between the alleged attitudes test and the behaviors test. Is the measure valid? From the

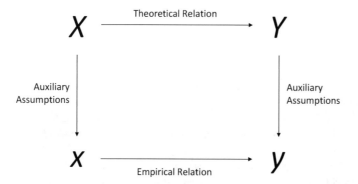

Figure 11.1 Figure illustrating the role auxiliary assumptions have in connecting constructs in a theoretical relation, with observable tests.

perspective of auxiliary validity, the alleged attitude measure is not valid because the auxiliary assumptions are wrong: the alleged attitudes test measures moods instead of attitudes. However, from the perspective of construct validity, the measure is valid. To see why, consider again that construct validity is about empirical relations matching theoretical relations. To use our symbols, the theory states that attitude (X) is supposed to cause behavior (Y): $X \to Y$. There is support for the empirical connection between the attitudes measure (x) and the behaviors measure (y), though the fact that the support is only correlational renders it weak. In any event, at the empirical level, we have support for $x \to y$. Thus, we have a matching of empirical with theoretical relations. There is empirical support for $x \to y$ and that maps well onto the theoretical relation $X \to Y$. The problem, of course, is that the empirical relation, $x \to y$, works for the wrong reason as the alleged attitudes test measures moods rather than attitudes. This is one reason why, although I respect construct validity, I believe auxiliary validity is conceptually superior.

Nor is this the only possible contrast. To return to an example from Chapter 3, feeling threatened is supposed to cause prejudice (Stephan & Stephan, 2000). Suppose a researcher attempts a threat manipulation but fails to influence scores on the prejudice measure. Finally, let us also imagine that we have certain knowledge that all auxiliary assumptions, including the tacit ones, are true. Are the tests valid? From the perspective of auxiliary validity, the truth of the auxiliary assumptions forces that the tests are valid and that blame for the empirical failure can be placed squarely on the theory. In contrast, from the perspective of construct validity, empirical relations fail to match theoretical relations. At the empirical level, the threat manipulation did not influence the prejudice test, whereas at the theoretical level threat is supposed to cause prejudice. As in the foregoing contrast, I believe that the auxiliary validity conception is superior to the construct validity conception.

How to Support Auxiliary Validity

Let us consider again whether an alleged test of attitudes really measures them. One way of making progress can be accomplished without data, simply by thinking. If presented with an article correlating attitudes with behaviors, it is possible to simply look at the tests and see whether the attitude items correspond with the behavior items with respect to the elements of action, target, time, and context. If not, and to this day most such research fails in this respect, then the measure is not valid. Nor does it matter whether the researcher reports an impressive Cronbach's alpha. As we saw in Chapter 9, an impressive Cronbach's alpha falls far short of establishing validity, and it is controversial whether it even establishes reliability (it does not!).

Another way to make progress without data is to mentally review the theory and review the tests. Sometimes it will be obvious that a test depends on questionable auxiliary assumptions. A caveat is that researchers are generally very lax about stating the auxiliary assumptions, and so some imagination might be required to figure out what the auxiliary assumptions might have been.

And data can help too. Many have suggested manipulation checks as the answer for those cases where there is a manipulation rather than a measure. Suppose a researcher performs an attitude manipulation in the hope of influencing behavior. A typical way to support that the manipulation really manipulates attitude is to have participants complete an attitude test. If mean attitudes are substantially greater in the pro attitude condition than in the other condition, researchers take that as positive evidence that the attitude manipulation really manipulates attitudes.

However, there are question marks. It is almost impossible to manipulate only one thing, and so even if the manipulation succeeds in manipulating attitudes, it almost certainly manipulates something else too. In turn, it could be the something else—such as mood—that is what is responsible for the effect on the dependent measure (e.g., behavior). Thus, the manipulation check is far from definitive. In terms of auxiliary assumptions, it is nice that the manipulation influences attitudes, but one of the implicit auxiliary assumptions is likely that the manipulation does not influence anything else that can affect the dependent variable. A manipulation check, by itself, cannot make a strong case here. In addition, it is possible that the mere act of completing the manipulation check can have an unintended effect on the experimental findings. I hasten to add, however, that if the experiment does not work, a failure on the manipulation check could be quite useful in helping diagnose the reason for the empirical failure. Thus, whether to use a manipulation check may depend, at least in part, on your confidence that the experiment will succeed.

Manipulation checks do not exhaust the possibilities. Let us return to the annoying possibility that the manipulation influences mood as well as attitude, thereby leaving it ambiguous whether the manipulation works because of attitude or because of mood. A way to reduce the ambiguity would be to include a test of mood. If the manipulation influences the attitude test, but does not influence the mood test, that constitutes a reasonably strong argument that the attitude manipulation (a) manipulates attitudes and (b) does not manipulate mood.

For a correlational study, where there is no manipulation, there is always the issue of whether the tests index the constructs of interest or whether they index something else. Here it can be helpful to establish that the measure correlates well with other tests of the construct (convergent validity) and that the measure does not correlate well with tests of plausible alternative constructs (divergent validity).

The larger point is that it is possible to make progress with respect to auxiliary validity through careful thinking or collecting relevant data that bears on competing alternatives to one's auxiliary assumptions. Although there is no way to prove, in a 100% fashion, that all of one's auxiliary assumptions are true, it is nevertheless possible to make a strong case.

Auxiliary Assumptions and Meaning

As we saw in Chapter 1 and Chapter 3, as well as earlier in the present chapter, theories contain nonobservational terms. That fact forces that there is ambiguity. There is no way to define most constructs that are of theoretical interest. There is no way to provide a definition of depression, love, threat, and so on that includes everything that we would agree fits the term and excludes everything that we would agree does not fit the term. Hence, it is fair to question how we know the meanings of such terms, despite our inability to provide definitions.

There are multiple answers. One answer is that although most terms of interest in the social sciences cannot be defined, that need not indicate that they are meaningless. There is much area between 'completely definable' and 'meaningless.' For instance, although I do not know how to define 'game' so that the definition includes everything that I think is a game and excludes everything that I think is not a game, I still know—at least to some extent—what a game is. As politicians sometimes say, "I cannot define pornography, but I know it when I see it!"

Of course, the quality of meaning described in the previous paragraph, though certainly not zero, is less than we hope for in science. Are there ways to add meaning? There are.

One way is to use examples, characterizations, and so on. Although there is no way to define depression, it is possible to give examples of depressed behavior, and the famous depression inventory by Beck is replete with these (see ismanet.org).

Another way to add meaning is to use the term of concern in a theory. We saw in Chapter 1 how Newton's theory helps give meaning to the nonobservational term, 'mass.' The way a nonobservational theory term connects with other theoretical terms helps provide additional meaning. The meaning of 'attitude' provides a nice social science example. In the threat theory, threat connects to prejudicial attitudes, and so we immediately understand attitude as having something to do with threat. In contrast, in the theory of reasoned action, attitudes connect to behavioral intentions and behaviors, so we immediately understand attitude as having something to do with behavior. These are very different meanings, and the contrast illustrates the importance of the theory in understanding what the individual terms mean.

Finally, there are auxiliary assumptions. You can tell a lot about the meaning of a theoretical term by looking at the auxiliary assumptions that connect it to an observational term. For example, in the theory of reasoned action, the auxiliary assumptions militate in the direction of attitudes being cognitive evaluations of behaviors. In contrast, in research on the effects of threat on prejudicial attitudes, the auxiliary assumptions militate in the direction of attitudes being feeling states about a group of people. And you can confirm these assertions merely by looking at attitude tests in the two areas. Thus, although auxiliary assumptions are crucial for testing theories, they also matter for imbuing theoretical terms with meaning. For both reasons, you should care about auxiliary validity.

Chapter Summary

We commenced with predictive validity. Although predictive validity is good to have, it is not sufficient because a test can predict a criterion for the wrong reason. Predictive validity might be considered a minimum necessary criterion for validity, but it is not sufficient.

We then moved to construct validity, which is easily the type of validity most bandied about. When researchers promote new tests of constructs, their main goal is to convince readers that they have established construct validity. A problem is that most substantive researchers believe construct validity is about a test measuring what it is supposed to measure, but this is incorrect. The truth is that construct validity is about demonstrating that empirical relations match theoretical relations. As construct validity increases, support for both the theory and the validities of the tests increases simultaneously. The more the empirical relations that can be matched with theoretical relations, the more extensive the nomological network, and the greater the support for construct validity.

Many researchers claim construct validity falsely. There is no way for empirical relations to match theoretical relations if there is no theory and, hence, no theoretical relations to match. Therefore, in those papers where there is no theory, construct validity is out of the question. In addition, even if there is a theory, typical methods such as factor analysis do not explore theoretical relations to any great extent. Rather, they focus on a single construct or multiple subconstructs, but fail to consider causal connections to criterion constructs. It is one thing, for example, to use factor analysis on threat items, and perhaps even identify potential dimensions of threat, but it is quite another thing to connect threat tests to prejudice tests. The extent to which factor analysis is sufficient for the former is controversial, but it certainly is insufficient for the latter. Any social scientist who depends exclusively on factor analysis is not demonstrating construct validity. More generally, before believing claims about construct validity, try to identify precisely what empirical relations have been uncovered that match theoretical relations. If you cannot do it, the article likely is misleading about having established construct validity.

The notion of auxiliary validity springs directly from an explicit recognition that there is no way to test theories without auxiliary assumptions. If you recall Chapter 3, there is also the issue of statistical and inferential assumptions, though these were ignored in the present chapter for the sake of simplicity. In any event, once we acknowledge that empirical tests of theories are impossible without auxiliary assumptions, we are led naturally to auxiliary validity. Tests have auxiliary validity to the extent that the auxiliary assumptions are true.

With both construct validity and auxiliary validity explained, they sometimes lead to contradictory conclusions. We discussed a case where the auxiliary assumptions are false so that empirical relations match theoretical relations, but for the wrong reason. In this case, there is an increase in construct validity but not in auxiliary validity. We also discussed a case where the auxiliary assumptions are correct, but the theory is wrong, and the wrongness of the theory causes a mismatch of empirical and theoretical relations. Due to the mismatch, there is a lack of construct validity, but there is auxiliary validity. Put more generally, it is possible to have a valid measure of a construct, even if the theory is wrong. To use a physics example, a theory about radioactivity can be disconfirmed by data obtained via a Geiger counter, but the mismatch between empirical and theoretical relations need not indicate that the Geiger counter is working poorly, especially if an independent test shows the Geiger counter works properly. It is crucial to recognize that valid measures, in the context of a wrong theory, can result in wrong conclusions or empirical relations that fail to match theoretical relations. This recognition is a strong point for auxiliary validity as superior to construct validity.

Finally, we briefly discussed the meaning of theoretical constructs. Although these cannot be defined, that problem need not indicate that theoretical constructs have no meaning. We discussed some methods for imbuing theoretical constructs with meaning. One of those methods is to use auxiliary assumptions. Because auxiliary assumptions are connected to theoretical constructs, meaning can flow from auxiliary assumptions to theoretical constructs, as well as in the more obvious direction. Thus, auxiliary validity is desirable not just from a theory testing standpoint, but also because better auxiliary assumptions may enhance the meanings of theoretical constructs.

12 Unit Validity and Why Units Matter

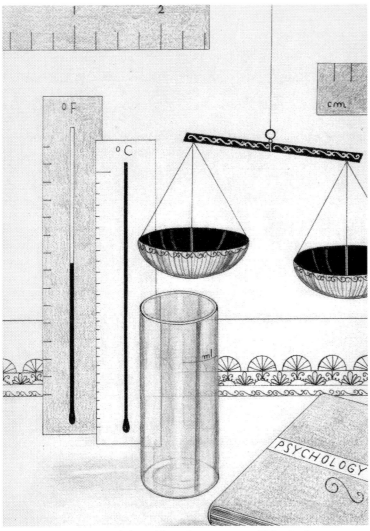

In Chapter 11, I argued that although construct validity is the most emphasized type of validity in the social sciences, the social sciences would be better off moving in the direction of auxiliary validity. In the present chapter, I will argue for yet another type of validity: unit validity.

DOI: 10.4324/9781003365167-14

I have published on this before (Trafimow, 2012b), but I will attempt to improve the clarity of the argument here.

Let us commence speaking generally. One difference between the physical sciences and the social sciences is that units are explicitly stated in the physical sciences but usually are not in the social sciences. The explicit statement of units lends greater specificity to the physical sciences which, in turn, renders theories more easily tested. Moreover, the last part of Chapter 11 considered the problem of the meanings of theoretical constructs. We pointed out that meaning can be imbued to theoretical constructs via the word itself, examples or characterizations, connections with other constructs in a theory, and connections with auxiliary assumptions. However, there is yet another way researchers can imbue theoretical constructs with meaning, and that is through units.

A physics example might be energy, which, literally, means "work within." But what does that vague characterization mean? As usual, meaning comes from many places but one of the places is units. To see that this is so, consider a typical physics equation:

$$E = \frac{1}{2}mv^2. \tag{12.1}$$

Stated in words, energy E equals one-half mass m times velocity squared v^2. Although the equation aids meaning because we now know energy connects with mass and velocity, it is possible to imbue even more meaning if we consider units. If we use the International System of Units, energy could be expressed as joules J, in honor of James Prescott Joule. But what is a joule?

To answer this question, let us return to Equation 12.1 but considering units. To remain with the International System of Units, we would index mass in kilograms kg and velocity in meters m per second s. Thus, in units, ignoring numbers, Equation 12.1 becomes Equation 12.2:

$$J = kg\left(\frac{m}{s}\right)^2. \tag{12.2}$$

Although energy remains a nonobservational term with a vague semantic definition, we now have a much better idea of what the term means than when we started. Equation 12.1 shows that energy is connected to mass and even more connected to distance and time (remember that velocity is squared). Further, using the International System of Units, we know that a meaning of mass is kilograms, a meaning of distance is meters, and a meaning of time is seconds, though these are not the only possible meanings. Putting all these together, we find that energy, in joules, is highly connected to kilograms and even more connected to meters and seconds. In sum, although we still do not have an independent definition of energy (independent, that is, from mass, distance, and time), we have imbued much more meaning than we had originally based on the vague "work within." Finally, the gain in meaning and specificity greatly aids with theory testing and with the progress of physics.

The vagueness in meaning of social science terms hides a further problem, a subtle kind of incoherency problem. To see the importance, consider that one characteristic of good theories is that they are internally coherent. Theories should not say self-contradictory things such as that the Moon orbits the Earth, and the Moon does not orbit the Earth. Although it may seem unlikely that any psychology theories suffer from an incoherency problem, I will argue to the contrary, that even some highly cited theories do suffer from an incoherency problem or that they are so vaguely stated that it is difficult to tell.

Examples

Most social science theories do not contain equations and so units are out of the question. This is problematic because, as we have just seen, when there are no units the meaning of the construct is vaguer. Theories about love, depression, prejudice, and so on tend to eschew equations and therefore eschew units too. A consequence is that it is more difficult to understand what these terms mean. This is not to say that the concepts are meaningless, as meaning can stem from other sources than equations or units within equations, only that there is a vagueness to these terms that is not there with energy. If we were to settle for energy meaning "work within," then energy would be every bit as vague as social science terms. But physicists do not thusly settle, and so energy carries with it clearer meaning than do psychology terms.

Theory of Reasoned Action: Attitudes

Although most social science theories do not involve equations, this is not to say that none of them involve equations. For an exception, let us consider the theory of reasoned action that featured in previous chapters (e.g., Ajzen & Fishbein, 1980; Fishbein, 1980; Fishbein & Ajzen, 1975; 2010). One of the equations in this theory is provided as Equation 12.3 below:

$$A = \sum b_i e_i. \tag{12.3}$$

The idea is that people have some beliefs about the probabilities of possible consequences of a behavior, that is, *i* beliefs about consequences, but they also have *i* evaluations about the goodness or badness of each of these consequences. According to Equation 12.3, an attitude A is the summation of the products of each belief b_i and its associated evaluation e_i.

Equation 12.3 is helpful, meaning-wise, because we now know that attitudes are connected to beliefs about consequences and evaluations of those consequences. But we are still in less good shape with respect to meaning than in the energy example. Consider three bullet-listed questions.

- What is a belief about a consequence unit?
- What is an evaluation unit?
- What is an attitude unit?

We have no way of answering the bullet-listed questions.

Let us imagine that there is such an entity as a belief unit b and an evaluation unit e. In that case, just as an energy unit includes kilograms, meters, and seconds, we would know that an attitude unit contains the belief unit and the evaluation unit. We might say that just as an energy unit (in joules) is a conglomeration of kilograms, meters, and seconds, an attitude unit is a conglomeration of beliefs and evaluations. Is this consistent with the verbal description of attitude? It is difficult to say because there are multiple descriptions. For example, an old-fashioned description is that an attitude is a combination of physical and mental readiness for action. Another description is that an attitude is a predisposition for behavior. Yet others would describe attitudes as including affect, cognition, and conation. And then there is the theory of reasoned action attitude description, which is that an attitude is an evaluation of a behavior. None accord well with the unit analysis description of an attitude including a belief unit and an evaluation unit. The theory of reasoned action description comes closest, because at least it includes the word, "evaluation." Even so, the discrepancy is obvious.

174 Measurement Issues

The larger point is that the lack of units causes a subtle kind of incoherence. If Equation 12.3 had included units, then doubtless the verbal description of attitudes would have included those units too, and all would be coherent, though not necessarily correct. But now we see that when we put the units in, there is incoherence because the verbal description mismatches the mathematical description.

It would be easy to interpret the foregoing as a scathing criticism of the theory of reasoned action, but that would not be justified. The only reason it was possible to make the point about a subtle kind of incoherence is because at least there is an equation, Equation 12.3, where we could insert units. And the theory has other equations too, and we will get to one momentarily. Note, however, the stark contrast to other social science theories that do not have any equations. Without equations, an analysis such as that performed here is impossible. Thus, there is no way to judge the subtle type of incoherence that is the present worry.

One way of handling the problem of units is to include a constant k. Modifying Equation 12.3 thusly results in Equation 12.4.

$$A = k \sum b_i e_i. \tag{12.4}$$

What units does the constant need to have? Suppose we make up a further unit—an evaluation of behavior unit—symbolized by e_b. Our constant then could have the following units: $\frac{e_b}{b \cdot e}$. In units, then, we would have the following: $1 e_b = 1 \frac{e_b}{b \cdot e} b \cdot e = 1 e_b$, and the theory would then have unit coherence. Of course, the theory of reasoned action would become a different theory, as the constant would now be an important component of it that would have to be treated seriously in empirical tests or applications. Then, too, it might be that the value of 1 that I used might be shown empirically to be false, with some other value for k superior.

In contrast to the theory of reasoned action, which has equations, there are no equations in the threat theory that has served as an example in previous chapters, where threat is theorized to cause prejudicial attitudes (Stephan & Stephan, 2000). Therefore, there is no way to know if there is incoherence between the verbal description of prejudicial attitudes and equations because there are no equations! Thus, the best we can say is that the degree of incoherence in threat theory is undetermined. We could, of course, run through a threat-and-prejudice exercise.

Suppose we attempt to make the theory more specific by including a constant. Thus, the new idea is that prejudicial attitudes Pa are a function of threat T but also a function of the constant k. Hence, we have the following: $Pa = kT$. Let us imagine a threat unit Tu and we already see a problem. That is, the verbal description of prejudicial attitudes as a negative feeling or evaluation of an outgroup does not include anything remotely resembling a threat (Tu) unit in its description. So, in our attempt to make the threat-and-prejudice theory more specific, we run into incoherence. We might attempt to fix it. For example, let us imagine a prejudice unit Pu and figure out what units the constant needs to have so that the two sides of the equation balance in units. We could say the constant has the following units: Pu/Tu. In that case, the equation works out: $Pa = kT$ stated in units is $1 Pu = 1 \frac{Pu}{Tu} Tu = 1 Pu$. Thus, the theory need not remain incoherent, but there is certainly a potential incoherency problem as things stand now.

In one way, it is a good strategy for psychology theories to be as vague as possible because there is then no way to disconfirm them or show that there is any incoherence. But that is more a sociology of science point than a science point. From a sociology of science perspective, having vague theories might be a good way to achieve career success. From a what-is-good-for-science perspective, such vagueness is clearly contraindicated because it is deleterious for understanding the meanings of theoretical constructs. It is difficult to connect high-quality auxiliary assumptions to theoretical terms one does not understand! And without high-quality auxiliary assumptions, there is an obvious failure to achieve auxiliary validity, and strong theory tests are out of the question. Thus, despite the incoherence, the theory of reasoned action comes off better than threat theory because, in the former case, we understand the theoretical terms well enough to derive the incoherence, whereas, in the latter case, our understanding of the terms is so incomplete that there is no way even to assess the possibility of incoherence save by much imagination.

Theory of Reasoned Action: Subjective Norms

According to the theory of reasoned action, subjective norms SN are based on beliefs about what important others think one should do, termed normative beliefs n, and motivations to comply with those normative referents m. Thus, there is an equation analogous to Equation 12.3, and it is Equation 12.5, below:

$$SN = \sum n_i m_i. \tag{12.5}$$

Let us perform a like exercise such as that performed with attitudes.

We can imagine a kind of normative belief unit n, and a motivation to comply unit m, in which case these units ought to figure into the definition of subjective norm. But the verbal definition of subjective norms is that they are what a person believes most people who are important to her think she should do. This verbal definition obviously falls short of the idea that subjective norms are summed belief-motivation to comply products. Thus, we again have incoherence that becomes clear once we start considering units.

We could fix the incoherence by including a constant such as we saw earlier. I will leave it to you to perform the exercise.

Are Social Science Tests Mathematical?

A potential problem with the foregoing argument about units is that, in physics, the constructs are assumed to have mathematical characteristics. Two seconds are twice the time of one second, the difference between three and two seconds is the same as the difference between 2 and 1 seconds, and so on. Even if we go to energy, which is more complex than mass, time, or distance, the mathematical nature continues. For example, two joules are twice the energy of one joule, the difference between three joules and two joules is the same as the difference between two joules and one joule, and so on. Do psychology measures meet these standards? And if not, would it not be misleading to impose units?

Reaction Time

In fact, social science measures differ widely. For example, consider the time it takes for participants to react to a stimulus, often called reaction time, and usually measured in milliseconds. Here, it seems we do have a dependent variable that has mathematical characteristics. Two milliseconds are twice one millisecond, the difference between three and two milliseconds is the same as the difference between two and one milliseconds, and so on. However, there is a potential issue. A researcher who measures reaction time in milliseconds usually is not interested in time, per se, but rather in making some sort of claim about the associative connection between two items. If, say, it takes more time to respond to 'nurse' after being primed with 'doctor' than to respond to 'banana' after being primed with 'doctor,' the typical researcher would conclude that the doctor–nurse association is stronger than the doctor–banana association.

However, moving from time, per se, to associative strength, may interfere with our previous happy conclusions about the mathematical characteristics of reaction time. Suppose that the mean reaction time for the doctor–nurse pairing is 600 milliseconds whereas the mean reaction time for the doctor–banana pairing is 1200 milliseconds. Would we be justified in concluding that the strength of the former associative connection is twice that of the latter one? Probably, we would not be. Or suppose a third pairing, 'doctor' and 'fool,' results in a mean reaction time of 1800 milliseconds. Would we be justified in concluding that the difference in associative strength with respect to the doctor–nurse pairing and the doctor–banana pairing equals the difference in associative strength between the doctor–banana pairing and the doctor–fool pairing? Again, probably we would not be justified, even though the difference is 600 milliseconds in both cases.

Thus, whether reaction time has mathematical properties depends on our interpretation. If we merely want to say that different word pairings result in different reaction times, then there is no problem. But if we want to compare word pairings with respect to the strength of their associative connection, there is a large problem. Or to restate in words pertaining to units, if the crucial unit is milliseconds, we are on firm mathematical ground, but if what we really care about is associative strength units, then we are wallowing in mathematical quicksand. In most published work, reaction time is not of interest for its own sake, but rather of interest as a conduit to something else, such as associative strength. Thus, even for reaction time, the issue of meaningful units can be troublesome.

This point can be stated in another and more general way. It is one thing to say that reaction time is the dependent variable and that it has mathematical properties so that millisecond units are sensible. It is quite another thing to say that the construct, such as associative strength, for which reaction time is supposed to serve as a stand-in, has similar mathematical properties.

Agree–Disagree Items

Many social science measures involve participants responding to agree–disagree items. They might indicate their agreement or disagreement that they are enthusiastic, talkative, or other items that load on an extraversion factor. Other so-called Big 5 factors are also measured with agree–disagree items. If Sally agrees that she is agreeable (score = +1) and Peter strongly agrees that he is agreeable (score = +2), does that imply that Peter is twice as agreeable as Sally? Certainly not, this would be a ridiculous conclusion. Or if Lina neither agrees nor disagrees (score = 0), it would be completely unwarranted to conclude that the distance between Peter and Sally (3 − 2 = 1) is the same as the distance between Sally and Linda (1 − 0 = 1). There is no reasonable way to argue that agree–disagree items have the requisite mathematical qualities. In turn, it is far from clear what to do about units. Even if we grant, for the sake of argument, that agree–disagree items are "good enough for government work," there remains a problem at the level of units.

Consider again enthusiasm and talkativeness items that, with other items, are supposed to give rise to an extraversion score. If we think of enthusiasm units, talkativeness units, and so on, why should we believe that if we somehow combine all these units we somehow end up with an extraversion unit? Of course, the factor analysis a researcher conducts may indicate that the various items are correlated with each other and correlated with the factor too, but that is far from showing, at the level of units, that if we were to have the various units, there would be any reason to expect them to combine to result in an extraversion unit. To make that go, it would be necessary to assume something like the following: 1 *enthusiasm · talkativeness ·...kth unit* = 1 *extraversion*. This seems a highly questionable assumption, at best.

We could include a constant to fix the problem. For example, we could imagine the combination of a constant that includes an extraversion unit and where the other units cancel, such as the following: $1\ extraversion = 1 \dfrac{extraversion}{enthusiasm \cdot talkativeness \cdot \ldots kth\ unit}$, $enthusiasm \cdot talkativeness \cdot \ldots kth\ unit = 1\ extraversion$. However, this might involve further problems such as justifying the constant in the first place. A critic might argue that instead of an unwieldy constant, an alternative is to assume that an enthusiasm item measures enthusiasm and that a talkativeness item measures talkativeness, and that neither measures extraversion. We will revisit this issue in Chapter 14.

A Counterargument: Physics Has Unitless Measures Too

Consider the notion of specific gravity in physics. It is a unitless measure of the density of a substance relative to water. Thus, the specific gravity of water is defined as equaling 1, whereas the specific gravity of other substances may be less than 1 for less dense substances, or greater than 1 for denser substances. Unitless measures in physics, such as specific gravity, open the door for a counterargument to the present focus on the importance of units. If a science as successful as physics can make do with unitless measures, why is it a crime for the social sciences to employ mostly unitless measures? Perhaps the present focus on units is misplaced.

To refute this counterargument, let us consider specific gravity in physics, with an exploration of why it is a unitless measure. To aid us in this exploration, let us consider the density of water: *density of water* $= 1 \dfrac{gm}{cm^3}$. In words, one gram of water takes up a volume of one cubic centimeter under standard conditions, which is its density. In contrast, mercury has a much greater density: $13.546 \dfrac{gm}{cm^3}$. Given that we know the density of water and we know the density of mercury, it is trivial to figure out the specific gravity of mercury which, again, is the density of mercury divided by the density of water: *specific gravity of mercury* $= \dfrac{13.546 \dfrac{gm}{cm^3}}{1 \dfrac{gm}{cm^3}} = 13.546$.

The example illustrates for us why specific gravity is unitless. Specific gravity is unitless because the density units, gm/cm^3, cancel out!

We are now in a good position to contrast the reasons why specific gravity versus prejudicial attitudes are unitless. In the case of specific gravity, there are units that cancel out, thereby

178   Measurement Issues

leaving a unitless measure that is both easily understood and coherent. In contrast, prejudicial attitudes are unitless because there were never any units there from the start. Thus, although specific gravity and prejudicial attitudes seem similar in their being unitless, the underlying reasons are vastly different. Consequently, we see that there is a vast gulf between unitless measures in physics and unitless measures in the social sciences.

Not All Social Science Measures Are Unitless

If units are desirable and the social sciences nevertheless are short on them, the obvious direction is for social scientists to specify their theories in greater detail, including units. A potential riposte is that social scientists do not have the capability to do that. Consequently, the present chapter is really a waste of time because it amounts to recommending a course of action that researchers are unable to take. Possibly the most powerful way to demonstrate that social scientists have the capability to include units in their theories would be to provide examples where they have done just that. The following subsections provide such examples.

A Theory of Social Decision Schemes

James (Jim) Davis, a former professor of mine, was concerned with addressing the issue of how people in a group combine their individual predilections into a group decision. Offhand, this seems like a difficult and perhaps intractable problem. Davis' brilliant insight was that it is possible to address the issue mathematically (Davis, 1973).

Although social decision schemes theory is applicable to many sorts of group tasks, let us consider six-person juries. Davis realized that it is possible to estimate the probability that a particular person would favor a verdict of guilty or not guilty simply by taking the proportion of participants who favor each. For example, if 140 out of 200 participants think the defendant is guilty, then the probability of a guilty preference is the following: $\frac{140}{200} = 0.7$. Of course, the probability of a not guilty preference would be 0.3. Given these base probabilities, it is also possible to use the binomial theorem to estimate the probability of various group distributions of preferences, such as that all six jury members will prefer a guilty verdict, that five will, and so on. This matrix of probabilities is called a pi matrix and symbolized by $\boldsymbol{\pi}$. The reason for the boldfacing is that the symbol refers to a matrix of probabilities as opposed to a single probability.

In addition, it is possible to propose theories in the form of matrices of probabilities. For example, a researcher might propose that if two-thirds or more of the participants support a particular verdict, that will be the group verdict, with a hung jury otherwise. Alternatively, a researcher might propose that if the two-thirds majority stipulation is not met, the probability that the jury will vote guilty or not guilty reflects the proportions of members who favor each verdict, with a hung jury only happening when the split is exactly equal. A third possibility is to propose simple proportionality, so that the probability of a guilty or not guilty verdict depends on the proportion of individual preferences for a guilty or innocent verdict. For example, if everyone prefers a guilty verdict, the probability would be 1.00 that the jury would vote to convict. If five people prefer a guilty verdict and one person prefers a not guilty verdict, the jury would have five-sixths (0.83) probability of a guilty verdict, and so on. And there are numerous other possible theories one can propose too. The point is that whatever competing theories a researcher wishes to test, all of these can be expressed as a matrix of probabilities of jury verdicts for different distributions of individual preferences. This matrix is called a decision schemes matrix or **D** matrix.

Finally, Davis (1973) showed that the probabilities of a jury verdict of guilty, not guilty, or hung, based on (a) the distribution of individual preferences and (b) which social decision schemes theory is of interest, can be obtained simply by multiplying the two matrices. Thus, the matrix of probabilities with which the jury will choose each option, for each prior distribution of juror preferences, is as follows: **P** = π**D**.

A nice characteristic of social decision schemes theory is that it provides an elegant way to choose between competing schemes. That is, using the π matrix, which can be calculated based on the proportions of individual preferences obtained from the data, and competing **D** matrices from various proposed decision schemes, competing **P** matrices follow mathematically. Thus, the winning theory is the theory that results in the **P** matrix that accords most closely with the actual data, with the other theories losing.

Of great importance for the present chapter, social decision schemes theory is unit coherent. The π matrix is in probability units, the competing **D** matrices are in units of transitional probabilities, and the competing **P** matrices, to be compared to the data, are in units of probabilities of group decisions. All is well with respect to units. No wonder social decision schemes became one of the most influential theories in the history of group research.

A Theory of Signal Detection

Swets, Tanner, and Birdsall (1961) argued against the notion of a single parameter for sensory detection, and proposed *signal detection theory* as an alternative. At the time, researchers believed that performance on detection tasks depended solely on how sensitive the participants were to the stimuli being presented. Swets et al. suggested that there were two parameters: sensitivity and decision criterion location. To understand the argument, suppose that participants are presented with various sounds, with the goal of detecting its presence or absence. There are four possibilities.

- Hit: the sound is there, and the participant detects it.
- Miss: the sound is there, and the participant fails to detect it.
- False alarm: the sound is not there, but the participant nevertheless detects it.
- Correct rejection: the sound is not there, and the participant appropriately does not detect it.

Based on the proportions of responses in the four categories, and assuming normal distributions, it is possible to calculate both sensitivity d' and criterion location cl (Macmillan and Creelman, 2005):

$$d' = z\big(p(Hits)\big) - z\big(p(False\ Alarms)\big),$$

$$cl = \frac{1}{2}\big(z\big(p(Hits)\big) - z\big(p(False\ Alarms)\big)\big).$$

These equations are unit coherent. The proportion of hits is the frequency of hits divided by the frequency of hits and misses; in other words, a frequency divided by a frequency. And the proportion of false alarms is likewise a frequency divided by a frequency. Thus, for both hits and false alarms, the frequency units cancel, leaving unitless indices. In addition, z-scores give the

180 *Measurement Issues*

difference in means, as a fraction of a standard deviation. Thus, z-scores are considered unitless, which is not precisely correct because they are in standard deviation units. Therefore, with all frequency units cancelling, d' and cl can be considered in standard deviation units, though they are usually presented as unitless.

That signal detection theory is unit coherent doubtless contributed to its having achieved a dominant position in the perception field. Nevertheless, as we saw in Chapter 10, although unit coherence is good to have, it does not necessitate that the theory is correct, and signal detection theory is not correct.

Potential Performance Theory

Recall Chapter 10 where we reviewed potential performance theory. It contains equations for determining the 'potential' cell scores based on observed cell scores and the correlation between entities (e.g., two people or one person versus an objective standard), adjusted for unreliability R. It is possible to estimate true cell frequencies based on R and based on the margin frequencies for row 1 R_1, row 2 R_2, column 1 C_1, and column 2 C_2. Let us rewrite, Equation 10.9 that gives the expected frequency for Cell A.

$$A = \frac{R\sqrt{R_1 R_2 C_1 C_2} + C_1 R_1}{R_1 + R_2}$$

Although the units are understood rather than written, it is easy to write them in. Remembering that R is unitless because it is a correlation coefficient (standardized covariance), and that we are only concerned with multiplication at the unit level (not addition), the frequency units, abbreviated as f play out as follows:

$$\text{units of } A = \frac{\sqrt{f \cdot f \cdot f \cdot f} + f + f}{f + f} = \frac{f^2}{f} = f.$$

Thus, the estimated potential frequency of cell A works out to the correct units. A similar statement is true of the other potential performance theory equations.

To summarize, the present section briefly describes social decision schemes theory, signal detection theory, and potential performance theory. In all cases, there are clear units, and the units balance out so that there is unit coherence. And there are additional social science examples too. These examples prove that it is possible to have unit coherence in the social sciences, though it is not easy.

Chapter Summary

We commenced by reminding ourselves of Chapter 11 and the focus on auxiliary validity. One advantage of auxiliary validity is that it helps add meaning to theoretical constructs. However, an additional way to add meaning is to have units. We saw this in the case of energy, where mass, distance, and time units aided in providing meaning to energy far beyond the vague verbal description of 'work within.'

We then switched to the theory of reasoned action, and the notion of attitude. An advantage of the theory of reasoned action, relative to many other social science theories, is that it has equations that render theoretical constructs easier to understand. However, we also saw that the theory of reasoned action falls short when it comes to units because it does not have any. We proceeded through the exercise of adding units and found that the verbal description of an attitude does not match well with the implication of the attitude equation after adding units. There is unit incoherence or a lack of unit validity. It is possible to fix the problem by including a constant in the attitude equation and endowing the constant with the requisite set of units to result in the verbal description matching the mathematical description. Of course, the addition of the constant changes the theory.

Although it is possible to criticize the theory of reasoned action for its deficit in unit validity, it compares well to other social science theories for which there are no equations. At least, for the theory of reasoned action, it is possible to deduce that there is unit invalidity, whereas for most social science theories, such as the threat-and-prejudice theory, there is no way even to assess it, though we went through a speculative exercise in that direction.

For good measure, we also briefly investigated the theory of reasoned action subjective norm equation. We saw that, in addition to the attitude unit validity problem, there is an analogous unit validity problem pertaining to subjective norms.

Then there is the thorny issue of whether social science constructs have mathematical properties. We briefly investigated reaction time and saw that our answer depends importantly on whether reaction time is considered of interest, for its own sake, or whether it is a stand-in for something else, such as associative strength. Although, in the former case, reaction time clearly has requisite mathematical properties and is a unit valid measure, in the latter case, the presence of requisite mathematical properties and unit validity are arguable. Moving to agree–disagree scales, the issues become even more problematic and controversial.

We subsequently discussed a potential objection, which is that some physics constructs, such as specific gravity, are unitless. In that case, why should we object to unitless constructs in psychology, such as threat, prejudicial attitudes, extraversion, and so on? To respond to the potential objection, we saw that in the case of specific gravity there are units, but they cancel out, thereby leaving a unitless measure. This contrasts with most social science constructs where there never were units in the first place. Thus, specific gravity has a clear meaning despite its lack of units, whereas most social science constructs do not have such clear meanings.

Finally, we addressed the issue of whether it is possible to have unit validity in psychology research. We saw that it is possible. Social decision schemes theory, signal detection theory, and potential performance theory all promote unit valid research. Therefore, unit validity is possible to achieve, though it remains difficult. Hopefully, future researchers will take up the challenge, and you might be one of them.

13 A Tripartite Parsing of Variance

In Chapter 3 we defined variance, and it is crucial to understand, on a conceptual level, why variance matters. Let us consider two experiments, each with two conditions, and with eight participants per condition. Obviously, the sample size is too small for ideally strong conclusions but let us ignore that. Scores for Experiment 1 are as follows.

Experimental condition: 2, 2, 2, 2, 2, 2, 2, 2.
Control condition: 1, 1, 1, 1, 1, 1, 1, 1.

The mean is 2 in the experimental condition and 1 in the control condition, and this is immediately obvious.

In contrast, let us consider Experiment 2.

Experimental condition: 0, –1, 4, 5, 0, 4, 5, –1.
Control condition: –1, –2, 2, 4, –1, 4, 4, –2.

Here, the mean again is 2 in the experimental condition and 1 in the control condition, but it is much more difficult to see. Variance complicates matters.

Also, variance can change the meanings of the differences. A mean difference of 1 is very impressive when there is no variance within each group. In contrast, a mean difference of 1 is less impressive when there is much variance within each group.

We can see this point in a more general way. We mentioned effect sizes in Chapter 3, but we can take the concept further here. Cohen's d is a typical effect size index for when there are two conditions, and we assume the same population standard deviations. Cohen's d is the difference in means divided by the standard deviation: $\frac{\mu_1 - \mu_2}{\sigma}$. To remain conceptual and avoid issues pertaining to samples, I used population means μ_1 and μ_2 as opposed to sample means, and the population standard deviation σ instead of the sample standard deviation. Now, suppose that the difference in population means equals 1, as in the example, but we let the standard deviation vary, so it is 1, 4, 7, or 10. Cohen's d is 1, 0.5, 0.14, or 0.10, respectively. As the standard deviation increases, the effect size decreases, and the decrease can be dramatic.

There are two ways to obtain a large effect size. One way is to have a large difference in means. Another way to say this is that we want scores *between* conditions, such as between the experimental and control condition, to be as different as possible—to vary a lot. Thus, variance between conditions can be considered "good" variance or the variance that we want to maximize.

The other way to obtain a large effect size is to have small variance *within* each condition. From an experimentalist's perspective, variance within conditions is undesirable because it reduces effect sizes. Thus, variance within conditions is called "error" variance, but we can call it "bad" variance too because it is variance that experimentalists wish to minimize. Therefore, to obtain large effect sizes, we wish to maximize good variance and minimize bad variance.

Given this backdrop, it might not surprise you to learn—if you do not already know it—that many statistical analyses are based on the idea of parsing good and bad variance; for example, the famous F statistic is good variance divided by bad variance and the famous T statistic is the square root of the F statistic. The point is for you to appreciate that researchers find it crucial to parse total variance into good and bad variance. And again, researchers wish to maximize good variance and minimize bad variance to obtain the largest effect sizes possible.

You might wonder why researchers wish to maximize effect sizes, other than to get statistically significant findings, as we discussed in Chapter 4. One reason is that large effect sizes provide a more convincing case for application than do small effect sizes. Another reason is that small effect sizes are more susceptible to alternative explanations than are large effect sizes. For example, if the effect size is only 0.10, it is quite plausible to attribute the effect to a slight imperfection in the random assignment of participants to conditions, to accidentally manipulating an unintended variable, and so on. Although such alternative explanations remain possible even for large effect sizes, they are less plausible. If the effect size is 0.90, it would be quite a stretch to assert that it is because of a mishap with respect to random assignment of participants to conditions, rather than that the manipulation was the cause.

An Ambiguity with Respect to Bad Variance

That which we are calling good variance is clear. Good variance is caused by the manipulation.

In contrast, bad variance is less clear. This is because bad variance can be caused by randomness, but it can also be caused by systematic factors other than the manipulated variable. Either way, such variance remains bad. We want randomness to contaminate our research to the smallest extent possible. And we want systematic factors, other than the manipulation, to likewise contaminate our research to the smallest extent possible. Thus, we see that bad variance can be attributed to randomness, but it can also be attributed to inconvenient systematic causes.

Because bad variance can be for random or systematic reasons, the thought may have occurred to you that it would be interesting to figure out a way to thusly parse that bad variance. There might be a way to estimate the portion of the bad variance that is random versus the portion of the bad variance that is systematic.

Or to push back on the suggestion, it is possible to argue that if the variance is bad, there is no reason to parse it further. It does not matter if the variance is bad for random or systematic reasons—either way, it remains bad!

To see why further parsing might be desirable, suppose that you are a researcher who has obtained a small effect size. Knowing that this is typical in the social sciences, an obvious issue—and one that faces many social science researchers—is whether to pursue future research to attempt to account for more variance in the dependent variable. Here is one place where parsing bad variance into random and systematic components can be helpful. Suppose that most of the bad variance is attributable to randomness, and very little to systematic factors. In that case, your search for additional systematic factors to account for more variance is unlikely to succeed. After all, the systematic variance to be accounted for is simply not there. In contrast, if much of the bad variance is systematic, then a search for new independent variables to account for it may be likely to succeed. At least there is a substantial amount of systematic variance there to be found. Hence, a potential gain to be had by parsing bad variance into that which is attributable to randomness or systematicity is to aid in determining the direction of future research. Bad variance that is systematic can potentially be converted to good variance, if the researcher is sufficiently insightful or fortunate to find the relevant independent variables in future research. However, bad variance that is random cannot be converted into good variance unless the dependent variable is changed.

How might the dependent variable be changed, while still measuring the construct you wish to measure? One way is to increase the reliability of the dependent variable. This might necessitate increasing the quality of the items, the quantity of the items, or both. It also could necessitate refining your understanding of the construct. If you can increase the reliability with which you measure the construct, then there may be more good variance in the first place, and more of the bad variance will be systematic as opposed to random. In turn, as we have seen, there is a possibility of converting systematic bad variance into good variance in future research.

Although the foregoing two paragraphs were concerned with future research, there are potential benefits with respect to interpreting the present study too. Suppose that there is 10% good variance and 90% bad variance, so that you are accounting for 10% of the variance in the dependent variable with your independent variable. In turn, suppose that 50% of the bad variance is random and 50% is systematic so that 45% of the total variance is random and 45% of the total variance is systematic. In addition to asking what percentage of the total variance you are accounting for with your independent variable, it is possible to ask how you are doing with respect to random bad variance or systematic bad variance. Although, in this example, the answers would come out similarly, it is possible to imagine a different example. Suppose that most of the bad variance is random, in which case an argument could be that although the independent variable accounts for very little of the total variance, relative to systematic bad variance, the good variance is quite substantial! Say that the systematic bad variance is 5%. In that case, the anemic looking 10% variance accounted for value translates into twice as much good variance as systematic bad variance, which may put a different spin on the research because the manipulation is accounting for an impressive portion of the variance that is capable of being accounted for.

To summarize thus far, there are good reasons to parse bad variance into a random portion and a systematic portion. Such parsing provides a strong clue as to the direction future research should take and can help, too, with interpreting the present study. In the next section, I will explain how to obtain a tripartite parsing of variance: good variance, systematic bad variance, and random bad variance. For more details, you can also consult my paper in *Educational and Psychological Measurement* (Trafimow, 2018c).

Two Derivations of How to Achieve a Tripartite Parsing of Variance

Imagine a correlational study where you have a test to measure X and a test to measure Y. Normally, if we wanted to know how much variance in X accounts for variance in Y, the best we could do is square the correlation coefficient to obtain that value. This would be the proportion of good variance and it can be converted into a percentage by multiplying by 100%. In turn, the percentage of bad variance would be 100% minus the percentage of good variance, and there would be no way to parse the bad variance further. But now, let us suppose that we have a measure of the reliability of the test measuring Y. In that case, consistent with what we learned about the classical measurement theory in Chapter 9, we can make further progress by taking reliability extremely seriously. The present chapter is based upon applying that insight to the issue of a tripartite parsing of variance.

We will imagine two scenarios. In the first scenario, the researcher conducts a correlational study, and we wish to obtain not just good and bad variance, but rather good variance, random bad variance, and systematic bad variance. In the second scenario, the researcher conducts an experiment and we again wish to have a tripartite parsing into good variance, random bad variance, and systematic bad variance.

Correlational Study

Let us start with the following symbols.

- Variance in the dependent variable accounted for by the independent variable: σ_{IV}^2.
- Proportion of variance in the dependent variable accounted for by the independent variable (proportion of good variance): ρ_{XY}^2.

186 *Measurement Issues*

- Total variance in the dependent variable: σ_Y^2.
- True score variance: σ_T^2 (recall this from Chapter 9).
- Random variance: σ_R^2.
- Systematic variance not accounted for by the independent variable: σ_O^2.
- Reliability of Y: $\rho_{YY'}^2$.

Let us start with what might be considered the basic assumption, which is that observed variance σ_Y^2 can be parsed into three components: good variance σ_{IV}^2, bad random variance σ_R^2, and bad systematic variance σ_O^2. Thus, what we might call the base equation is as follows:

$$\sigma_Y^2 = \sigma_{IV}^2 + \sigma_R^2 + \sigma_O^2. \qquad \text{(Base Equation)}$$

The issue now is to figure out how to obtain σ_{IV}^2, σ_R^2, and σ_O^2 from variables that can be estimated from data. We can start with figuring out how to get σ_{IV}^2. Let us first multiply the proportion of good variance ρ_{XY}^2 by the total variance σ_Y^2 to obtain the amount (not proportion) of good variance σ_{IV}^2, as shown in Equation 13.1:

$$\sigma_{IV}^2 = \rho_{XY}^2 \sigma_Y^2. \qquad (13.1)$$

Note that both ρ_{XY}^2 and σ_Y^2 can be estimated directly from the data, so we have already completed one-third of our task.

Let us now employ the classical definition of reliability from Chapter 9, which is true score variance in Y divided by total variance in Y:

$$\rho_{YY'}^2 = \frac{\sigma_T^2}{\sigma_Y^2}. \qquad (13.2)$$

Algebraic manipulation of Equation 13.2 provides Equation 13.3 or how to estimate true score variance:

$$\sigma_T^2 = \rho_{YY'}^2 \sigma_Y^2. \qquad (13.3)$$

If we have tested the reliability of Y, we can use the obtained sample value to estimate the population reliability. And with total variance in Y estimated from the data, there is no problem calculating true score variance even though it cannot be observed directly.

Then too, total variance can be partitioned into true score variance and random variance, as Equation 13.4 shows. This equation also features in Chapter 9:

$$\sigma_Y^2 = \sigma_T^2 + \sigma_R^2. \qquad (13.4)$$

Equation 13.4 can be algebraically rearranged to elicit random variance:

$$\sigma_R^2 = \sigma_Y^2 - \sigma_T^2 \tag{13.5}$$

And we can substitute Equation 13.3 into Equation 13-5 to obtain Equation 13-6.

$$\sigma_R^2 = \sigma_Y^2 - \rho_{YY'}^2 \sigma_Y^2 = \left(1 - \rho_{YY'}^2\right)\sigma_Y^2. \tag{13.6}$$

We now have equations for estimating good variance (Equation 13.1) and random bad variance (Equation 13.6) in terms of variables we can estimate from data, and our task is two-thirds completed. But what about systematic bad variance?

We now can use our Base Equation and substitute Equation 13.1 (good variance) and Equation (13.6) (random bad variance) into the appropriate places to arrive at Equation 13.7.

$$\sigma_Y^2 = \rho_{XY}^2 \sigma_Y^2 + \sigma_Y^2 - \rho_{YY'}^2 \sigma_Y^2 + \sigma_O^2. \tag{13.7}$$

After some algebraic rearrangement, we arrive at Equation 13.8:

$$\sigma_O^2 = \sigma_Y^2 - \sigma_Y^2 - \rho_{XY}^2 \sigma_Y^2 + \rho_{YY'}^2 \sigma_Y^2 \tag{13.8}$$

And simplifying renders Equation 13-9.

$$\sigma_O^2 = \rho_{YY'}^2 \sigma_Y^2 - \rho_{XY}^2 \sigma_Y^2 = \sigma_Y^2 \left(\rho_{YY'}^2 - \rho_{XY}^2\right) \tag{13.9}$$

Our task is now finished. We can obtain good variance σ_{IV}^2, bad random variance σ_R^2, and bad systematic variance σ_O^2 based on variables we can estimate directly from data (the observed correlation, the observed variance, and the observed reliability). We only need employ Equation 13.1 for good variance, Equation 13.6 for random bad variance, and Equation 13.9 for systematic bad variance.

Experiment

The previous section assumed a correlational study and the present section will assume an experiment. Although the equations amount to the same thing in both sections, researchers who perform experiments are used to *T*-statistics, so I provide another derivation that features *T*-statistics.

To commence, Harris (1994) showed how to obtain variance accounted for from *T*-statistics, written below as Equation 13.10:

$$\rho_{XY}^2 = \frac{T^2}{T^2 + df}, \text{ where } df \text{ refers to degrees of freedom.} \tag{13.10}$$

188 *Measurement Issues*

Multiplying the right side of Equation 13.10 by total variance gives the amount of variance in the dependent variable accounted for—or in this case hopefully caused—as it is an experiment, by the independent variable. This is shown via Equation 13.11:

$$\sigma_{IV}^2 = \frac{T^2}{T^2 + df} \sigma_Y^2. \tag{13.11}$$

As we already know how to get σ_R^2 from Equation 13.6, two-thirds of our work in this section is already finished. It only remains to obtain σ_O^2 on terms of variables estimable from the data. We can use the Base Equation for this purpose, substituting Equations 13.6 and 13.11 for the random bad variance σ_R^2 and good variance σ_{IV}^2 to obtain Equation 13.12:

$$\sigma_Y^2 = \frac{T^2}{T^2 + df} \sigma_Y^2 + \sigma_Y^2 - \rho_{YY'}^2 \sigma_Y^2 + \sigma_O^2. \tag{13.12}$$

Algebraic rearrangement gives Equation 13.13:

$$\sigma_O^2 = \sigma_y^2 - \sigma_y^2 + \rho_{YY'}^2 \sigma_Y^2 - \frac{T^2}{T^2 + df} \sigma_Y^2. \tag{13.13}$$

And simplifying gives Equation 13.14:

$$\sigma_O^2 = \rho_{YY'}^2 \sigma_Y^2 - \frac{T^2}{T^2 + df} \sigma_Y^2 = \sigma_Y^2 \left(\rho_{YY'}^2 - \frac{T^2}{T^2 + df} \right). \tag{13.14}$$

Thus, in experimental terms, we have good variance σ_{IV}^2, random bad variance σ_R^2, and systematic bad variance σ_O^2, from Equations 13.11, 13.6, and 13.14, respectively. I include all these in a convenient table (Table 13.1).

Examples

Imagine a correlational study, where the total variance in the dependent variable is 100, the correlation between the two variables is 0.40, and the reliability of the dependent variable is 0.70. Thus, based on observed data, we have the following estimates:

- $est\ \sigma_Y^2 = 100$,
- $est\ \rho_{XY} = 0.40$, so $\rho_{XY}^2 = 0.16$,
- $est\ \rho_{YY'}^2 = 0.70$.

Table 13.1 A table of equations for obtaining good variance σ_{IV}^2, random bad variance σ_R^2, and systematic bad variance σ_O^2, from variables estimable from observable data

Type of Study	Equations
Correlational Study	
Good Variance	$\sigma_{IV}^2 = \rho_{XY}^2$
Random Bad Variance	$\sigma_R^2 = \sigma_Y^2 - \rho_{YY'}^2 \sigma_Y^2$ or $\sigma_R^2 = \sigma_Y^2(1 - \rho_{YY'}^2)$
Systematic Bad Variance	$\sigma_O^2 = \rho_{YY'}^2 \sigma_Y^2 - \rho_{XY}^2 \sigma_Y^2$ or $\sigma_O^2 = \sigma_Y^2(\rho_{YY'}^2 - \rho_{XY}^2)$
Experiment	
Good Variance	$\sigma_{IV}^2 = \dfrac{T^2}{T^2 + df} \sigma_Y^2$
Random Bad Variance	$\sigma_R^2 = \sigma_Y^2 - \rho_{YY'}^2 \sigma_Y^2$ or $\sigma_R^2 = \sigma_Y^2(1 - \rho_{YY'}^2)$
Systematic Bad Variance	$\sigma_O^2 = \rho_{YY'}^2 \sigma_Y^2 - \dfrac{T^2}{T^2 + df} \sigma_Y^2$ or $\sigma_O^2 = \sigma_Y^2\left(\rho_{YY'}^2 - \dfrac{T^2}{T^2 + df}\right)$

Instantiating these into the first three equations in Table 10.1, provides our answers.

- $\text{est } \sigma_{IV}^2 = \rho_{XY}^2 \sigma_Y^2 = 0.16 \cdot 100 = 16,$
- $\text{est } \sigma_R^2 = \sigma_Y^2(1 - \rho_{YY'}^2) = 100(1 - 0.70) = 30,$
- $\text{est } \sigma_O^2 = \sigma_Y^2(\rho_{YY'}^2 - \rho_{XY}^2) = 100(0.70 - 0.16) = 54.$

As a check, we would hope that the three component variances would add to the total variance, and they do: $16 + 30 + 54 = 100$.

Or consider an experimental study, where observed data provide the following estimates:

- $\text{est } \sigma_Y^2 = 500,$
- $\text{est } T = 3.00$ and $df = 1000$, so $T^2 = 9.00,$
- $\text{est } \rho_{YY'}^2 = 0.80.$

Instantiating these into the last set of three equations in Table 10.1 provides the following answers.

- $\text{est } \sigma_{IV}^2 = \dfrac{T^2}{T^2 + df} \sigma_Y^2 = \dfrac{9.00}{9.00 + 1000} 500 = 4.46$

- $\text{est } \sigma_R^2 = \sigma_Y^2 \left(1 - \rho_{YY'}^2\right) = 500(1 - 0.80) = 100$

- $\text{est } \sigma_O^2 = \sigma_Y^2 \left(\rho_{YY'}^2 - \dfrac{T^2}{T^2 + df} \right) = 500\left(0.80 - \dfrac{9.00}{9.00 + 1000} \right) = 395.54.$

Let us check whether the component variances add to the total variance, and they do: $4.46 + 100 + 395.54 = 500$.

In the correlational example, the total variance was at the convenient value of 100, so the component variances we found also equal the percentages of good variance, random bad variance, and systematic bad variance. In the experimental example, this is not so, as the total variance was 500 and not 100. Therefore, the findings do not reflect the percentages of good variance, random bad variance, or systematic bad variance. However, it is easy to make the conversion simply by dividing each by the total variance and multiplying by 100%. I performed these operations below.

- *percentage of good variance* $= \dfrac{4.46}{500} 100\% = 0.892\%.$

- *percentage of bad random variance* $= \dfrac{100}{500} 100\% = 20\%.$

- *percentage of bad systematic variance* $= \dfrac{395.54}{500} 100\% = 79.108\%.$

The three bullet-listed percentages should add up to 100%, and they do: $0.892\% + 20\% + 79.108\% = 100\%$.

A caveat on the examples is that estimates obtained from samples can be biased, and so slight modifications might be advisable for your actual research (see Trafimow, 2017c). However, as this book is conceptual, the modifications will not be described here. In any event, it matters little if the sample size is sufficiently large and you can review Chapter 6 on calculating sample sizes.

Planning Future Research

A standard operating procedure for researchers interested in accounting for variance is to keep performing studies—and keep publishing articles—where each article adds another predictor variable, with the net effect of accounting for an increment in variance relative to previous articles. For example, there are thousands of articles in the theory of reasoned action tradition where researchers have added a touted variable to the list of predictor variables, with a slight increase in variance accounted for in either behavioral intentions or actual behaviors. The foregoing equations can be used in such a multiple predictor—or multiple regression—research paradigm.

Let us consider an example but also consider the implications for future research. Imagine a study where the researcher has a set of predictor variables and where the estimated total variance is 100. In addition, the estimated reliability of the dependent variable is 0.30. Also, suppose that the estimated multiple correlation between all the predictor variables and the dependent variable equals 0.20, so that the variance accounted for is 0.04. As the researcher has only accounted for 4% of the variance in the dependent variable with the whole set of predictor variables, common sense may suggest the advisability of searching for more predictor variables to account for the other 96% of the variance. With common sense in mind, let us crunch the numbers but using the symbol ρ^2_{XY} to refer to the variance accounted in the dependent variable by all the predictor variables, rather than a single predictor variable, as in a previous example. To continue, we have the following values.

- $est\ \sigma^2_Y = 100$,

- $est\ \rho_{XY} = 0.20$, so $\rho^2_{XY} = 0.04$,

- $est\ \rho^2_{YY'} = 0.30$.

Instantiating these values into the top three equations from Table 10.1 renders the following results.

- $est\ \sigma^2_{IV} = \rho^2_{XY}\sigma^2_Y = 0.04 \cdot 100 = 4$,

- $est\ \sigma^2_R = \sigma^2_Y(1 - \rho^2_{YY'}) = 100(1 - 0.30) = 70$,

- $est\ \sigma^2_O = \sigma^2_Y(\rho^2_{YY'} - \rho^2_{XY}) = 100(0.30 - 0.04) = 26$.

As usual, it is good to make sure the component variances sum to the total variance, and they do: $4 + 70 + 26 = 100$.

The good variance is only 4. Because the total variance is 100, we can say, too, that the good variance is 4% of the total variance. Similarly, the percentage of systematic bad variance is 26% whereas the random bad variance is a whopping 70%. Thus, we see that the actual numbers run counter to what may have seemed commonsensical. With only 26% of systematic bad variance to account for with future research, such research is unlikely to result in big dividends. In contrast, because there is so much random variance, potentially much larger research dividends might come about by devising a more reliable dependent variable.

To see how that might work, suppose that the researcher, after careful thought and perhaps the collection of additional data, creates a new dependent variable but this time with reliability equal to 0.80. This would obviously be a considerable increase from the 0.30 value we had before. What would the variance components be in this case?

For illustration, suppose that we keep the good variance the same at 4, and the systematic bad variance the same at 26. The interesting issue is what happens to the random bad variance, which obviously decreases with a more reliable dependent variable. Recalling Equation 13.3, we know the following, using numbers from the example and where reliability was 0.30: $\sigma^2_T = \rho^2_{YY'}\sigma^2_Y = 0.3 \cdot 100 = 30$. Suppose we keep true score variance σ^2_T constant at 30 and apply Equation 13.3 to the new reliability coefficient of 0.8: $\sigma^2_T = \rho^2_{YY'}\sigma^2_Y$. It follows that $\sigma^2_Y = \dfrac{\sigma^2_T}{\rho^2_{YY'}}$, and the new value for total variance is: $\sigma_Y^2 = \dfrac{30}{0.80} = 37.5$. Thus, we now have all the pieces needed to get the new random variance: $est\ \sigma_R^2 = \sigma_Y^2\left(1 - \rho_{YY'}^2\right) = 37.5(1-0.80) = 7.5$.

Now, let us figure the new variance accounted for by each component, remembering that the new total variance is 37.5 as opposed to 100 as before. Again, this is because increasing reliability greatly reduces random variance, which is a component of total variance. The values are bullet-listed below.

- $\text{percentage of good variance} = \dfrac{4.00}{37.5}100\% = 11\%$.

- $\text{percentage of bad random variance} = \dfrac{7.5}{37.5}100\% = 20\%$.

- $\text{percentage of bad systematic variance} = \dfrac{26.00}{37.5}100\% = 69\%$.

The percentages should add to 100%, and they do: $11\% + 20\% + 69\% = 100\%$. The main point, however, is that the previous picture has now changed dramatically. First, simply by increasing the reliability of the test, we have reduced the percentage of random bad variance from 70% to 20%. In addition, reducing the random bad variance also reduced the total variance, so that the percentage of good variance increased substantially from 4% to 11%. Finally, the percentage of systematic bad variance increased from 26% to 69%. Increasing the reliability of the dependent variable betters both the percentage of good variance and the percentage of systematic bad variance.

Now, what are the implications for future research? In contrast to before, when we concluded that there just was not enough systematic bad variance there to make it worthwhile to search for new independent variables that could account for it, we now see that there is a strong percentage of systematic bad variance with the more reliable measure. Thus, with 69% systematic bad variance there to be accounted for by future independent variables, it now makes much more sense to search for them. The search has much better possibilities for paying off impressively. More generally, the ability to provide researchers with a good idea of whether future research efforts are better devoted towards increasing reliability, or better devoted to finding new independent variables, is a strong plus for tripartite parsing.

Implications of Tripartite Parsing for Evaluating the Worth of an Independent Variable

Consider again the example from the previous section where reliability was only 0.30, total variance was 100, and the correlation between the predictor variables and the dependent variable was only 0.2, so the variance accounted for was 0.04. In this case, we saw that the percentage of good variance was only 4%, thereby suggesting that the researcher has failed miserably to find good predictor variables. However, there is another way to look at it. Consider that the percentage of random bad variance was 70% and the percentage of systematic bad variance was 26%. Because the percentage of random bad variance was so ridiculously large, there was obviously not a lot of room for the predictor variables to do well. Thus, the anemic value of 4% good variance might not be as pessimistic as it might seem, in the following sense. As the percentage of good variance is 4% and the percentage of systematic bad variance is 26%, the total percentage of nonrandom (systematic) variance is 4% + 26% = 30%. Well, then, if we consider the percentage of good variance as a fraction of the percentage of nonrandom variance, we have the following: $\frac{4\%}{30\%} = 13.33\%$. Obviously, the value of 13% seems more impressive than the value of 4%, which suggests that perhaps the independent variables are not so badly chosen as appearances suggest. And we can take this one step further in the next section.

Don't Ignore the Reliability of the Predictor Variable

Thus far, although the reliability of the dependent variable has played an important role in our tripartite parsing of variance, we have not considered the reliability of the independent variable. For easy calculations, we can restrict ourselves to a single independent variable and a single dependent variable. Suppose that the reliability of the dependent variable is very large but the correlation between the independent and dependent variable is nevertheless extremely low, so that the independent variable only accounts for a trivial percentage of variance in the dependent variable. It might seem we are stuck because the reliability of the dependent variable is already impressive, and little we can do is likely to increase it very much. It might seem obvious then, as we saw in a foregoing section, that the way to make progress is to find better independent variables, and if we were to crunch the numbers as previously, the results would doubtless bear us out. However, the purpose of the present section is to place a large qualification on that conclusion, because we have not considered the reliability of the independent variable.

If the independent variable accounts for very little good variance in a reliable dependent variable, there are two candidate reasons for why. The most obvious reason is that we simply chose a poor independent variable for accounting for variance in the dependent variable. However, a less obvious—but nevertheless possibly crucial—possibility, is that we chose the independent variable well but have an unreliable measure of it. Let us play this out by supposing that the reliability of the dependent variable is at the respectable value of 0.8, the true correlation coefficient is 0.6, and the reliability of the independent variable is either 0.1 or 0.9. These latter values, especially the 0.1 value, might not be realistic, but it will provide a dramatic illustration. Recall from Chapter 9 the attenuation formula, that I copied again here as Equation 13.15:

$$\rho_{XY} = \rho_{T_X T_Y} \sqrt{\rho_{XX'} \rho_{YY'}}. \tag{13.15}$$

Hopefully, Equation 13.15 looks familiar!

Anyway, let us run out the consequences, instantiating our values into Equation 13.15.

- The 0.1 case: $\rho_{XY} = \rho_{T_X T_Y} \sqrt{\rho_{XX'} \rho_{YY'}} = 0.6\sqrt{0.10 \cdot 0.80} = 0.17$.
- The 0.9 case: $\rho_{XY} = \rho_{T_X T_Y} \sqrt{\rho_{XX'} \rho_{YY'}} = 0.60\sqrt{0.90 \cdot 0.80} = 0.51$.

The bullet-listed examples show the surprising effects that independent variable reliability can have on its ability to account for variance in the dependent variable. When the reliability of the independent variable is set at 0.10, the correlation is only 0.17, and so the independent variable only accounts for approximately 3% of the variance in the dependent variable. But when the reliability of the independent variable is set at 0.90, the correlation is 0.51, and so the independent variable accounts for approximately 26% of the variance in the dependent variable. The difference between 3% and 26% is obviously huge and exemplifies the gains to be had by considering reliability in the independent variable, as well as reliability in the dependent variable.

Thus, the moral of the story is, do not forget to look at the reliability of the independent variable!

Chapter Summary

We commenced at the conceptual level, with an explanation of good variance and bad variance. Although this distinction has proven useful in the social sciences, a potential limitation is that bad variance can be random or systematic. Thus, there are really three categories of variance, not two. And these are good variance, random bad variance, and systematic bad variance. An advantage of the tripartite variance parsing is that having good estimates of all three types of variance aids in making decisions about future research. If most of the bad variance is random, and not much of it is systematic, then future research to discover new independent variables to account for more variance is unlikely to result in a big payoff for the researcher. There just is not enough systematic bad variance there to be accounted for. In contrast, if most of the bad variance is systematic, then the likelihood of finding new independent variables that account for substantial proportions of it increases. If the researcher succeeds in finding new independent variables that account for more systematic bad variance, then that systematic bad variance is thereby transformed into good variance.

A tripartite variance parsing also can aid in interpreting the present study because it is possible to assess the percentage of good variance with respect to either the percentage of random bad variance or the percentage of systematic bad variance. In turn, even if there is very little good variance, the good variance might nevertheless be a substantial portion of all systematic variance (good variance plus systematic bad variance), which suggests that the researcher did a better job than it otherwise might seem in choosing effective independent variables.

Following the conceptual discussion, we proved the Equations in Table 10.1 for estimating good variance, random bad variance, and systematic bad variance. And we derived the equations from either a correlational perspective or an experimental perspective.

Subsequently, we proceeded through examples to clarify how to use the Equations in Table 10.1. However, the examples also showed that how good variance, random bad variance, and systematic bad variance come out can indicate quite different conclusions. We also saw an example of how dependent variable unreliability can dramatically alter these variances with different conclusions for the conduction of future research.

Next, we saw that even with respect to the present study, not worrying about future research, the tripartite parsing of variance suggests conclusions. For example, seemingly trivial good variance might not be trivial if compared to all systematic variance as opposed to total variance that includes the random variance component.

Finally, I showed that although the reliability of the independent variable does not figure into the equations in Table 10.1, it nevertheless influences good variance. And there was an example of how the amount of good variance can change dramatically, depending on the reliability of the independent variable.

Hopefully, in your own work, you will not settle for contrasting good variance against bad variance. Instead, you should consider both types of bad variance, random and systematic, with the possibility of contrasting good variance against each, or contrasting the two kinds of bad variance against each other to aid in decisions regarding future research.

14 Shocking Measurement Implications

Consider again a matter that has concerned us throughout, which is that effect sizes in the social sciences, whether in an experimental or correlational study, tend to be small. This is problematic for multiple reasons (Trafimow et al., under submission). Perhaps the most obvious reason is that

DOI: 10.4324/9781003365167-16

if the effect size is small, it fails to provide a convincing reason for intervention or policy change. For example, suppose a researcher finds that a manipulation decreases prejudice, but the effect size is small. Given that a large-scale implementation carries with it significant financial costs, not to mention the political difficulties involved, the implementation would be a difficult sell.

Nor does switching from an applied perspective to a basic research perspective help much. If a study that purports to test a theory finds a small effect size, alternative explanations are quite plausible. Perhaps the randomization was slightly imperfect. Perhaps the manipulation affected something else, in addition to (or instead of) the touted independent variable, and it is the something else that was responsible for the effect on the dependent variable. And so on. Of course, these alternative explanations are possible even if the effect size is large, but they are more plausible if the effect size is small. In turn, that increased plausibility undermines the empirical case for the theory. It is unfortunate that the dominance of the null hypothesis significance testing procedure has caused many researchers to take a dichotomous view, where the effect is "there" or "not there," whereas researchers ought to be concerned with the size of the effect as one, though far from the only, way to address the issue of alternative explanations.

Once we acknowledge the importance of the size of the effect, there comes the inevitable question: Why are social science effect sizes mostly small? Although there are multiple answers, the answer to be addressed in this chapter is that poor measurement in the social sciences is responsible, in important part, for small effect sizes. Put simply, if our tests of constructs are unreliable or otherwise problematic, then small effect sizes are statistically inevitable. The ideas to be presented come from a paper that I recently submitted with my colleagues Mike Hyman and Alena Kostyk (Trafimow, Hyman, & Kostyk, submitted manuscript).

Reliability Reminders

Hopefully, you recall the lessons learned in Chapter 9, one of which is that reliability sets an upper limit on the ability of a test of a construct to predict anything. If not, it may pay for you to return to Chapter 9 and review before proceeding. In addition, as was explained in Chapter 9, there are many ways of indexing reliability, though they may not all be equally justified.

Another point made in Chapter 9 is that by far the most popular reliability index in substantive social science research is Cronbach's alpha. And we saw that Cronbach's alpha depends on two entities: the interitem correlations and the number of items. Thus, one can obtain an impressive value for Cronbach's alpha by having items that correlate well with each other, by having many items even if the items do not go well together, or both. Most researchers consider a Cronbach's alpha of 0.70 or greater to be acceptable, though a few researchers prefer setting the threshold at 0.80. Either way, it is not particularly difficult to obtain a value for Cronbach's alpha that exceeds the threshold.

However, Chapter 9 covered the lack of clarity about whether Cronbach's alpha functions as a reliability index (the usual position), an internal consistency index, or both. The position in Chapter 9 is that Cronbach's alpha functions as neither. But for now, let us suppose that the position advocated in Chapter 9 is wrong, and that Cronbach's alpha really does provide a high-quality index of the reliability of the test. If Cronbach's alpha provides a high-quality index for the reliability of the test, we would expect that, keeping the number of items constant, increasing the interitem correlations ought to increase the ability of the test to predict criterion variables. Here is the logic. We know from the attenuation and dis-attenuation equations in Chapter 9, that the greater the reliability, the greater the ability of a test to predict scores on a criterion measure. In turn, according to the interpretation of Cronbach's alpha as a high-quality reliability index, increasing interitem correlations increases reliability. It follows unavoidably that increasing a test's interitem correlations increases the ability of that test to predict a criterion measure. But is this so? In addition, what is the effect of adding items on a test's ability to predict a criterion variable?

The Effects of Interitem Correlations, and Adding Items on Prediction

It would be convenient if we had an equation that describes, simultaneously, the effects of interitem correlations and number of items on the ability of a test to predict scores on a criterion measure. Fortunately, Guilford and Fruchter (1973) supplied the equation in their famous book (p. 386): *Fundamental statistics in psychology and education*. It is described as Equation 14.1 below and will play a crucial role for the argument to be made here:

$$r_{cs} = \frac{\sum r_{ci}\sigma_i}{\sqrt{\sum \sigma_i^2 + 2\sum r_{ij}\sigma_i\sigma_j}}. \qquad (14.1)$$

Equation 14.1 has the following components:

- r_{cs} is the correlation between the test and the criterion,
- r_{ci} is the correlation between any one-item X_i and the criterion,
- σ_i is the item's standard deviation,
- r_{ij} is the correlation between X_i and any other item X_j, with j greater than i.

For the sake of clarity, I expanded Equation 14.1 for tests with one, two, three, four, or five items. These expanded equations appear in Table 14.1. Finally, in Equation 14.1, the components are weighted equally. Guilford and Fruchter also supplied an equation for when the components are weighted unequally, but the simpler equation for unweighted components is sufficient for present purposes.

Equation 14.1 suggests two crucial implications. One of these implications is that adding items influences the ability of a test to predict a criterion variable. The second is that the size of the interitem correlation coefficients also influences the ability of a test to predict a criterion variable. Let us explore these implications in detail by creating Figure 14.1, based on the equations in Table 14.1.

Consider Figure 14.1, where all interitem correlation coefficients are kept the same, but that value ranges from 0.1 to 0.9. There are five curves, representing when the test includes five items, four items, three items, two items, or one item, from top to bottom. Finally, the item-criterion correlations were kept constant at 0.45.

The figure illustrates important points. One of these is that adding items increases the ability of a test to predict a criterion, as is demonstrated by the heights of the different curves. A caveat, however, is that adding items is not always good, if the added items poorly predict the criterion. We will see this later.

Secondly, and crucially, Figure 10.1 addresses the question we had asked about whether having large interitem correlation coefficients is good or bad for predicting a criterion. According to the combined implications of the classical theory and Cronbach's alpha, if we keep the number of items constant, such as each of the curves in the figure, the larger the interitem correlations

198 Measurement Issues

Table 14.1 Expansions of Equation 3 for tests with one, two, three, four, or five components

Number of Components	Equation
1	$r_{cs} = r_{c1}$
1 and 2	$r_{cs} = \dfrac{r_{c1}\sigma_1 + r_{c2}\sigma_2}{\sqrt{\sigma_1^2 + \sigma_2^2 + 2r_{12}\sigma_1\sigma_2}}$
1, 2, and 3	$r_{cs} = \dfrac{r_{c1}\sigma_1 + r_{c2}\sigma_2 + r_{c3}\sigma_3}{\sqrt{\sigma_1^2 + \sigma_2^2 + \sigma_3^2 + 2(r_{12}\sigma_1\sigma_2 + r_{13}\sigma_1\sigma_3 + r_{23}\sigma_2\sigma_3)}}$
1, 2, 3, and 4	$r_{cs} = \dfrac{r_{c1}\sigma_1 + r_{c2}\sigma_2 + r_{c3}\sigma_3 + r_{c4}\sigma_4}{\sqrt{\sigma_1^2 + \sigma_2^2 + \sigma_3^2 + \sigma_4^2 + 2(r_{12}\sigma_1\sigma_2 + r_{13}\sigma_1\sigma_3 + r_{14}\sigma_1\sigma_4 + r_{23}\sigma_2\sigma_3 + r_{24}\sigma_2\sigma_4 + r_{34}\sigma_3\sigma_4)}}$
1, 2, 3, 4, and 5	$r_{cs} = \dfrac{r_{c1}\sigma_1 + r_{c2}\sigma_2 + r_{c3}\sigma_3 + r_{c4}\sigma_4 + r_{c5}\sigma_5}{\sqrt{\sigma_1^2 + \sigma_2^2 + \sigma_3^2 + \sigma_4^2 + \sigma_5^2 + 2\begin{pmatrix} r_{12}\sigma_1\sigma_2 + r_{13}\sigma_1\sigma_3 + r_{14}\sigma_1\sigma_4 + r_{15}\sigma_1\sigma_5 + r_{23}\sigma_2\sigma_3 \\ + r_{24}\sigma_2\sigma_4 + r_{25}\sigma_2\sigma_5 + r_{34}\sigma_3\sigma_4 + r_{35}\sigma_3\sigma_5 + r_{45}\sigma_4\sigma_5 \end{pmatrix}}}$

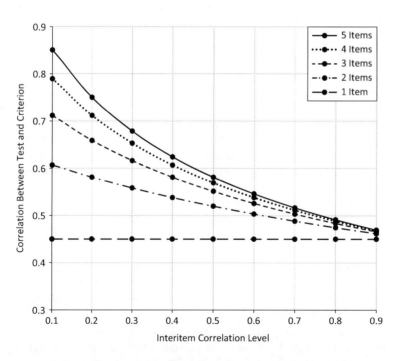

Figure 14.1 The correlation between the whole test and the criterion ranges along the vertical axis as a function of the interitem correlation level along the horizontal axis. The curves represent tests with five items, four items, three items, two items, or one item, from top to bottom.

the better the prediction of the criterion. However, Figure 14.1 shows the opposite! As the interitem correlations increase, the ability of the test to predict the criterion decreases. Thus, having large interitem correlations, what everyone wishes to achieve given the dominance of Cronbach's alpha, harms prediction.

In Figure 14.1, the item–criterion correlation coefficients were kept constant so that all added items were 'good' items in the sense that they correlated as well as the first item with the criterion. But what if we add 'bad' items that do not correlate as well as the first item with the criterion? For example, we could set the correlation between the first item and the criterion at 0.55, and then add items that correlate at a much lower level with the criterion, say at the 0.10 level. Figure 14.2 runs out the consequences of adding poor items.

Figure 14.2 illustrates what happens when poor items are added. In one way it contrasts dramatically with Figure 14.1 and in another way it supports Figure 14.1. The obvious contrast is provided by the fact that, this time, the top curve represents one-item tests, and the bottom curve represents five item tests. This time, adding items is bad, whereas previously, adding items was good. The reason, of course, is that previously we added good items and this time we are adding bad items. Thus, the mantra of "add more items" does not work if the items are bad ones.

However, Figure 14.2 supports Figure 14.1 in a crucial respect, which is that the curves proceed downward as the interitem correlation coefficients decrease. Large interitem correlation coefficients remain bad if the researcher's goal is to predict a criterion.

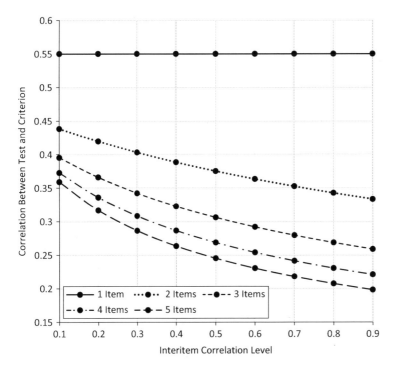

Figure 14.2 The correlation between the whole test and the criterion ranges along the vertical axis as a function of the interitem correlation level along the horizontal axis. The top curve represents tests with one item where the item–criterion correlation equals 0.55. The other curves represent the addition of more items, where the added items correlate only at the 0.1 level with the criterion.

There are two conclusions. Adding items aids in prediction or harms prediction, depending on how well the added items correlate with the criterion. In addition, and perhaps more important, large interitem correlations harm prediction.

The conclusion that large interitem correlation coefficients harm prediction bears on a longstanding controversy in the social sciences. Although the majority position has been that it is best to have large interitem correlation coefficients, there has been a contrary position that large interitem correlation coefficients are bad due to their potentially indicating that the test fails to cover the construct. A counterargument to the contrary position is that small interitem correlation coefficients indicate that the construct is really two or more constructs that should not be amalgamated. To my knowledge, the only experimentally (not based on correlation coefficients) obtained data of relevance is the result of my own research on the notion of perceived behavioral control (Ajzen, 1988). Normally, perceived behavioral control is considered a person's perceived ability to control whether they perform the behavior of interest, and it is measured with items such as "Performing the behavior is under my control (not under my control)" or "Performing the behavior is easy (difficult)." However, it is possible to argue that these are not the same, as it is possible for a behavior to be difficult to perform but still under one's control. I and some colleagues performed a set of experiments where we used separate measures of control and difficulty (Trafimow et al., 2002). In one experiment, we performed a manipulation that influenced responses to items measuring control but not difficulty; and in another experiment we performed a manipulation that influenced responses to items measuring difficulty but not control. Thus, we demonstrated that what seemed a unitary construct—perceived behavioral control—is really two constructs, which are perceived control and perceived difficulty. This finding suggests two items. Firstly, perceived behavioral control measures tend to be highly reliable, according to Cronbach's alpha, but we now see that there are nevertheless two constructs. Secondly, we can ask a pointed question: If even reasonably intercorrelated items can be shown to measure two constructs rather than a single construct, how much more suspicious should we be of tests with small interitem correlation coefficients?

And yet, Figures 14.1 and 14.2 show that large interitem correlations harm prediction. This seems to support the position that it really is best to have small interitem correlations. Is there a way out? There is, but it is necessary to move to a new idea.

To Aggregate or Not, That Is the Question!

Until now, we have assumed that researchers wish to aggregate items to have multiple item tests. And the assumption is so true that it is a cliché. However, that everyone desires to aggregate items to have multiple item tests need not indicate that this is what they ought to desire. There is another option, which is to keep the items separate or dis-aggregated. An obvious counterargument is that Figure 14.1 shows clearly that if one has good items, it is better to have more of them than fewer of them. However, there is a way to dis-aggregate and nevertheless have multiple items. And the way to do this is to use multiple regression, entering each item as a separate predictor variable. I will demonstrate by considering a test with two items that are either aggregated or dis-aggregated. The lesson to be learned can be generalized to more items, but then the multiple regression equation gets more complicated, and the complication is unnecessary for explanatory purposes.

The formula for obtaining a multiple correlation coefficient, that is, the ability to predict a criterion from two test items, is given by Equation 14.2 below.

$$R_{c.12} = \sqrt{\frac{r_{c1}^2 + r_{c2}^2 - 2r_{c1}r_{c2}r_{12}}{1 - r_{12}^2}}. \tag{14.2}$$

The symbols are as follows.

- $R_{c.12}$ is the multiple correlation between the two test items and the criterion.
- r_{c1} is the squared correlation between the first item and the criterion.
- r_{c2} is the correlation between the second item and the criterion.
- r_{12} is the correlation between the first item and second item.

Note that as in the equations in Table 14.1, we still have the item–criterion correlation coefficients r_{c1} and r_{c2}, and we also have the interitem correlation coefficient r_{12}.

Recalling that in aggregated tests, large interitem correlation coefficients are bad for prediction, what about when we dis-aggregate as in Equation 14.2? Figure 14.3 shows that much depends on the spread in the ability of the test items to predict the criterion.

Figure 14.3 shows what happens to the ability of two test items to predict a criterion depending on (a) whether they are aggregated into a single test (Equation 14.1) or dis-aggregated (Equation 14.2) and (b) whether the spread between the two-item–criterion correlation coefficients is large or small. Commencing with a small spread, the two black curves are extremely close together, indicating that aggregation versus dis-aggregation matters very little with only

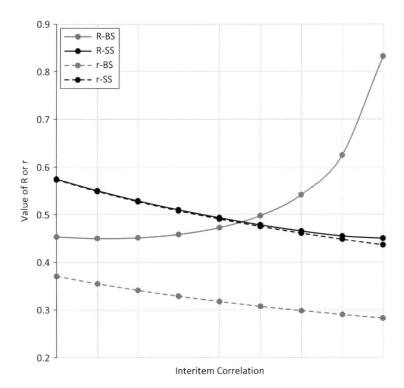

Figure 14.3 The value of the multiple correlation coefficient or bivariate correlation coefficient ranges along the vertical axis as a function of the interitem correlation along the horizontal axis. Curves are in gray for a big spread (BS) in item–criterion correlation coefficients (0.45 versus 0.1) or a small spread (SS) in item–criterion correlation coefficients (0.45 versus 0.4). Solid curves represent multiple correlation coefficients (R), and dashed curves represent bivariate correlation coefficients (r).

202 *Measurement Issues*

a very slight advantage for dis-aggregation (solid black curve) over aggregation (dashed black curve). However, when there is a large spread, the two gray curves show that dis-aggregation (solid gray curve) potentially has a huge advantage over aggregation (dashed gray curve). Let us consider aggregation when there is a large spread in item–criterion correlation coefficients. In this case, as Figure 10.2 showed, predictive ability is decreased by the inclusion of a bad item. There is no surprise here.

However, the curve representing a large spread in item–criterion correlation coefficients, under dis-aggregation, provides a big surprise. Here, in contrast to the other three curves, there is *better*, not worse, prediction as the interitem correlation coefficient increases. Moreover, if the interitem correlation coefficient is quite large, prediction can be truly impressive. Possibly, this is because of the ability of each item to suppress error variance in the other.

And so, we have a solution to our dilemma. On the one hand, it seems as if large interitem correlation coefficients ought to be good because they increase the likelihood that all the items are measuring the same construct and the Trafimow et al. (2002) demonstration casts suspicion on any tests with interitem correlation coefficients that are not large. On the other hand, Figures 14.1 and 14.2 indicate that large interitem correlation coefficients decrease the ability to predict a criterion. But we are not stuck. By switching from aggregation (Equation 14.1 and Table 14.1) to dis-aggregation (Equation 14.2), we see that finally, a large interitem correlation coefficient can be good. In fact, as Figure 14.3 shows, it can be excellent! What's more, the fact that each solid curve (dis-aggregation) is higher in the figure than its corresponding dashed curve (aggregation) shows that one never loses in predictive ability by dis-aggregating. But does the issue of whether to aggregate or dis-aggregate make a difference with respect to real data as opposed to mathematical simulations?

Real Data

Fortunately, my very good friend and colleague, Mike Hyman, furnished me with some old data he had collected that are perfect for empirically testing the foregoing implications (Hyman et al., 2002). The sample size was 725 participants, substantially larger than most social science studies.

Hyman and his colleagues had conducted a consumer lifestyle study with a focus on consumer affluence that included questions about many consumer-related constructs. They measured affluence with a single affluence item (i.e., "I think I have an affluent lifestyle"). They also measured materialism, using the following six agree–disagree items obtained from Richins (1987), with the last item reverse-scored (Cronbach's $\alpha = 0.71$).

- It's really true that money can buy happiness.
- It is important to me to have really nice things.
- I would like to be rich enough to buy anything I want.
- I'd be happier if I could afford to buy more things.
- It sometimes bothers me quite a bit that I can't afford to buy all the things I want.
- People place too much emphasis on material things. (*reverse-scored*)

Our goal is to predict affluence from materialism but trying both aggregating and dis-aggregating to see which enables the best prediction.

Let us now attempt to predict the affluence item from the materialism items. When the materialism items are aggregated, the test–criterion correlation coefficient is only 0.12. If we use the single best item (the second one), the coefficient rises to 0.26. Finally, under dis-aggregation, the multiple correlation jumps to 0.38, even after adjusting for the number of materialism items. In summary, dis-aggregating wins, and by a lot!

Or consider additional data that Hyman et al. (2002) collected pertaining to predicting an item termed fashion innovativeness from items measuring fashion consciousness (Darden & Perreault, 1976; Lumpkin & Darden, 1982). The fashion innovativeness item is, 'I am among the first to try a new fashion.' The six items measuring fashion consciousness are bullet-listed below (Cronbach's α = 0.86).

- I usually have one or more outfits that are of the very latest style.
- A person should try to dress in style.
- When I must choose between the two I usually dress for fashion, not for comfort.
- An important part of my life and activities is dressing smartly.
- I often try the latest hairdo styles when they change.
- It is important that my clothes be of the latest style.

Let us again test dis-aggregating the items versus aggregating them to predict fashion innovativeness.

Given the obvious relatedness of the fashion consciousness and fashion innovativeness constructs, we would expect better prediction than before. The aggregated scale works well, resulting in a correlation of 0.66. The single best item (the last one) predicts even better, and the correlation jumps to 0.70. However, consistent with Figure 14.3, dis-aggregating yields the best prediction, where the multiple correlation coefficient equals 0.75, controlling for the number of fashion innovativeness items. Again, aggregating performs worst and dis-aggregating performs best.

There is another way to assess the foregoing correlation coefficients, which is to square them to obtain the variance accounted for in the criterion from the test items. Let us first engage in this exercise to consider the prediction of perceived affluence from materialism. The percentages of variance accounted for by aggregation and dis-aggregation are 1% and 14%, which differ by approximately 13%. For predicting fashion consciousness from fashion innovativeness, these values are 44% and 57% for aggregation and dis-aggregation, respectively. This difference also equals approximately 13%.

Conceptual Considerations and Implications

The foregoing quantitative analyses suggest important conceptual implications: items need not measure the same thing, even if they load on the same factor; the meaning of constructs could be unclear, and often is, when researchers propose tests that ostensibly measure them; and single item measures might be better than aggregation.

Items Need Not Measure the Same Thing, Even If They Load on the Same Factor

A typical social science assumption is that all items that load on a factor are indicators of the same construct. However, this is not necessarily so. Researchers typically focus on interitem correlation coefficients, but not item–criterion correlation coefficients. And yet, if item–criterion correlation coefficients differ substantially, then that suggests that no matter how impressive the interitem correlation coefficients, the items nevertheless are not equally good indicators of the construct the test was designed to measure. And worse yet, the items may not even be measuring the same construct. We have already seen an example where ostensible perceived behavioral control items were experimentally shown to really be indicating two different concepts: perceived control and perceived difficulty.

Let us consider an example of items shown to load on the same factor in factor analysis, but that nevertheless may be measuring different constructs. The so-called Big 5 personality traits, which can be remembered easily using the acronym, OCEAN, are openness to experience, conscientiousness, extraversion, agreeableness, and neuroticism (see John, Naumann, & Soto, 2008 for a review). Let us consider what might be the most popular of these: extraversion. Participants indicate the extent of their agreement with items such as the two bullet-listed below.

- Person X is talkative.
- Person X generates a lot of enthusiasm.

The question: Do the two bullet-listed items measure the same construct?

On the one hand, researchers consistently find that the items correlate and load on the same factor, usually labeled 'extraversion.' On the other hand, a quick look at the items themselves suggests otherwise; it is possible for people to be talkative without being enthusiastic and to be enthusiastic without being talkative. Rather than assume that both items measure extraversion, a more plausible assumption is that the item pertaining to being talkative measures talkativeness and the item pertaining to being enthusiastic measures enthusiasm. Moreover, if we were to use both items to predict various criterion behaviors, there is little reason to believe that the item–criterion correlation coefficients would be similar. For example, the talkativeness item likely would better predict the amount of talking people do at parties than would the enthusiasm item. In turn, if there are different item–criterion correlation coefficients, Figure 14.3 suggests that dis-aggregating them would result in far better prediction than typical aggregation.

Or consider the materialism items used in one of the foregoing empirical demonstrations. I repeat the first two of them here.

- It's really true that money can buy happiness.
- It is important to me to have really nice things.

Remember that the inclusion of these items on the materialism factor is because they have been shown to load on the same factor.

Nevertheless, it seems self-evident that whether "money can buy happiness" is different from "owning nice things." The former item is broader than the latter item and whereas "nice things" represent physical objects, people can "buy happiness" by purchasing services (a massage) or experiences (an exotic vacation). We could go back over all the ostensible materialism items and make similar comments about their dissimilarities. Finally, of course, recall the empirical demonstration that dis-aggregation resulted in dramatically superior prediction of affluence than did aggregation, thereby indicating substantial differences in item–criterion correlation coefficients. In turn, substantial differences in item–criterion correlation coefficients support that which is obvious upon merely looking at the items: they do not measure the same construct!

In addition, recall the fashion consciousness items, considered previously to predict fashion innovativeness, and that load on the same factor. I repeat two of them here.

- I usually have one or more outfits that are of the very latest style.
- A person should try to dress in style.

Recall that the fashion consciousness items not only load on the same factor but score an impressive value for Cronbach's alpha equal to 0.86.

But upon looking at the items, despite the strongly positive evidence from factor analysis and Cronbach's alpha, we can see they are quite different. One item is about the clothing people have, whereas the other item is about clothing people should wear. It is quite possible for people to think they should wear clothing but not have it. They might not be able to afford to buy the clothing they think they should wear. Or they might not care enough to buy the clothing they think they should wear. Either way, there would be a discrepancy between the two items, suggesting they are not measuring the same construct. Going back over all the other fashion consciousness items results in similar discrepancies that continue to cast doubt on the items measuring the same construct. And, of course, we have seen empirical evidence too, in the form of accounting for 13% more variance in fashion innovativeness with dis-aggregating than with aggregating. Thus, we see that the item–criterion correlation coefficients are substantially dissimilar, thereby supporting our qualitative assessment that the items seem to be measuring different constructs.

The Meaning of Constructs

We saw in Chapter 1 that most theoretical constructs, such as extraversion, materialism, fashion consciousness, and so on cannot be defined. There is no way to supply a definition that includes everything that we feel ought to be included and exclude everything we feel aught to be excluded. There was discussion in previous chapters about how meaning nevertheless accrues to constructs in a variety of ways. These include connections with other constructs in the theory, auxiliary assumptions connecting constructs with the items designed to measure them, and units in those few cases in the social sciences where researchers have specified them. A crucial implication is that having a well-specified theory can go a long way towards enhancing prediction. The better we understand what a construct means, by dint of its connections with other constructs, the better the auxiliary assumptions we can make linking the construct to specific items designed to measure it. Better theory and auxiliary assumptions might even lead the researcher to include units, thereby increasing specificity of meaning and further leading to better measurement. And, with better measurement, prediction ought to be enhanced even under aggregation.

Furthermore, if the theory specifies the constructs that are supposed to cause, be caused, or otherwise relate to the focal construct, then it ought to be easier to create items that maximize item–criterion correlation coefficients.

The bottom line is that well-specified theories can substantially improve prediction. And yet, social science researchers rarely devote much effort to specifying how their constructs of interest are theoretically connected to other constructs. There is so much focus on measuring the construct itself, that the theory, if there is one at all, is an afterthought with poorly specified connections between constructs. For instance, consider the foregoing demonstrations regarding the prediction of affluence from materialism without any strong theoretical connection, and the prediction of fashion innovativeness from fashion consciousness, again without any strong theoretical connection. Although dis-aggregating clearly was superior to aggregating in both cases, how much better would the correlations have been combining dis-aggregation with tests based on a strong theoretical understanding of the constructs and their relations?

Tests with One Item

I showed that items that load on the same factor need not measure the same construct, even when the factor loadings are augmented by an impressive value for Cronbach's alpha. Then, too, without a strong theory, there is even further reason to doubt that multiple items bear on the same construct. Perhaps the most obvious and simple solution is to have one-item tests. As a further reason to have one-item tests, recall that the single best item in the empirical demonstrations outperformed aggregated tests, though dis-aggregation easily outperformed both the single best item and aggregated tests. A caveat is that the evidence for the single best item over aggregation might be capitalizing on chance, and so cross-validation would be desirable. Despite the caveat, however, there is substantial empirical support in a variety of domains that single items predict criteria approximately as well as aggregated tests for reasonably concrete constructs (e.g., Abdel-Khalek, 1998; Bergkvist & Rossiter, 2007; Cheah et al., 2018; Graf et al., 2018).

The usual argument against one-item measures is that aggregation provides opportunities for random error associated with scores on the different items to cancel each other, thereby rendering a more accurate total test score. However, the apparent simplicity of this argument may hide a more complex issue. In Chapter 9 we learned that, according to the classical theory, the cancelation of random errors leaves the person's true score T. However, we also learned that a person's true score need not equal a person's score on a psychological construct, and there need not even be a psychological construct. For those who insist on a psychological construct, the person's standing on it is often symbolized by θ (theta). The point here, and substantive researchers rarely understand it, is that θ, even assuming there is a θ, need not equal T, so $\theta \neq T$.

If a person's standing on a construct does not equal that person's true score on a test, then we have potentially contradictory notions of what constitutes error. From a true score point of view, all errors are random deviations of observed scores from true scores: $O = T + E$, so $E = O - T$. In contrast, from a theta point of view, errors are deviations from θ: $O = \theta + E$, so $E = O - \theta$. However, if $\theta \neq T$, then we have a self-contradictory conclusion: $E \neq E$! The way out is to understand that E in the classical sense refers to random error whereas E in the theta sense refers to random and systematic error. Thus, it is unclear how well the alleged cancellation of errors works under the assumption that one is measuring a theta, such as materialism, fashion consciousness, and so on.

Although there is literature supporting that one-item tests predict criterion variables as well as aggregating does for relatively concrete constructs, aggregation is often superior for vaguer constructs. Nor is that surprising as Figure 14.1 showed that aggregating more items can improve prediction. But this positive outcome is predicated on the added items not being too much lower in their item–criterion correlation coefficients than the original items. Now, consider that sometimes the ability of any of the items to predict the criterion may not be very impressive. In that case, added items may not be substantially worse, not because they are good items, but because the poorness of the original items with respect to item–criterion correlation coefficients provides such a low bar. In that case, adding even poor items will increase prediction, but the overall ability of the test to predict the criterion may nevertheless be unimpressive. And remember that, although we have good reason to suspect whether multiple items measure the same construct, in general, that suspicion becomes overwhelming for extremely vague constructs. Ironically, there may be many cases where aggregation works better than do one-item scales, but for a bad reason. Added items may measure constructs other than that which they are supposed to measure and that correlate with the criterion too. In that case, we would expect improved prediction of the criterion, under Equation 14.1, but for the wrong theoretical reason.

An obvious argument in favor of aggregation over one-item tests is that there are cases where the added items aid in prediction, just as Figure 14.1 illustrates. From a purely predictive point of view, and not considering anything else, this fact seems to favor aggregation in those cases where it applies. However, a nice characteristic of dis-aggregation is that, remaining with a purely predictive perspective, it works better than aggregation. And we have seen empirical examples where the difference is impressive. Therefore, if all we care about is prediction, dis-aggregation is better than aggregation; having multiple one-item tests is better than aggregating the items into a single test.

Alternatively, we might also care about theoretical coherence. But if multiple items are not measuring the same construct, then aggregation all but guarantees that the whole test invalidly measures the construct. An exception might be if all items are synonymous. Therefore, we again see that dis-aggregating is superior to aggregating.

Well, then, if we take a purely predictive standpoint, dis-aggregating is better than aggregating. And if we take a theoretical standpoint, dis-aggregating is better than aggregating. Therefore, it is safe to say that speaking generally, dis-aggregating is better than aggregating.

Multicollinearity

A potential counterargument stems from standard multiple regression advice not to have predictor items that are too correlated with each other. From that perspective, it might seem that the present advice, to dis-aggregate, is contraindicated. However, remember that multicollinearity is only a problem if you wish to interpret regression coefficients, that is, the coefficients associated with each of the predictor variables. But the goal here is not to interpret regression coefficients, but rather to maximize the multiple correlation coefficient. Thus, multicollinearity need not discommode us. On the contrary, multicollinearity can be strongly positive in the dis-aggregation context, as Figure 14.3 illustrates and as the empirical examples support.

Chapter Summary

We commenced by commiserating over the small effect sizes that seem to be the rule in the social sciences. Small effect sizes are problematic for application because they suggest the application is not likely to make much of a difference. Small effect sizes are problematic for basic research because they are extremely susceptible to alternative explanations. Small effect sizes are caused, in large part, by poor measurement.

One part of the problem is the dominance of Cronbach's alpha. Although most researchers believe it indexes reliability, and others believe it indexes internal consistency, I argued that it indexes neither.

A quantitative way to address the issue is to consider Equation 14.1, which takes both the number of items and the interitem correlation coefficients into account. If Cronbach's alpha indicates reliability, then keeping the number of items constant, greater interitem correlation coefficients should imply greater prediction of the criterion. But Figures 14.1 and 14.2 show that the opposite is so!

Figures 14.1 and 14.2 show, too, that the number of items matters. If the added items correlate reasonably well with the criterion, adding items benefits prediction (Figure 14.1). But if the added items are much more poorly correlated with the criterion than the original items, adding them harms prediction (Figure 14.2).

The demonstration that larger interitem correlations are harmful for prediction is at odds with the seemingly obvious notion that items measuring the same construct ought to correlate well with each other. Fortunately, dis-aggregation provides a way out. Instead of aggregating items into a single test, and then correlating the test with the criterion, an alternative is to have each item as a separate entry into a multiple regression equation; that is, dis-aggregating. Rather than use the bivariate correlation between an aggregated test and a criterion as indicating the degree of prediction, it is possible to use the multiple correlation of all items and the criterion as indicating the degree of prediction. When we switch from aggregating items, to dis-aggregating them, large interitem correlation coefficients imply better prediction of the criterion. Moreover, dis-aggregating always either equals or outperforms aggregating, as Figure 14.3 illustrates. Thus, dis-aggregation should become the general methodology, replacing aggregation.

After making these points, I used data Mike Hyman provided to pit aggregation against dis-aggregation. The tests showed that dis-aggregation was far superior to aggregation.

The quantitative demonstrations and empirical pitting of aggregation against dis-aggregation suggest conceptual implications. Even when test items load on the same factor in a factor analysis, and result in an impressive value for Cronbach's alpha, they may not measure the same construct. In fact, they probably do not. Secondly, to have better measures, including having items that do measure the same construct, it is important to have better theory. Better theory would aid researchers in understanding the meaning of the construct, and in creating effective auxiliary assumptions linking the construct to the items that purport to measure it. Better yet, if the theory includes relations to criterion constructs, the items created would be more likely to correlate with them.

Finally, once we acknowledge that dis-aggregating is far superior to aggregating, an option is to conceive items as separate one-item tests. We discussed advantages of one-item tests. We also discussed disadvantages of one-item tests but also why the disadvantages are not necessarily sufficient to overcome the advantages.

From a prediction standpoint, dis-aggregating is better than aggregating. And from a theoretical standpoint, the lack of confidence we can have that test items measure the same construct also supports dis-aggregating over aggregating. Either way, then, we should dis-aggregate. Hopefully, this will become the new methodology.

References

Abdel-Khalek, A. M. (1998). Single-versus multi-item scales in measuring death anxiety. *Death Studies*, *22*(8), 763–772. https://doi.org/10.1080/074811898201254

Ajzen, I. (1988). *Attitudes, personality and behavior*. Chicago, IL: Dorsey Press.

Ajzen, I., & Fishbein, M. (1980). *Understanding attitudes and predicting social behavior*. Englewood Cliffs, NJ: Prentice-Hall.

Ajzen, I., & Fishbein, M. (2005). The influence of attitudes on behavior. In D. Albarracin, B. T. Johnson, & M. P. Zanna (Eds.), *The handbook of attitudes* (pp. 173–221). Mahwah, NJ: Lawrence Erlbaum.

Azzalini, A. (2014). *The skew-normal and related families*. New York, NY: Cambridge University Press.

Baron, R., & Kenny, D. A. (1986). The moderator–mediator variable distinction in social psychological research: Conceptual, strategic, and statistical considerations. *Journal of Personality and Social Psychology*, *51*(6), 1173–1182. https://doi.org/10.1037=0022-3514.51.6.1173

Bergkvist, L., & Rossiter, J. R. (2007). The predictive validity of multiple-item versus single item measures of the same constructs. *Journal of Marketing Research*, *44*(2), 175–184. https://doi.org/10.1509/jmkr.44.2.175

Berk, R. A., & Freedman, D. A. (2003). Statistical assumptions as empirical commitments. In T. G. Blomberg & S. Cohen (Eds.), *Law, punishment, and social control: Essays in honor of Sheldon Messinger* (2nd ed., pp. 235–254). New York, NY: Aldine de Gruyter.

Blanca, M. J., Arnau, J., López-Montiel, D., Bono, R., & Bendayan, R. (2013). Skewness and kurtosis in real data samples. *Methodology: European Journal of Research Methods for the Behavioral and Social Sciences*, *9*(2), 78–84. https://doi.org/10.1027/1614-2241/a000057

Bradley, M. T., & Brand, A. (2016). Significance testing needs a taxonomy: Or how the Fisher, Neyman-Pearson controversy resulted in the inferential tail wagging the measurement dog. *Psychological Reports*, *119*(2), 487–504.

Brinberg, D., & McGrath, J. E. (1985). *Validity and the Research Process*. Beverly Hills, CA: SAGE Publishing.

Campbell, D. T., & Stanley, J. C. (2015/1963). *Experimental and quasi-experimental designs for research*. Ravenio Books.

Cao, L., Wang, C., Wang, T., & Trafimow, D. (2021). The APP for estimating population proportion based on skew normal approximations and the Beta-Bernoulli process. *Communications in Statistics – Simulation and Computation*, https://doi.org/10.1080/03610918.2021.2012192

Cao, L., Tong, T., Trafimow, D., Wang, T., & Chen, X. (2022). The a priori procedure for estimating the mean in both log-normal and gamma populations. *Methodology: European Journal of Research Methods for the Behavioral and Social Sciences*, *18*(1), 24–43. https://doi.org/10.5964/meth.7321

Cartwright, N. (2007). *Hunting causes and using them: Approaches in philosophy and economics*. Cambridge, UK: Cambridge University Press.

Cheah, J. H., Sarstedt, M., Ringle, C. M., Ramayah, T., & Ting, H. (2018). Convergent validity assessment of formatively measured constructs in PLS-SEM: On using single-item versus multi-item measures in redundancy analyses. *International Journal of Contemporary Hospitality Management*, *30*(11), 3192–3210. https://doi.org/10.1108/IJCHM-10-2017-0649

Chen, X., Trafimow, D., Wang, T., Tong, T., & Wang, C. (2021). The APP procedure for estimating Cohen's effect size. *Asian Journal of Economics and Banking*, *5*(3), 289–306. https://doi.org/10.1108/AJEB-08-2021-0095

Cohen, J. (1994). The earth is round (*p* < . 05). *American Psychologist*, *49*(12), 997–1003. https://doi.org/10.1037/0003-066X.49.12.997

Cohen, J. (1988). *Statistical power analysis for the behavioral sciences* (2nd ed.). Hillsdale, NJ: Lawrence Erlbaum.

Cronbach, L. J. (1951). Coefficient alpha and the internal structure of tests. *Psychometrika*, *16*(3), 297–334. https://doi.org/10.1007/bf02310555

Cronbach, L. J., & Meehl, P. E. (1955). Construct validity in psychological tests. *Psychological Bulletin*, *52*(4), 281–302. https://doi.org/10.1037/h0040957

Darden, W. R., & Perreault, Jr., W. D. (1976). Identifying interurban shoppers: Multiproduct purchase patterns and segmentation profiles. *Journal of Marketing Research*, *13*(1), 51–60. https://doi.org/10.1177/002224377601300107

Davidson, A. R., & Jaccard, J. (1979). Variables that moderate the attitude–behavior relation: Results of a longitudinal survey. *Journal of Personality and Social Psychology*, *37*(8), 1364–1376. https://doi.org/10.1037/0022-3514.37.8.1364

Davis, J. H. (1973). Group decision and social interaction: A theory of social decision schemes. *Psychological Review*, *80*(2), 97–125. https://doi.org/10.1037/H0033951

Duhem, P. (1954). *The aim and structure of physical theory* (P. Wiener, Trans.). New York, NY: Atheneum. (Original work published 1914)

Earp, B. D., & Trafimow, D. (2015). Replication, falsification, and the crisis of confidence in social psychology. *Frontiers in Psychology*, *6*(621), 1–11. https://doi.org/10.3389/fpsyg.2015.00621

Einstein, A. (1961). *Relativity: The Special and the General Theory*, Robert W. Lawson, Trans., New York, NY: Crown Publishers.

Fishbein, M. (1980). Theory of reasoned action: Some applications and implications. In H. Howe, & M. Page (Eds.), *Nebraska Symposium on Motivation* (Vol. 1979, pp. 65–116). Lincoln, NE: University of Nebraska Press.

Fishbein, M., & Ajzen, I. (1975). *Belief, attitude, intention and behavior: An introduction to theory and research*. Reading, MA: Addison-Wesley.

Fishbein, M., & Ajzen, I. (2010). *Predicting and changing behavior: The reasoned action approach*. New York, NY: Psychology Press (Taylor & Francis).

Freud S. (1955). Group psychology and the analysis of the ego. In J. Strachey (Ed. and Trans.), *The standard edition of the complete psychological works of Sigmund Freud* (Vol. 18, pp. 169–175). London: Hogarth. (Original work published 1922)

Freud, S. (1959). Character and anal eroticism. In J. Strachey (Ed. and Trans.), *The standard edition of the complete psychological works of Sigmund Freud* (Vol. 9, pp. 67–143). London: Hogarth. (Original work published 1908)

Galilei, Galileo. (1632/1953). *Dialogue concerning the two chief world systems, Ptolemaic & Copernican*. (Stillman Drake, Trans.). Berkeley, CA: University of California Press.

Graf, L. K., Mayer, S., & Landwehr, J. R. (2018). Measuring processing fluency: One versus five items. *Journal of Consumer Psychology*, *28*(3), 393–411. https://doi.org/10.1002/jcpy.1021

Gische, C., West, S. G., & Voelkle, M. C. (2020). Forecasting causal effects of interventions versus predicting future outcomes. *Structural Equation Modeling: A Multidisciplinary Journal*, 1–18. https://doi.org/10.1080/10705511.2020.1780598

Greenland, S. (2019). Valid P-values behave exactly as they should: Some misleading criticisms of P-values and their resolution with S-values. *The American Statistician*, *73*(sup1), 106–114. https://doi.org/.1080/00031305.2018.1529625.

Greve, W. (2001). Traps and gaps in action explanation: Theoretical problems of a psychology of human action. *Psychology Review*, *108*(2), 435–451. https://doi.org/10.1037/0033-295X.108.2.435

Grice, J. W., Cohn, A., Ramsey, R. R., & Chaney, J. M. (2015). On muddled reasoning and mediation modeling. *Basic and Applied Social Psychology*, *37*(4), 214–225. https://doi.org/10.1080/01973533.2015.1049350

Guilford, J. P., & Fruchter, B. (1973). *Fundamental statistics in psychology and education.* New York, NY: McGraw-Hill.

Gulliksen, H. (1987). *Theory of mental tests.* Hillsdale, NJ: Lawrence Erlbaum.

Harris, R. J. (1994). *ANOVA: An analysis of variance primer.* Itasca, IL: F. E. Peacock.

Hays, W. L. (1994). *Statistics* (5th ed.). Fort Worth, TX: Harcourt Brace College.

Hempel, C. G. (1965). *Aspects of scientific explanation and other essays in the philosophy of science.* New York, NY: The Free Press.

Hirschauer, N., Grüner, S., Mußhoff, O., Becker, C., & Jantsch, A. (2020). Can *p*-values be meaningfully interpreted without random sampling? *Statistics Surveys, 14,* 71–91. https://doi.org/10.1214/20-SS129

Ho, A. D., & Yu, C. C. (2015). Descriptive statistics for modern test score distributions: Skewness, kurtosis, discreteness, and ceiling effects. *Educational and Psychological Measurement, 75*(3), 365–388. https://doi.org/10.1177/0013164414548576

Hyman, M. R., Ganesh, G., & McQuitty, S. (2002). Augmenting the household affluence construct. *Journal of Marketing Theory & Practice, 10*(3), 13–31. https://doi.org/10.1080/10696679.2002.11501917

Hyman, M. R., Kostyk, A., & Trafimow, D. (2023). True consumer autonomy: A formalization and implications. *Journal of Business Ethics, 183,* 841–863. https://doi.org/10.1007/s10551-022-05114-0

John, O. P., Naumann, L. P., & Soto, C. J. (2008). Paradigm shift to the integrative big-five trait taxonomy: History, measurement, and conceptual issues. In O. P. John, R. W. Robins, & L. A. Pervin (Eds.), *Handbook of personality: Theory and research* (pp. 114–158). New York, NY: Guilford Press.

Kahneman, D. (2011). *Thinking, fast and slow.* New York, NY: MacMillan.

Kline, R. B. (2015). The mediation myth. *Basic and Applied Social Psychology, 37*(4), 202–213. https://doi.org/10.1080/01973533.2015.1049349

Kuhn T. S. (1962). *The structure of scientific revolutions.* Chicago, IL: University of Chicago Press.

Kuhn, M. H., & McPartland, T. (1954). An empirical investigation of self-attitudes. *American Sociological Review, 19*(1), 58–76. https://doi.org/10.2307/2088175

Lakatos, I. (1978). *The methodology of scientific research programmes.* Cambridge, UK: Cambridge University Press.

Lederman, L. (1993). *The god particle: If the universe is the answer, what is the question?* New York, NY: Houghton Mifflin.

Li, H., Trafimow, D., Wang, T., Wang, C., & Hu, L. (2020). User-friendly computer programs so econometricians can run the a priori procedure. *Frontiers in Management and Business, 1*(1), 2–6. https://doi.org/10.25082/FMB.2020.01.002

Lin, H., Werner, K. M., & Inzlicht, M. (2021). Promises and perils of experimentation: The mutual-internal-validity problem. *Perspectives on Psychological Science, 16*(4), 854–863. https://doi.org/10.1177/1745691620974773

Lord, F. M., & Novick, M. R. (1968). *Statistical theories of mental test scores.* Reading, MA: Addison-Wesley.

Lumpkin, J. R., & Darden, W. R. (1982). Relating television preference viewing to shopping orientations, lifestyles, and demographics. *Journal of Advertising, 11*(4), 56–67. https://doi.org/10.1080/00913367.1982.10672822

Macmillan, N. A., & Creelman, D. (2005). *Detection theory: A user's guide* (2nd ed.). Mahwah, NJ: Lawrence Erlbaum.

Manzi, J. (2012). *Uncontrolled: The surprising payoff of trial-and-error for business, politics, and society.* New York, N. Y.: Basic Books.

McQuitty, S. (2004). Statistical power and structural equation models in business research. *Journal of Business Research, 57*(2), 175–183. https://doi.org/10.1016/ S0148-2963(01)00301-0.

McQuitty, S. (2018). Reflections on "Statistical power and structural equation models in business research". *Journal of Global Scholars of Marketing Science, 28*(3), 272–277. https://doi.org/10.1080/21639159.2018.1434806.

Meehl, P. E. (1967). Theory-testing in psychology and physics: A methodological paradox. *Philosophy of Science, 34,* 103–115. https://doi.org/10.1086//288135

Meehl, P. E. (1990). Appraising and amending theories: The strategy of Lakatosian defense and two principles that warrant using it. *Psychological Inquiry*, *1*(2), 108–141. download;jsessionid=E2E98 557E78260208125135C1C3CFF4F (psu.edu)

Micceri, T. (1989). The unicorn, the normal curve, and other improbable creatures. *Psychological Bulletin*, *105*(1), 156–166. https://doi.org/10.1037/0033-2909.105.1.156

Michell, J. (1999). *Measurement in psychology: A critical history of a methodological concept*. New York, NY: Cambridge University Press.

Michell, J. (2011). Qualitative research meets the ghost of Pythagoras. *Theory & Psychology*, *21*(2), 241–259. https://doi.org/10.1177/0959354310391351

Morris, S. D., Grice, J. W., & Cox, R. A. (2017). Scale imposition as quantitative alchemy: Studies on the transitivity of neuroticism rating. *Basic and Applied Social Psychology*, *39*(1), 1–18. https://doi.org/10.1080/01973533.2016.1256288

Narita, K., Hoshide, S., Fujiwara, T., Kanegae, H., & Kario, K. (2020). Seasonal variation of home blood pressure and its association with targe organ damage: The J-HOP study (Japan morning surge-home blood pressure. *American Journal of Hypertension*, *33*, 620–628. https://doi.org/10.1093/ajh/hpt290

Nickerson, R. S. (2000). Null hypothesis statistical testing: A review of an old and continuing Controversy. *Psychological Methods*, *5*(2), 241–301. https://doi.org/10.1037//1082-989X.5.2.21

Open Science Collaboration (2015). Estimating the reproducibility of psychological science. *Science*, *349*(6251), aac4716. https://doi.org/10.1126/science.aac4716

Oyserman, D., & Lee, S. W. S. (2008). Does culture influence what and how we think? Effects of priming individualism and collectivism. *Psychological Bulletin*, *134*(2), 311–342. https://doi.org/10.1037/0033-2909.134.2.311

Pearl, J., & Bareinboim, E. (2011). Transportability of causal and statistical relations: A formal approach. In *Proceedings of the 25th AAAI Conference on Artificial Intelligence*. AAAI Press.

Pearl, J., & Mackenzie, D. (2018). *The book of why*. New York, NY: Basic Books.

Pedhazur, E. J. (1997). *Multiple regression in behavioral research: Explanation and prediction* (3rd ed.). New York, NY: Holt, Rinehart & Winston.

Popper, K. R. (1963). *Conjectures and refutations*. London: Routledge.

Popper, K. R. (1972). *Objective knowledge*. Oxford, UK: Oxford University Press.

Quine, W. V. O. (1952). *The dogmas of empiricism*. Reprinted from "A logical point of view," Cambridge, MA: Harvard University Press.

Rice, S. & Trafimow, D., & Hunt, G. (2010). Using PPT to analyze sub-optimal human–automation performance. *Journal of General Psychology*, *137*(3), 310–329. https://doi.org/10.1080/00221301003645236

Richins, M. L. (1987). Media, materialism, and human happiness. In M. Wallendorf & P. Anderson (Eds.), *Advances in consumer research*, Vol. 14 (pp. 352–356). Provo, UT: Association for Consumer Research.

Richters, J. E. (2021)Incredible utility: The lost causes and causal debris of psychological science. *Basic and Applied Social Psychology*, *43*(6), 366–405. https://doi.org/10.1080/01973533.2021.1979003

Rohrer, D., Pashler, H., & Harris, C. R. (2019). Discrepant data and improbable results: An examination of Vohs, Mead, and Goode (2006). *Basic and Applied Social Psychology*, *41*(4), 263–271. https://doi.org/10.1080/01973533.2019.1624965.

Rosenthal, R., & Rosnow, R. L. (1991). *Essentials of behavioral research: Methods and data analysis*. New York, NY: McGraw-Hill.

Rosenthal, R., & Rubin, D. B. (1979). A note on percent variance explained as a measure of the importance of effects. *Journal of Applied Social Psychology*, *9*(5), 395–396. https://doi.org/10.1111/j.1559-1816.1979.tb02713.x

Rosenthal, R., & Rubin, D. B. (1982). A simple general purpose display of magnitude of experimental effect. *Journal of Educational Psychology*, *74*(2), 166–169. https://doi.org/10.1037/0022-0663.74.2.166

Sarnoff, C. (1976). *Latency*. Lanham, MD: Jason Aronson.

Saylors, R., & Trafimow, D. (2021). Why the increasing use of complex causal models is a problem: On the danger sophisticated theoretical narratives pose to truth. *Organizational Research Methods*, *24*(3), 616–629. https://doi.org/10.1177/1094428119893452

Schwartz, S., Gatto, N. M., & Campbell, U. B. (2011). Transportability and causal generalization. *Epidemiology*, *22*(5), 745–746. https://doi.org/10.1097/EDE.0b013e3182254b8f

Spearman, C. (1904). The proof and measurement of association between two things. *American Journal of Psychology*, *15*(1), 72–101. www.jstor.org/stable/1412159

St Quinton, T., Morris, B., & Trafimow, D. (2021). Untangling the theory of planned behavior's auxiliary assumptions and theoretical assumptions: Implications for predictive and intervention studies. *New Ideas in Psychology*, *60*, 100818. https://doi.org/10.1016/j.newideapsych.2020.100818.

Stephan, W. G., & Stephan, C. W. (2000). An integrated threat theory of prejudice. In S. Oskamp (Ed.), *Reducing prejudice and discrimination* (pp. 23–45). Mahwah, NJ: Lawrence Erlbaum.

Swets, J. A., Tanner, W. P., Jr., & Birdsall, T. G. (1961). Decision processes in perception. *Psychological Review*, *68*(5), 301–340. https://doi.org/10.1037/h0040547

Tate, C. U. (2015). On the overuse and misuse of mediation analysis: It may be a matter of timing. *Basic and Applied Social Psychology*, *37*(4), 235–246. https://doi.org/10.1080/01973533.2015.1062380

Thoemmes, F. (2015). Reversing arrows in mediation models does not distinguish plausible models. *Basic and Applied Social Psychology*, *37*(4), 226–234. https://doi.org/10.1080/01973533.2015.1049351

Tong, T., Trafimow, D., Wang, T., Wang, C., Hu, L., & Chen, X. (2022a). The a priori procedure (APP) for estimating regression coefficients in linear models. *Methodology: European Journal of Research Methods for the Behavioral and Social Sciences*, *18*(3), 203–220. https://doi.org/10.5964/meth.8245

Tong, T., Wang, T., Trafimow, D., & Wang, C. (2022b). The probability of being better or worse off, and by how much, depending on experimental conditions with skew normal populations. In W. Y. E. S. Sriboonchitta & V. Kreinovich (Eds.), *Credible asset allocation, optimal transport methods, and related topics* (pp. 141–149). New York, NY: Springer-Verlag.

Trafimow, D. (2003). Hypothesis testing and theory evaluation at the boundaries: Surprising insights from Bayes's theorem. *Psychological Review*, *110*(3), 526–535. https://doi.org/10.1037/0033-295X.110.3.526

Trafimow, D. (2005). The ubiquitous Laplacian assumption: Reply to Lee and Wagenmakers. *Psychological Review*, *112*(3), 669–674. https://doi.org/10.1037/0033-295X.112.3.669

Trafimow, D. (2009). The theory of reasoned action: A case study of falsification in psychology. *Theory & Psychology*, *19*(4), 501–518. https://doi.org/10.1177/0959354309336319

Trafimow, D. (2012a). The role of auxiliary assumptions for the validity of manipulations and measures. *Theory & Psychology*, *22*(4), 486–498. https://doi.org/10.1177/0959354311429996

Trafimow, D. (2012b). The concept of unit coherence and its application to psychology theories. *The Journal for the Theory of Social Behaviour*, *42*(2), 131–154. https://doi.org/10.1111/j.1468-5914.2011.00483.x

Trafimow, D. (2015a). Introduction to the special issue on mediation analyses: What if planetary scientists used mediation analysis to infer causation?, *Basic and Applied Social Psychology*, *37*(4), 197–201. https://doi.org/10.1080/01973533.2015.1064290

Trafimow, D. (2015b). Artificial enhancement of motivation is typically not a bioethical problem. *American Journal of Bioethics: Neuroscience*, *6*(1), 44–45. https://doi.org/10.1080/21507740.2014.995319

Trafimow, D. (2015c). On retiring the TRA/TPB without retiring the lessons learned: Commentary on Sniehotta et al. *Health Psychology Review*, *9*(2), 168–171. https://doi.org/10.1080/17437199.2014.884932

Trafimow, D. (2017a). Implications of an initial empirical victory for the truth of the theory and additional empirical victories. *Philosophical Psychology*, *30*(4), 411–433. https://doi.org/10.1080/09515089.2016.1274023

Trafimow, D. (2017b). Using the coefficient of confidence to make the philosophical switch from *a posteriori* to *a priori* inferential statistics. *Educational and Psychological Measurement*, *77*(5), 831–854. https://doi.org/10.1177/0013164416667977

Trafimow, D. (2017c). The probability of simple versus complex causal models in causal analyses. *Behavior Research Methods*, *49*(2), 739–746. https://doi.org/10.3758/s13428-016-0731-3

Trafimow, D. (2018a). Confidence intervals, precision and confounding. *New Ideas in Psychology, 50,* 48–53. https://doi.org/10.1016/j.newideapsych.2018.04.005

Trafimow, D. (2018b). An *a priori* solution to the replication crisis. *Philosophical Psychology, 31*(8), 1188–1214. https://doi.org/10.1080/09515089.2018.1490707

Trafimow, D. (2018c). Some implications of distinguishing between unexplained variance that is systematic or random. *Educational and Psychological Measurement, 78*(3), 482–503. https://doi.org/10.1177/0013164417691573

Trafimow, D. (2019a). A taxonomy of model assumptions on which P is based and implications for added benefit in the sciences. *International Journal of Social Research Methodology, 22*(6), 571–583. https://doi.org/10.1080/13645579.2019.1610592

Trafimow, D. (2019b). Why successful replications across contexts and operationalizations might not be good for theory building or testing. *Journal for the Theory of Social Behaviour 49*(3), 359–368. https://doi.org/10.1111/jtsb.12211

Trafimow, D. (2020). A taxonomy of major premises and implications for falsification and verification. *International Studies in the Philosophy of Science, 33*(4), 211–229. https://doi.org/10.1080/02698595.2021.1964845

Trafimow, D. (2021). The underappreciated effects of unreliability on multiple regression and mediation. *Applied Finance and Accounting, 7*(2), 14–30. https://doi.org/10.11114/afa.v7i2.5292

Trafimow, D. (in press). A new way to think about internal and external validity. *Perspectives on Psychological Science.*

Trafimow, D. (in press). Distinguishing between models and hypotheses: Implications for significance testing. Meta-Psychology.

Trafimow, D., Bromgard, I. K., Finlay, K. A., Ketelaar, T. (2005). The role of affect in determining the attributional weight of immoral behaviors. *Personality and Social Psychology Bulletin, 31*(7), 935–948. https://doi.org/10.1177/0146167204272179

Trafimow, D., Brown, J., Grace, K., Thompson, L., & Sheeran, P. (2002). The relative influence of attitudes and subjective norms from childhood to adolescence: Between-participants and within-participants analyses. *The American Journal of Psychology, 115*(3), 395–414. https://doi.org/10.2307/1423424

Trafimow, D. T., Hyman, M. R., & Kostyk, A. (2020). The (im)precision of scholarly consumer behavior research. *Journal of Business Research, 114,* 93–101. https://doi.org/10.1016/j.jbusres.2020.04.008

Trafimow, D., Hyman, M. R., & Kostyk, A. (2023). Are structural equation models theories and does it matter? *Journal of Global Scholars of Marketing Science, 33*(2), 248–263. https://doi.org/10.1080/10.1080/21639159.2022.2048960

Trafimow, D. T., Hyman, M. R., & Kostyk, A. (under submission). Enhancing predictive power by unamalgamating multi-item measures.

Trafimow, D., Hyman, M. R., Kostyk, A., Wang, C., & Wang, T. (2021). The harmful effect of null hypothesis significance testing on marketing research: An example. *Journal of Business Research, 125,* 39–44. https://doi.org/10.1016/j.jbusres.2020.11.069

Trafimow, D., Hyman, M. R., Kostyk, A., Wang, Z., Tong, T., Wang, T., & Wang, C. (2022). Gain-probability diagrams in consumer research. *International Journal of Market Research, 64*(4), 470–483. https://doi.org/10.1177/14707853221085509

Trafimow, D., Li, H., Wang, T., Hu, L., Wang, C., & Rodriguez, A. (2020). Expanding the a priori procedure (APP) to address proportions. *Journal of Asian Economics, Accounting and Finance, 1*(2), 117–134. www.esijournals.com

Trafimow, D., MacDonald, J. A., & Rice, S. (2012). Using PPT to account for randomness in perception. *Attention, Perception, & Psychophysics, 74*(6), 1355–1365. https://doi.org/10.3758/s13414-012-0319-7

Trafimow, D., & Marks, M. (2015). Editorial. *Basic and Applied Social Psychology, 37*(1), 1–2. https://doi.org/10.1080/01973533.2015.1012991

Trafimow, D., & Myüz, H. A. (2019). The sampling precision of research in five major areas of psychology. *Behavior Research Methods, 51*(5), 2039–2058. https://doi.org/10.3758/s13428-018-1173-x

Trafimow, D., & Osman, M. (2022). Editorial: Barriers to converting applied social psychology to bettering the human condition. *Basic and Applied Social Psychology, 4*(1), 1–11. https://doi.org/10.1080/01973533.2022.2051327

Trafimow, D., & Rice, S. (2008). Potential performance theory (PPT): A general theory of task performance applied to morality. *Psychological Review, 115*(2), 447–462. https://doi.org/10.1037/0033-295X.115.2.447

Trafimow, D., & Rice, S. (2009). Potential performance theory (PPT): Describing a methodology for analyzing task performance. *Behavior Research Methods, 41*, 359–371. https://doi.org/10.3758/BRM.41.2.359

Trafimow, D., Rodriguez, A., Myüz, H. A., Wang, C., & Wang, T. (2019). The precision of research in three top medical journals. *Mental Health & Human Resilience International Journal, 3*(1), 000131. https://doi.org/10.23880/mhrij-16000131

Trafimow, D., & Sheeran, P. (1998). Some tests of the distinction between cognitive and affective beliefs. *Journal of Experimental Social Psychology, 34*(4), 378–397. https://doi.org/10.1006/jesp.1998.1356

Trafimow, D., Sheeran, P., Conner, M., & Finlay, K. A. (2002). Evidence that perceived behavioral control is a multidimensional construct: Perceived control and perceived difficulty. *British Journal of Social Psychology, 41*(1), 101–121. https://doi.org/10.1348/014466602165081

Trafimow, D., Triandis, H. C., & Goto, S. G. (1991). Some tests of the distinction between the private self and the collective self. *Journal of Personality and Social Psychology, 60*(5), 649–655. https://doi.org/10.1037/0022-3514.60.5.649

Trafimow, D., & Uhalt, J. (2020). The inaccuracy of sample-based confidence intervals to estimate *a priori* ones. *Methodology: European Journal of Research Methods for the Behavioral and Social Sciences, 16*(2), 112–126. https://doi.org/10.5964/meth.2807

Trafimow, D., Wang, T., & Wang, C. (2019). From a sampling precision perspective, skewness is a friend and not an enemy! *Educational and Psychological Measurement, 79*(1), 129–150. https://doi.org/10.1177/0013164418764801

Trafimow, D., Wang, C., & Wang, T. (2020). Making the a priori procedure (APP) work for differences between means. *Educational and Psychological Measurement, 80*(1), 186–198. https://doi.org/10.1177/0013164419847509

Valentine, J. C., Aloe, A. M., & Lau, T. S. (2015). Life after NHST: How to describe your data without "p-ing" everywhere. *Basic and Applied Social Psychology, 37*(5), 260–273. http://dx.doi.org/10.1080/01973533.2015.1060240

Vazire, S., Schiavone, S. R., & Bottesini, J. G. (2022). Credibility beyond replicability: Improving the four validities in psychological science. *Current Directions in Psychological Science, 31*(2), 162–168. https://doi.org/10.1177/09637214211067779

Vohs, K. D., Mead, N. L., & Goode, M. R. (2006). The psychological consequences of money. *Science (New York, N.Y.), 314*(5802), 1154–1156. https://doi.org/10.1126/science.1132491

Wang, C., Wang, T., Trafimow, D., & Chen, J. (2019). Extending a priori procedure to two independent samples under skew normal settings. *Asian Journal of Economics and Banking, 3*(2), 29–40. http://ajeb.buh.edu.vn/Home

Wang, C., Wang, T., Trafimow, D., Li, H., Hu, L., & Rodriguez, A. (2021). Extending the a priori procedure (APP) to address correlation coefficients. In N. Ngoc Thach, V. Kreinovich, & N. D. Trung (Eds.), *Data Science for Financial Econometrics: Studies in Computational Intelligence*, vol. 898. Cham, Switzerland: Springer. https://doi.org/10.1007/978-3-030-48853-6_10

Wang, C., Wang, T., Trafimow, D., & Myüz, H. A. (2019). Necessary sample sizes for specified closeness and confidence of matched data under the skew normal setting. *Communications in statistics—Simulation and Computation, 51*(5), 2083–2094. https://doi.org/10.1080/03610918.2019.1661473

Wang, C., Wang, T., Trafimow, D., & Talordphop, K. (2020). Extending the a priori procedure to one-way analysis of variance model with skew normal random effects. *Asian Journal of Economics and Banking, 4*(2), 77–90. https://ajeb.buh.edu.vn/en/article/extending-the-a-priori-procedure-to-one-way-analysis-of-variance-model-with-skew-normal-random-effects

References

Wang, C., Wang T., Trafimow, D., & Xu, Z. (2021). A priori procedure (APP) for estimating the scale parameter in gamma populations for known shape parameter. In S. Sriboonchitta, V. Kreinovich, & W. Yamaka (Eds.), *Quantum computing in econometrics and quantum economics*. NewYork, NY: Springer-Verlag.

Wang, Z., Wang, T., Trafimow, D., & Xu, Z. (2022). A different kind of effect size based on samples from two populations with delta log-skew-normal distributions. In N. Ngoc Thach, D. T. Ha, N. D. Trung, & V. Kreinovich (Eds.), *Prediction and causality in econometrics and related topics*. ECONVN 2021. Studies in Computational Intelligence, vol. 983. Springer, Cham. https://doi.org/10.1007/978-3-030-77094-5_10

Wang, C., Wang, T., Trafimow, D., & Zhang, X. (2019). Necessary sample size for estimating the scale parameter with specified closeness and confidence. *International Journal of Intelligent Technologies and Applied Statistics*, *12*(1), 17–29. https://doi.org/10.6148/IJITAS.201903_12(1).0002

Wei, Z., Wang, T., Trafimow, D., & Talordphop, K. (2020). Extending the a priori procedure to normal Bayes models. *International Journal of Intelligent Technologies and Applied Statistics*, *13*(2), 169–183. https://doi.org/10.6148/IJITAS.202006_13(2).0004

Wicklund, R. A. (1990). *Zero-variable theories and the psychology of the explainer*. New York, NY: Springer-Verlag.

Wuellner, B. W. (1956). *Dictionary of scholastic philosophy*. Milwaukee, WI: Bruce.

Index

a priori procedure 74, 76–77, 80–81, 84, 86, 87–88, 90, 105
Abdel-Khalek, A. M. 206, 209
Ajzen, I. 3, 14, 42, 116–117, 165, 173, 200, 209–210
Aloe, A. M. 91, 215
Aristotle 17, 19, 22, 26–27, 29, 67, 111
assumptions: auxiliary 9–16, 22, 27–29, 31–32, 37, 39, 41–42, 45–46, 51, 61–63, 67, 69–70, 76, 118, 120, 125, 126, 164–170, 172, 175, 205, 208; inferential 37, 39, 44–46, 51, 63, 69, 118, 169; statistical 31, 37, 39, 43, 45–46, 51, 63, 69, 118, 169; theoretical 16, 37, 39, 46, 63, 205
attenuation 132, 137, 140, 193, 196
autonomy 157–160
Azzalini, A. 36, 209

bad variance 184–192, 194
Baron, R. 114–115, 209
Bayes 58, 60–61
Beck A. T., 168
Bergkvist, L. 206, 209
Berk, R. A. 38, 209
Big Five personality traits 204
Birdsall, T. G. 154, 179, 213
binomial distribution 81, 83
binomial theorem 178
Blanca, M. J. 36, 52, 77, 209
Bottesini, J. G. 39, 215
Bradley, M. T. 51, 209
Brand, A. 51, 209
Brinberg, D. 40, 209

Campbell, D. T. 40, 209
Cao, L. 83, 85, 87, 209
Cartwright, N. 40, 209
causation 140
central limit theorem 78
Cheah, J. H. 206, 209
Chen, X. 79, 83, 210, 215
Cohen, J. 48, 83–84, 87, 90, 210
Cohen's d 183
classical theory 125, 127–128, 136, 140, 185, 206

confidence 56–57, 61, 79–88, 90, 104, 113, 116, 163, 168, 180
consistency coefficient 143
Copernicus, N. 24, 26
covariance 141–143, 163
covariance law 129
Cox, R. A. 139, 212
Creelman, D. 179, 211
Cronbach, L. J. 162, 210, 210
Cronbach's alpha 134–136, 140, 167, 196–197, 199–200, 202–205, 207–208

Darden, W. R. 203, 210–211
Davidson, A. R. 165, 210
Davis, J. H. 178–179, 210
de Lacaille, N–L. 31
decision schemes matrix 179
delta lognormal distribution 99
dis-attenuation 132–133, 140, 143, 147–148, 154, 159, 196
Duhem, P. 12, 31, 210

Earp, B. D. 69, 210
effect size 26–27, 53, 55–56, 60, 64, 71, 72, 83, 85, 87, 90, 95, 101, 104–105, 119, 183–184, 195–196, 207
efficient cause 121, 111–112, 121
Einstein, A. 6–8, 15–17, 22, 24, 110, 210
empirical hypothesis 9–11, 16, 31–32, 37, 39, 43, 162
empirical laws 19, 21–23, 28
Eratosthenes 21, 28

factor analysis 163–164, 169, 177, 205, 208
falsification 6–9, 11–16
Fishbein, M. 3, 14, 16, 42, 116–117, 165, 173, 209–210
Freedman, D. A. 38, 209
Freud, S. 13–14, 16, 210
Fruchter, B. 197, 211

gain-probability 89, 91, 93, 94, 96–98, 100, 101–105

Galileo, G. 22–28, 68, 210
gamma distributions 85, 87
Gische, L. K. 119, 210
good variance 184–185, 187, 189–194
Goto, S. 66, 215
Graf, L. K. 206, 210
Greenland, S. 51, 54–55, 210
Greve, W. 14, 210
Grice, J. 111–112, 121, 139, 210, 212
Guilford, J. P. 197, 211
Gulliksen, H. 125, 129, 211

Halley, E. 31–32, 37
Harris, R. J. 187, 211
Hempel, C. G. 17, 211
Hirschauer, N. 38, 211
Ho, A. D. 36, 52, 77, 211
homogeneity 119, 139–140
Hunt, G. 153, 212
Hyman, M. R. 86, 95, 99, 116, 159, 196, 202–203, 208, 211, 214

incommensurability 6–8
inferential hypothesis 37–39, 63
interitem 198, 200–203, 207–208
internal consistency 136, 140
Inzlicht, M. 40, 211
item-criterion 197–199, 201–202, 204–206

Jaccard, J. 165, 210
John, O. P. 204, 211

Kahneman, D. 69, 211
Kenny, D. A. 114–115, 209
Kline, R. B. 113–114, 116, 121, 211
Kostyk, A. 86, 116, 159, 196, 211, 214
Kuhn, M. H. 66, 211
Kuhn, T. S. 6–8, 15, 211

Lakatos, I. 12, 31, 211
Laplace's demon 44, 75
Lau, T. S. 91, 215
Lederman, L. 16, 211
Lee, S. W. S. 67, 212
Li, H. 76, 211, 214
Lin, H. 40, 211
location 36–37, 43–44, 76–80, 87, 91–92, 95, 98, 102, 179
lognormal distributions 85, 91, 98, 101, 104
Lord, F. M. 125, 128, 211
Lumpkin, J. R. 203, 211

margin frequencies 150–152, 159, 180
Mackenzie, D. 40, 212
Macmillan, N. A. 179, 211
Manzi, J. 40, 211
Marks, M. 48, 214
MacDonald, J. A. 155, 214

McGrath, J. E. 40, 209
McPartland, T. 66, 211
McQuitty, S. 116, 211
measurement implication 195
mediation 106–120, 138, 140
Meehl, P. E. 12, 113, 162, 210–211
Micceri, T. 36, 52, 77, 212
Michell, J. 138–139, 212
modus tollens error 48–49, 56–57, 61
morality 146–147, 152–153, 157, 160
Morey, R. 60
Morris, B. 166, 213
Morris, S. D. 139, 212
multicollinearity 207
multiple correlation 200–201, 203, 207–208
multiple regression 81, 200, 207

Narita, K. 101, 212
Naumann, L. P. 204, 211
Newton, I. 6–8, 15–17, 23, 25–26, 28, 31–32, 126, 168
Neyman, J. 60, 61
Nickerson, R. A. 48, 212
nomological network 163, 169
nonobservational terms 9–11, 16–17, 19, 26, 30–31, 37, 39, 69–70, 126, 162, 168–169, 172
nonstandard tables 149–152, 159
normal distributions 35–36, 71, 76–79, 81, 83–86, 91–92, 99, 104–105,
Novick, M. R. 125, 128, 211
null hypothesis 38, 47–53, 56, 58, 60–61, 63–64, 84, 86–88, 91, 105, 113–114, 121

observational terms 9–11, 16–17, 31, 37, 39, 69–70, 125, 162, 169
observed correlation coefficient 147
observed performance 149, 150, 155–158
observed reliability coefficient 147
observed score 128, 149, 206
observed score variance 133, 140, 186–187
Open Science Collaboration 53, 68–69, 212
Osman, M. 52, 119, 214
Oyserman, D. 67, 212

parsing variance 185–186
path coefficients 108, 112–116,
Pearl, J. 40, 119, 212
Pedhazur, E. J. 107, 212
Perreault, W. D. 203, 210
phi coefficient 146–147, 159
pi matrix 178
Popper, K. 6, 212
potential performance 150, 156, 158–160,
potential performance theory 145–146, 153–155, 157, 159–160, 180–181
power analysis 86, 88, 115
precision 57–58, 61, 75–79, 80–88, 104,

Quine, W. V. O. 31, 212

received view 40–43, 45–46
regression to the mean 53
reliability 125, 126, 128–136, 140, 142 145–159, 184–187, 191–194, 196, 207: dependent variable 188; path coefficients 136–138; regression coefficients 136–138; task performance 145, 153–154; unreliability 132, 136–137, 140, 145, 153–154, 180, 194
replication 62–67, 70, 72–73: conceptual 65, 68; crisis 68, 75; exact 65, 70, 73; failures 68–69, 71–73; issue 70–71; successful 71–72; quasi-exact 65, 68, 70
Rice, S. 145, 148, 151, 153, 155, 212, 214–215
Richins, M. L. 202, 212, 214
Richters, J. 119, 139, 212
Rohrer, 65, 68–69, 212
Rosenthal, R. 148, 212
Rosnow, R. L. 148, 212
Rossiter, J. R. 206, 209
Rubin, D. B. 148, 212

Sarnoff, C. 13, 212
Saylors, R. 111, 212
scale 36, 77, 79, 80, 87, 91, 92, 95–96, 98, 99, 102, 138–139, 203
Schiavone, S. R. 39, 215
Schwartz, S. 119, 212
Sense 1 40–46
Sense 2 40–46
shape 36, 43, 77–79, 80, 83–84, 87–88, 91–92, 95, 98, 102
Sheeran, P. 14, 214–215
signal detection theory 154, 159, 179–181
significance test 37–38, 47–56, 59–61, 63–65, 68, 71, 73, 75, 78, 90, 95, 105, 113, 115–116, 196
skewness 32, 36–37, 43, 77–80, 83, 85, 88, 91, 98, 101, 104–105,
skew normal distributions 91, 95, 102
social decision schemes 178–181
Soto, C. J. 204, 211
Spearman, C. 132, 134, 140, 213
Spearman-Brown 134
standard tables 148–149, 150, 152, 159
St Quinton, T. 166, 213
Stanley, J. C. 40, 209
Statistical: hypothesis 37–39, 63; indistinguishability 114, 121; significance 51, 53–54, 68, 85, 86, 90, 100–101
S-value 55–56
Stephan, C. 31, 167, 174. 213
Stephan, W. 31, 167, 174, 213
Swets, J. A. 154, 179, 213

Talordphop, K. 87, 215–216
Tanner, W. P. 154, 179, 213
TASI taxonomy 39–42, 45–46, 51–52, 63, 118
Tate, C. U. 114–115, 121, 213
theoretical assumptions 37, 39, 46
theory of reasoned action 42, 173–175, 180–181
Thoemmes, F. 114, 213
Tong, T. 81, 91, 95, 115, 209, 214–215
Trafimow, D. 8, 12, 14, 27, 31, 36, 39, 48, 51–52, 55, 58–59, 69, 70, 81–82, 86, 87, 90–91, 95, 99, 109, 111, 116, 119–120, 128, 137–138, 145, 148, 151, 153, 155, 158–159, 165–166, 172, 185, 196, 200, 202, 209, 210–216
transitivity 139
transportability 119, 121
Triandis, H. C. 66, 215
tripartite 192, 194
true correlation coefficient 138, 147
true score 127–128, 140–143, 206
true score variance 133, 136, 186

Uhalt, J. 58, 215
unfalsifiable theory 13–14, 16,
unit coherence 179–180
unit incoherence 181
unitless constructs 181
unitless measures 177–178

Valentine, J., 91, 215
validity 125, 126, 129, 130, 133, 140, 161, 163, 167, 169, 207: auxiliary 161, 165–167, 170–171, 175, 180; construct 162–166, 168–171; convergent 164, 168; discriminant 163; divergent 168; external 39–46; internal 39–46; predictive 130, 140, 162, 169; unit 171, 181
Vazire, S. 39, 215
verification 9, 12
Vohs, K. D., 65, 68–69, 215

Wang, C. 77–83, 85, 87, 91, 95, 209–210, 214–216
Wang, T. 77–83, 85, 87, 91, 95, 99, 209–210, 214–216
Wang, Z. 95, 99, 214
Wei, Z. 87, 206
Werner, K. M. 40, 211
Wicklund, R. 22, 216
Wuellner, B. W. 111, 216

Xu, Z. 99, 215–216

z-score 76, 180

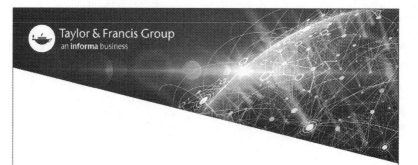

Printed in the United States
by Baker & Taylor Publisher Services